ARCHITECTURE
OF
SEGREGATION

The Hierarchy of Spaces and Places

JEREL McCANTS

Copyright © 2024 JEREL McCANTS

Two Penny Publishing
850 E. Lime Street #266
Tarpon Springs, Florida 34688

TwoPennyPublishing.com
info@TwoPennyPublishing.com

All rights reserved. This book or parts thereof may not be reproduced in any form, stored in any retrieval system, or transmitted in any form by any means—electronic, mechanical, photocopy, recording, or otherwise—without prior written permission of the publisher, except as provided by United States of America copyright law.

Scripture quotations marked (KJV) are from The Authorized (King James) Version. Rights in the Authorized Version in the United Kingdom are vested in the Crown. Reproduced by permission of the Crown's patentee, Cambridge University Press.

For permission requests and ordering information, email:
info@twopennypublishing.com

Hardback ISBN: 979-8-9901524-3-4
eBook also available

FIRST EDITION

For information about this author, to book event appearance, or media interview, please contact the author representative at:
info@twopennypublishing.com

Two Penny Publishing is a partnership publisher of a variety of genres. We help first-time and seasoned authors share their stories, passion, knowledge, and experiences that help others grow and learn. Please visit our website: TwoPennyPublishing.com if you would like us to consider your manuscript or book idea for publishing.

ABSTRACT

In *Architecture of Segregation*, the intricate interplay between architecture and societal divisions is meticulously explored, providing a comprehensive analysis of how built environments have shaped and reflected racial, ethnic, and social segregation throughout history. This groundbreaking work delves deep into the historical contexts of segregation, from the indigenous peoples of North America to the African diaspora through the Triangular Slave Trade to the Holocaust, uncovering how architecture played a pivotal role in the subjugation of marginalized communities. This book navigates through pivotal moments like the Nuremburg Race Laws, Plessy v. Ferguson Supreme Court decision, the establishment of Jim Crow segregation laws, and subsequent immigration acts and restrictions, shedding light on how legal frameworks influenced architectural design, policy and urban planning. It also examines the enduring legacies of segregation on contemporary society, demonstrating the profound and lasting impact of architectural decisions. *Architecture of Segregation* ultimately calls for a reevaluation of the role architects play in perpetuating or dismantling these divisions, challenging readers to consider the ethical implications of design and its potential to foster equality and inclusion in the built environment.

*This book is dedicated to my mom and dad,
the best parents in the world.*

PREFACE

As a child, I have always had an interest in spaces and how each space or place within a home, church, school, office building, hotel, etc., had particular needs that were required to allow a building to function properly. This interest in creating spaces led my career path to becoming an architect and operating my own firm. Stories from my family influenced my thoughts and meditations on architecture, especially listening to stories from my elders' experiences in life, community, and in the built environment. Given the time frame, their experience was drastically different from my own, and my brother, sisters, and cousins. These stories stayed with me throughout my formative years, matriculation through college, and in my professional life.

While attending higher educational institutions, I learned of other experiences classmates had in their communities and in other parts of the world. Their experiences vastly differed from mine, and each other's cultural backgrounds and ethnicities contributed to many perspectives. While traveling to countries in Europe, Asia, Africa, and South America, I experienced how societies other than mine approached cultural divides and formations of buildings at different periods in history, how this affected their ideals on the built environment, and how these districts, areas, and regions functioned to serve their specialized needs.

As an inquisitive person, I pose questions and then seek solutions to provide an understanding of what people endured, how they interacted with each other, and what provisions were accepted as commonplace law in order to keep the peace. This book is a culmination of shared experiences and the outcome or fallout from decisions about creating public, private, and governed spaces. I hope you gain a different perspective on how to look at the importance of spaces and how we use them each and every day.

TABLE OF CONTENTS

Introduction 9
01   "What and Why?" 13
     Definition and Significance of Segregation
02   Entomology of Segregation. 21
     Segregation and the Built Environment
03   Psychological Aspects of Architecture. 33
     Psychology of Segregation
04   "Who…Me?" 51
     Architect as Collaborator
05   Architect as Decider 87
     Architecture's Role in the Development of Civilizations
06   On Earth As It Is in Heaven. 119
     Segregation in Biblical Times
07   When We Were Gods 149
     Architect's Royal Position in Ancient Times
08   Segregation in Early Civilizations. 209
09   Architect as Nation Builder. 249
     Formation of Nations and Segregation
10   A Brave New World 265
     The Architecture of Institutionalized Racism
11   Architect as Cultural Identity 285
     Rize of the Nazi's and Jewish Isolationism
12   Architect as Destroyer. 299
     White Nationalism and the Pursuit of Racial Segregation

13	**Architect as Enforcer**.................................	317
	Legalized Segregation and Architecture	
14	**Architect as Policymaker**.............................	341
	The Third Wave of Migration	
15	**Architect as Gatekeeper**	369
	Socioeconomic Segregation	
16	**Architect as Integrator**	377
	"Who Got It Right?"	
17	**Conclusion**	393
	The New Republic	
References...		403

INTRODUCTION

As a child, my father would have the family visit our Grandparents in a small town in Alabama. As we drove to see our extended relatives, he would talk about his childhood and where he ventured to. There was one story that has stayed with me until this day. As we passed an old, dilapidated, moss-stained building that was once a bustling doctor's office, I listened intently as my father spoke of the building's history—how blacks had to enter the rear of the building, and how they had to wait until all the white patients were seen by the doctor first. This impacted me so deeply as to why and how this small shack could house such a strict procedure to separate the prevailing races at that time.

While imaging and attempting to illustrate its once divided spaces—one for whites, one for blacks—I tried to formulate the divided corridors, the separate examination rooms, and the duplicates of every amenity, all engineered to maintain racial segregation. In my spare time as a child, I would sit at my desk and draw for hours and hours, creating floor plans and revising them until I felt they were perfect. Because I needed to problem solve, my mind was fixated on spatial relationships and experiences one would encounter while circulating through a building, retail space, or educational institution. This realization came to me slowly that this building wasn't just wood siding and framed walls; it was a symbol of societal division, a testament to a time when architecture was used to reinforce an ugly reality.

These stories from my parents, aunts, and uncles informed me of a lifestyle that was very unfamiliar to my understanding and comprehension. These stories were about segregation in the Deep South. As a young man, my curiosity about architecture and its impact on society was formulated by these stories. This curiosity ignited a life-long passion to dig into the hidden recesses of history and unveil how the built environment was and continues to be a protagonist in our societal narratives. From personal anecdotes, original blueprints, and historical events to biblical tales, my journey took me on a path less traveled - a path that explored the intersection of architecture, history, and the human condition. This book, *Architecture of Segregation*, is the culmination of that journey.

It peels back the layers of time to delve into the origins of segregation, and the significant role architecture played in designing divisions. It travels through the avenues of ancient civilizations, analyzes aspects of the Roman Empire, braves the tumultuous waters of the colonial era, and traipses through present-day urban landscapes. It decodes the "Principles of Order in Architecture"—the underlying design guidelines that resulted in these segregated spaces, and investigates the psychological impact they had on people who were forced to navigate through them.

This book isn't just about how architects contributed to segregation; it's an exploration of the symbiotic relationship between architecture and society. It details how societal prejudices dictated the shape and form of our built environments and how these environments, in turn, cemented the biases, codifying them into our everyday existence. It's a reflection on our past but also a look into our future, where I hope we architects can learn from history to shape spaces that unite rather than divide.

Architecture of Segregation seeks to fill a gap in the existing literature by revealing the interconnected relationship between architecture and segregation. It also underscores the urgent need for a paradigm shift—from designing for segregation to designing for unity. I hope this book will provoke thought, spur dialogue, and inspire a more inclusive perspective on architecture and its significant impact on society. Architecture is not just bricks and mortar; it is a tangible embodiment of our societal narratives.

Let's start this journey together to uncover the hidden blueprints of our shared history and ponder upon the architectural methodology that has shaped the world we inhabit. I hope to present new ideals in design that can encourage integration. For the sake of clarity, I propose to concentrate on the history and development of segregation in terms of its influence on the built environment. Analyses of original blueprints of public facilities will be presented to show the careful and diligent order that was maintained to make segregation 'real' for its participants.

01

"Every man is the architect of his own fate."

Mahavir Jain

"WHAT AND WHY?"

DEFINITION AND SIGNIFICANCE OF SEGREGATION

Segregation, in its most basic form, is the act of separating or setting apart people or things from others. It's a word that's loaded with history, brimming with implications of inequality and isolation, and a potent reminder of our societal failures. However, if we're going to have a real, sincere, and comprehensive conversation about it, it's vital we understand what it truly signifies.

> *Origin of Segregation - mid 16th century: from Latin word segregat- "separated from the flock," and from the verb segregare, from se- "apart" + grex, greg- "flock."*

By formal definition, segregation is the enforced separation of different racial groups in a country, community, or establishment. It's an institutionalized system of discrimination where social relations and interactions between races are limited or nonexistent.[1]

This definition, though accurate, only scratches the surface of the vast iceberg that segregation truly is. Segregation is more than the visible physical barriers between groups of people. It's the invisible walls that exist in the minds of those on both sides. It's the quiet, unspoken understanding that 'this place' or 'that facility' is meant for 'those people.'

The significance of segregation goes far beyond its effects on the lives of those directly impacted by it. Segregation shapes society's very fabric and structure. It impacts the distribution of resources, wealth, opportunities, and power. It influences the development and growth of cities, towns, and neighborhoods.[2]

However, there is a critical aspect of segregation that often goes unnoticed—its influence on the built environment. Architecture and segregation have a long, intertwined history that's seldom examined. As I have earlier stated in the introduction of this book, buildings and public spaces are more than just brick and mortar; they are reflections of our values, desires, fears, and biases. They shape our experiences and interactions, subtly reinforcing societal norms and divisions.

The built environment's design and layout can be a powerful tool for segregation. Whether through "Whites only" signs in the Jim Crow South or through the 'invisible' walls of gated communities, the design and structure of our buildings and public spaces are often used to enforce separation and maintain social hierarchies.

Recognizing and understanding the role of architecture in promoting or perpetuating segregation is crucial. This understanding can help us challenge existing norms, encourage dialogue, and inspire us to envision a built environment that is more inclusive, equitable, and just. It is this journey that we will embark on, examining how we have used architecture to divide and asking how we might use it to unite.

OVERVIEW OF THE BUILT ENVIRONMENT, ARCHITECTURE, AND ITS ROLE

The built environment refers to human-made surroundings that provide the settings for our activities. These surroundings range from our homes, schools, workplaces, and parks to the neighborhoods, towns, cities, and regions that encompass them. Each of these spaces is designed with a purpose, and that purpose is often communicated and achieved through architecture.

Architecture is the art and science of designing and constructing buildings, structures, and spaces that serve various human needs.[3] The buildings we live in, the offices we work in, and the public spaces we gather in are architectural constructs that shape and influence our lives.

Architecture plays an essential role in how we perceive and interact with our environment. It provides a physical manifestation of the cultural, economic, and social aspects of our societies. The design and structure of buildings and spaces can convey power, evoke emotions, and guide behavior. The use of space, light, color, materials, and scale can all influence our experiences and interactions within a built environment.

The layout and design of our communities, cities, and public spaces also influence how we move, interact, and connect with each other. The built environment can facilitate or restrict these interactions, affecting our access to resources, our sense of community, and even our health and well-being.

In essence, architecture has the power to shape our societies. It can create spaces that encourage interaction and inclusivity, or it can construct barriers that isolate and segregate. The design of our built environment can reflect our values and biases, often encoding them into the very fabric of our cities and communities.

However, architecture is not just a tool for shaping society; it is also shaped by it. The design and structure of our built environment are influenced by a variety of factors, including economics, politics, culture, and social norms. These factors can impact architectural decisions, leading to the creation of spaces that reflect and reinforce existing social hierarchies and divisions.

As we will explore throughout this book, one of the most striking and enduring manifestations of this dynamic is the role of architecture in enforcing segregation. Whether through overt racial segregation laws or subtler forms of socioeconomic segregation, the built environment has often been used as a tool to separate, divide, and isolate. Understanding this aspect of architecture and its impact on our societies is a critical step toward creating a more equitable and inclusive future.

IMPORTANCE OF UNDERSTANDING THE PSYCHOLOGICAL ASPECTS OF ARCHITECTURE IN RELATION TO SEGREGATION

In the study of architecture and segregation, it is crucial to consider the psychological aspects and effects of built environments. The physical layout and design of a space can significantly influence the behavior, emotions, and mental well-being of its inhabitants. This influence becomes even more profound when applied to the context of segregated spaces.

- **Gestalt Psychology:** A psychology of mind that was derived from the Berlin School of Experimental Psychology. The word Gestalt translates into the word "shape or form" and is an attempt to rationalize and derive thoughtful perceptions in a chaotic world.[4] The whole (referring to the concept that drives the entire design process of a building) has a reality of its own, independent of the parts that make up the whole. This means that the whole is something different than the sum of its parts. When an architect designs a building, there is that initial concept that drives the entire design process. This creative thought or conception could be construed as Gestalt. Once this design is developed further, the individual parts take on a different purpose or task that contributes to the whole. These separate parts have their own purpose and function, sometimes anonymously from other parts and even the whole. Suppose an architect creates a building with thoughts of separating or segregating spaces to keep activities, security, functionality, and people within their respective areas. These forms can be seen in highly sensitive buildings such as prisons, maximum detention facilities, weapons vaults, classified storage warehouses, and high-hazard compartment chambers. With the focus of this chapter, how does segregation of peoples make its way into this thinking, and shaping or formulation of space making associated with Gestalt? We contend that since the architect, during whichever period he or she lived, was influenced by the culture and sentiments at that time. They would create buildings with an inherent bias and propagate those beliefs onto the final structure. If said architect designed for a private, public, or governmental agency, there would be a need to justify that design to the Owner. The architect has a conscience and should utilize that faculty when a building is in the design phase, but even at the highest level of technology and intelligence, the human has failed to lean towards that moral high ground. This was obvious in the King's courts, Jewish Ghettos, stepped temples, slave quarters, and immigrant holding facilities.

- **Perception and Experience of Space:** The way we perceive and experience a space can be largely shaped by architectural design. For instance, the use of light, color, materials, and spatial layout can all affect how welcoming or threatening a space feels. In the context of segregation, this may mean that certain areas are designed to be intentionally off-putting or uncomfortable for specific groups, acting as psychological barriers that reinforce physical ones.
- **Influence on Behavior:** Architecture can subtly guide or influence behavior. For example, the placement of pathways, the layout of rooms, or the height of ceilings can encourage or discourage certain activities. In segregated environments, these design choices can often subtly reinforce segregation by guiding different social groups into separate spaces.
- **Identity and Belonging:** Architecture plays a critical role in establishing a sense of identity and belonging. Buildings and spaces

often serve as a reflection of the cultural, social, and historical context of a community. When architecture is used to segregate, it can exclude certain groups from these shared spaces and histories, creating a strong sense of "us versus them."

- **Psychological Well-Being:** Lastly, the design of the built environment has a direct impact on mental health. Research has shown that factors such as access to natural light and green spaces, the presence of noise and pollution, and the availability of communal spaces can all significantly affect mood, stress levels, and overall mental well-being. Segregation in architecture often results in unequal access to positive design elements, leading to disparities in mental health outcomes.

Understanding these psychological aspects of architecture provides crucial insights into how segregation operates and is experienced on a day-to-day basis. It highlights how architecture is not just a passive backdrop to our lives but an active participant that shapes our experiences, behaviors, and well-being. By incorporating this understanding, architects and urban planners can better work towards creating spaces that promote inclusivity, well-being, and social equity.

02

"You must unlearn what you have learned."

Yoda

ENTOMOLOGY OF SEGREGATION

SEGREGATION AND THE BUILT ENVIRONMENT

EARLY FORMS OF SEGREGATION AND THEIR IMPACT ON THE BUILT ENVIRONMENT

The origins of segregation stretch back to ancient times, with numerous societies creating explicit or implicit spatial divisions based on factors such as social status, profession, gender, and ethnic group. This practice has taken two primary forms:

De Jure Segregation: This is segregation enforced by law with certain areas or facilities designated for use by specific groups. It has been a tool for maintaining power structures and enforcing social hierarchies.[1]

De Facto Segregation: This form of segregation arises naturally from societal behavior and customs rather than legislation. It can be just as pervasive and difficult to overcome as de jure segregation, particularly when ingrained societal biases and prejudices are present.[2]

Understanding these types of segregation helps to clarify how they have shaped the built environment throughout history.

SEGREGATION IN ANCIENT CIVILIZATIONS AND EXAMPLES OF SPATIAL DIVISIONS IN ANCIENT CITIES

The earliest known examples of urban planning in ancient civilizations display clear signs of segregation. Ancient civilizations, such as the Romans, Greeks, and Egyptians, often separated their cities into distinct districts for different functions and classes. The elite usually resided in the city center, close to temples and public buildings, while workers and slaves were housed in the periphery. This form of segregation was predominantly de facto, driven by socioeconomic factors rather than explicit laws.

One example of spatial divisions in ancient cities is the city of Rome. During the Roman Empire, the city was divided into "insulae," or city blocks, with varying types of housing.³ Wealthy citizens resided in "domus," large, spacious homes, usually in the city center. The lower classes, on the other hand, lived in crowded "insulas," or apartment buildings on the outskirts of the city.

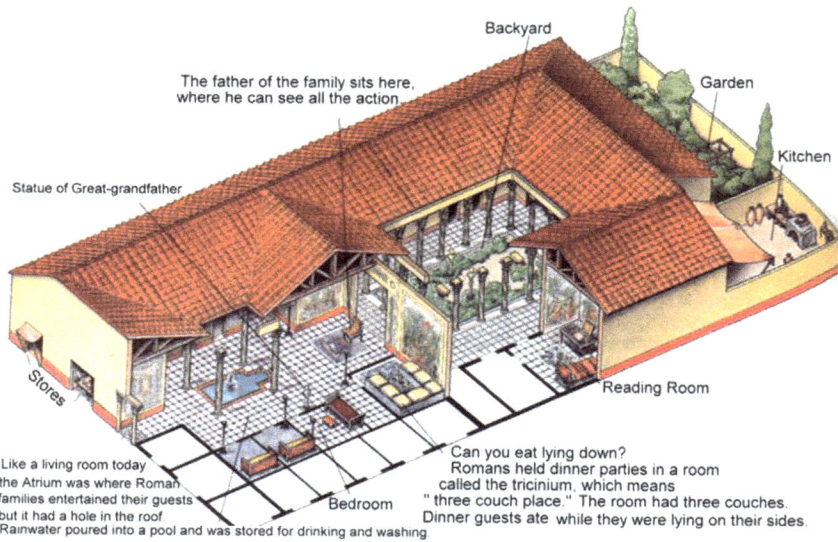

A cut-away image of a typical Roman domus. By JFJP. Wikipedia and Worldhistory.org

A typical insula dating from the early 2nd century AD. Credit: Zor. Forums.spacebattles.com

Another example is the ancient city of Miletus, in what is now Turkey. The city was divided into distinct districts for residential, commercial, and religious purposes, with additional separation based on the social status of inhabitants.[4]

Miletus, Turkey 1837. Wikimedia.

These early forms of segregation have had a significant impact on the built environment. They laid the foundations for city planning and architecture, influencing the way societies structure their cities and buildings. They also contributed to socioeconomic inequalities, as access to public goods, services, and opportunities often depended on where one lived within the city.

RACIAL AND SOCIAL SEGREGATION IN COLONIAL CITIES

The period of colonial expansion, particularly by European powers from the 15th to the 20th century, led to an intensification of segregation along racial and social lines. This was especially evident in colonial cities in the Americas, Africa, and Asia, where urban planning was used as a tool to establish and maintain control over colonized populations.

In these cities, separation was often based on race, with colonizers residing in central areas while indigenous populations and slaves were forced to live in peripheral regions. This was a form of de jure segregation, with colonial authorities using legislation to enforce these divisions. Social segregation was also rampant, as the built environment reflected and reinforced the hierarchies that privileged the colonizers over the colonized.

ARCHITECTURAL MANIFESTATIONS OF SEGREGATION DURING THE COLONIAL ERA

During the colonial era, architecture became a potent tool to express power, control, and racial supremacy. Segregation was evident in the layout of cities and the design of buildings, which often mirrored the social and racial hierarchies of the time.

In colonial cities, European quarters were typically characterized by well-planned streets, grand public buildings, and spacious villas. These areas were designed to replicate the architecture of the colonizers' home countries, serving as a constant reminder of their cultural and racial dominance.

On the other hand, the districts where the indigenous populations and slaves lived were often poorly planned and equipped, with cramped housing and limited access to essential facilities. These architectural disparities further entrenched social and economic inequalities.

An example is the city of Cape Town in South Africa, where the "City Bowl" area, located at the foot of Table Mountain, housed the Dutch colonial administrators and settlers, while the outlying townships were populated by indigenous Africans and imported slaves.

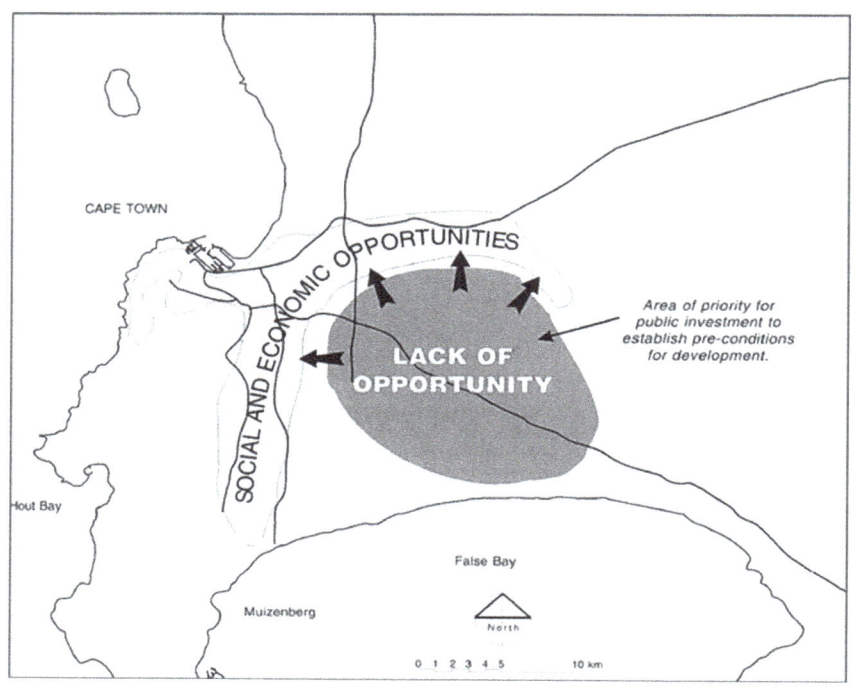

Cape Town's uneven development. Source: David Damiel's conference presentation, April 1993. Social Inequality and Spatial Segregation. ResearchGate.net

The City Bowl area of Cape Town and Table Mountain are seen from the roof of the Strand South Hotel. Photographed by Daniel Case, July 2018. Wikipedia.

Similarly, in cities like Delhi, India, and Hanoi, Vietnam, the colonizers (British and French, respectively) built spacious, planned districts with all the amenities for themselves, while the local populations were pushed to less desirable areas.

The French Governor of Tonkin residence in Hanoi, Vietnam in 1945. Wikipedia.

INDUSTRIALIZATION AND URBANIZATION

Emergence of Segregated Neighborhoods and City Planning

With the advent of the Industrial Revolution in the late 18th century, cities experienced significant growth and transformation. Industrialization brought about an immense demand for labor, leading to rural-urban migration and rapid urbanization. As cities grew in size and complexity, so did the social and economic disparities among their residents.

The growth of industries in urban areas led to the concentration of factories in certain districts, and poor working-class families, often immigrants, lived in overcrowded and squalid conditions near these industrial zones. Meanwhile, the middle and upper classes moved to cleaner, more spacious suburbs, marking the beginnings of modern urban segregation.

City planning emerged as a discipline during this period, partly as a response to the challenges presented by rapid urbanization. Many planners at the time held the belief that the physical environment could influence the behavior and health of city dwellers. Hence, they used city planning as a tool to manage the "social disorder" associated with industrialization.

The plan for Paris by Baron Haussmann in the mid-19th century, for example, aimed to eliminate overcrowded and disease-ridden areas of the city. However, it also effectively displaced the poor and pushed them to the city's outskirts. These city transformations, while often lauded for improving living conditions, inadvertently reinforced and institutionalized segregation by creating distinct neighborhoods based on class and economic status.[5]

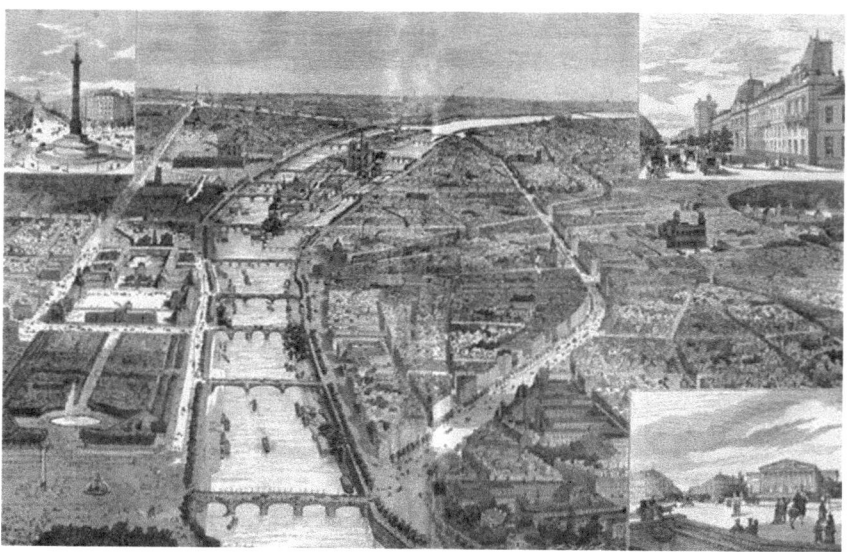

Bird's-eye view of Paris (1878) with the new Boulevard Saint-Germain on the right. From the Brown University Library. Wikipedia.

The Rue du Jardinet on the Left Bank, demolished by Haussmann to make room for the Boulevard Saint Germain, circa 1853 - 1870. By Charles Marville. Wikimedia.

Case Studies of Urban Planning Influenced by Segregation

1. Chicago, USA

Chicago, a major industrial city in the USA, serves as a vivid example of urban planning influenced by segregation. Following the Great Chicago Fire in 1871, the city was rebuilt with a distinct division between the working-class and the wealthy neighborhoods. Later, during the Great Migration of African Americans from the rural South to the industrial North between 1916 and 1970, racial segregation became further entrenched in the city's layout.

"White flight" was a phenomenon where white residents moved to the suburbs due to an influx of non-white residents, exacerbating segregation.[6] Predatory housing policies like redlining (refusing loans or insurance within specific geographic areas, generally racially determined) and restrictive covenants (agreements prohibiting property owners from selling to certain racial or ethnic groups) further entrenched this racial segregation.

2. Johannesburg, South Africa

The apartheid regime in South Africa led to one of the most extreme examples of urban planning influenced by segregation. Racial segregation was legislated and meticulously implemented in urban areas. Johannesburg, the country's largest city, was divided into distinct racial zones: white areas were situated in desirable locations, while black Africans were displaced to townships on the city's outskirts like Soweto, often far from work and with limited services. This spatial segregation, enforced by the Group Areas Act of 1950, deeply impacted the city's social and economic structure, the effects of which are still visible today.

Through these case studies, we can clearly observe how urban planning has been utilized as a tool for segregation, whether based on class, race, or economic status. The built environment, as a product of this planning, thus carries the imprint of these socio-political dynamics. How does this affect human behavior and perceived stigma?

03

"We live in a rainbow of chaos."

Paul Cezanne

PSYCHOLOGICAL ASPECTS OF ARCHITECTURE

PSYCHOLOGY OF SEGREGATION

Principles of Order in Architecture

Before we delve into the individual aspects of architecture and their psychological impact in the context of segregation, it is crucial to understand the guiding principles of order in architecture. These principles, which include axis, symmetry, hierarchy, transformation, datum, rhythm, pattern, and repetition, underpin how architectural spaces are designed and subsequently perceived and experienced.[1] They are integral to creating order, coherence, and meaning in the built environment.

Axis: This principle refers to an imaginary line used to organize a design or connect different architectural elements. In both monumental architecture and urban planning, the axis has often been used to create a sense of direction or to highlight significant views or structures.

Symmetry: The mirroring of elements on either side of an axis. It is a common feature in architecture, often used to convey balance, harmony, and stability. Symmetry can also serve to highlight the importance of the central axis and the elements along it.

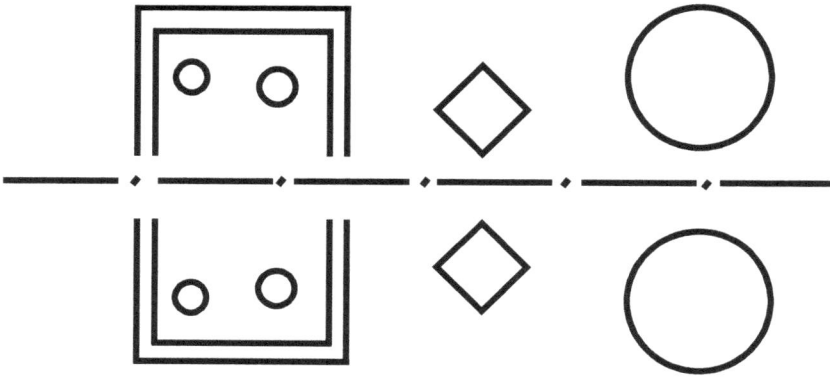

Hierarchy: In architecture, hierarchy involves the arrangement of elements in a way that signifies their relative importance. This can be achieved through differences in size, placement, style, or color among other factors. It is a powerful tool to indicate the prominence or priority of architectural spaces or elements.

Transformation: This refers to the adaptation or evolution of a basic architectural element or motif. By adjusting its scale, orientation, or other characteristics, architects can create variety and dynamism while maintaining a sense of unity in a design.

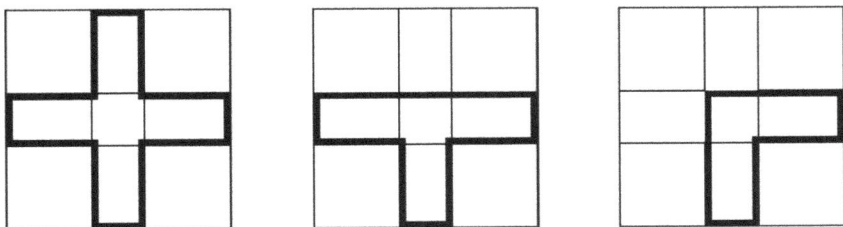

Datum: In architecture, a datum is a reference point or line that helps organize the layout of a building or a group of buildings. It can provide a sense of order and orientation, helping users to navigate and understand the space.

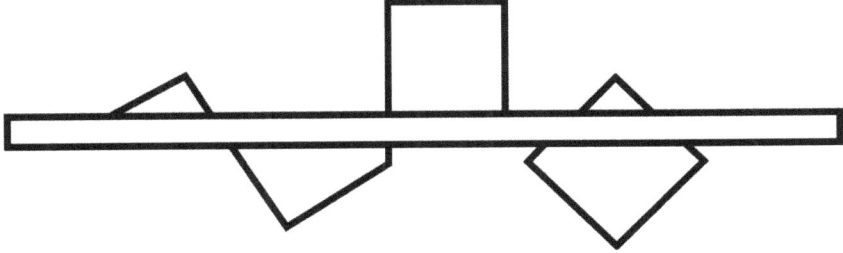

Rhythm: Rhythm in architecture is the repeated use of elements with an interval or sequence. It can create a sense of movement or flow in a building or urban landscape.

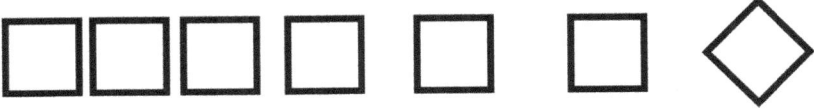

Pattern: Patterns involve repetition or arrangement of elements in a predictable manner. They can contribute to the visual interest, unity, and identity of a design.

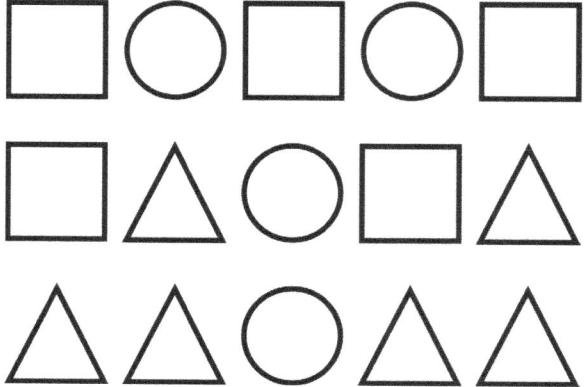

Repetition: Repetition involves using the same elements or motifs multiple times throughout a design. It can create a sense of unity, order, and rhythm.

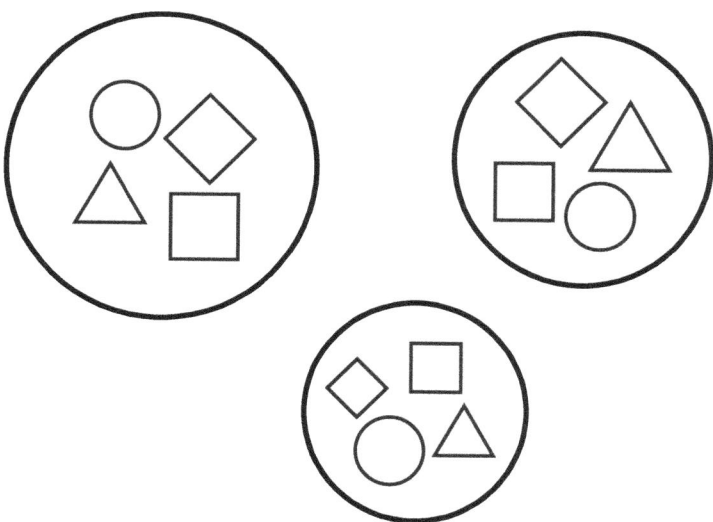

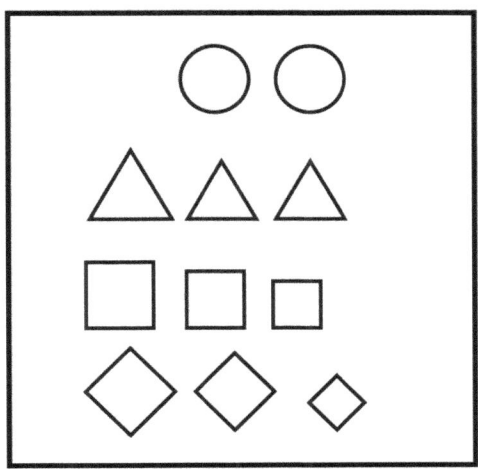

Images from "Architecture, Form, Space and Order" by Francis D.K. Ching (2007).

Understanding these principles is essential as they subtly shape how people interact with and perceive architectural spaces. For instance, a prominently placed, large-scale building on a central axis may convey a sense of importance and authority, potentially intimidating or excluding certain social groups.

Segregated communities often feature built environments that reinforce the social and economic disparities between them. The use of hierarchy, axis, and datum in architecture can psychologically reinforce these divisions. For example, the axis might lead to monuments or important buildings that are accessible to only one section of the community, reinforcing the notion of exclusion. Datum can also be applied to the construction of the Eisenhower Federal-Aid Highway Act of 1956. U.S. Highway and Interstate System, whereas in the name of Urban Renewal, sought to provide a more accessible route to connect and stitch together a more efficient way to transport the booming automobile revolution.

The Clay Committee submitted its report to President Eisenhower on January 11, 1955, offering recommendations regarding the funding of a nationwide interstate highway system. U.S. department of Transportation.

Since railroad service was the predominant mode of moving large quantities of people, goods, and services throughout the U.S., the need to modify and expand this new method of transportation—which would include people commuting to work and transporting of commodities, goods, and materials[2]—needed to be more organized. Although this system was held as a successful feat of ingenuity and construction technologies, these routes were often designed to seize land and occupy areas of towns that were primarily African American central business districts and neighborhoods.

Aerial photo of San Francisco on July 2, 1959: Highway 101 and Interstate 280 Interchange still under construction. Duke Downey/ The Chronicle 1959.

The effects of the interstate system on minority communities were deeply felt; they destroyed many of those communities' legacies and their heritage by being permanently dismantled.

Symmetry can be used to create an illusion of fairness and balance, while hiding imbalances in access and opportunities. Repetition and pattern in housing units might reflect monotony and a lack of individuality, often associated with marginalized or lower-income communities.

These principles of order do not inherently lead to segregation, but when used without thoughtful consideration of the broader social context, they can inadvertently contribute to it.

A. Perception and Psychological Impact of Segregated Spaces

The built environment profoundly influences our perceptions, behaviors, and overall well-being. Its impact becomes more evident when we consider the architecture of segregated spaces and its psychological effects on the occupants.

The example of St. Elizabeth's Hospital, as detailed in the article "Architecture of an Asylum,"[3] provides a compelling illustration of how architectural decisions and the subsequent changes in the built environment impact those inhabiting the space. This historical case illustrates the potential and the pitfalls of using architecture as a tool for treatment.

Initially, the hospital was designed with a profound understanding of the therapeutic value of architecture. The emphasis on natural light and outdoor views was meant to enhance patients' well-being and help them feel connected to society. This architectural intent showcases how spaces can be designed to influence positive social behavior and attitudes.

The Center Building at St. Elizabeth's, pictured circa 1900. Image courtesy of The National Building Museum.

However, segregation within the hospital—racial and gender-based—disrupted this intent. Despite the design's general focus on humane treatment, African American patients and women had access to inferior facilities compared to their white and male counterparts.[4] This is a poignant example of how architectural spaces can reflect and perpetuate social inequalities and biases.

1. Influence of Architecture on Social Behavior and Attitudes

Architecture can subtly influence our social behavior and attitudes. An inviting, open space can promote interaction and social cohesion, while a restrictive, oppressive environment can promote exclusion and division.

In the case of St. Elizabeth's, the segregated spaces within the hospital likely had a significant impact on the patients' social behavior and attitudes. The physical segregation mirrored and possibly reinforced the social and racial divisions of the broader society, exacerbating feelings of inequality and isolation among the marginalized patients.

2. Impact of Physical Barriers on Mental Health and Well-Being

Physical barriers in the built environment, like walls or fences, have more than just a practical impact; they also have a psychological one. These barriers can symbolize and enforce separation, division, and inequality, leading to feelings of isolation, stigmatization, and alienation.

Overcrowding and the subsequent neglect at St. Elizabeth's, fueled by shifts in mental health treatment and reduced government support, further illustrate how the built environment can negatively impact mental health. The conditions within the hospital likely contributed to the stress and discomfort experienced by the patients, undermining the healing and recovery process.

The story of St. Elizabeth's serves as a stark reminder of the psychological effects that architecture and the built environment can have, particularly within segregated contexts. Understanding these effects can inform more empathetic, inclusive design strategies that consider the well-being of all users, regardless of their social, racial, or economic status.

Symbolism and Power Dynamics in Architectural Design

Architecture is more than just creating functional spaces for people; it is also about communicating ideas, beliefs, and power structures. Buildings and their designs can serve as powerful symbols that reflect and reinforce the prevailing societal hierarchies and power dynamics.

In segregation, these power dynamics become even more apparent as architecture is often used as a tool to exert control, divide, and create and maintain boundaries. The segregation of spaces is not just a reflection of social and racial divides but also a reinforcement of the power structures that uphold these divisions.

Seven Ideals in Modern and Present-Day Structures

Modern and present-day architectural design is guided by several key principles or ideals.

- **Hierarchy:** In architecture, hierarchy refers to the way elements and spaces are arranged to indicate importance. This can be achieved through size, positioning, design, or the use of distinctive features. In a city, a towering skyscraper may denote economic power, while in a home, a large, centrally located family room might denote the importance of communal living.

Empire State Building, New York, by Shreve, Lamb, & Harmon (1931). Weebly.com

- **Approach:** Approach refers to the way a person moves towards and enters a building. The approach is significant as it sets the tone for the overall experience of the building. It can range from a grand, imposing entrance to a discreet, understated one, each conveying different emotions and responses.

Water Temple is home to the oldest sect of Tantric Buddhism in Japan completed in 1991. Architect: Tadao Ando. This sense of arrival begins when approaching the temple from the dense forest and hills and seeing the concrete wall, which informs where to travel to the procession. Wikiarquitectura.

Psychological Aspects of Architecture

- **Proportion:** Proportion concerns the balance between the different elements of a structure. Good proportion contributes to the aesthetic harmony of a building, making it pleasing to the eye and comfortable to inhabit.

Drayton Hall Plantation House, Charleston, SC. Author: Goingstuckey. Wikimedia.

- **Light:** Light plays a vital role in architecture, influencing the mood, perception, and functionality of a space. The manipulation of natural and artificial light can drastically alter the experience of a building.

Chapel of Notre Dame du Haut, Ronchamp, France. Architect: Le Corbusier. Photo by Ed Tyler. Ribaj.com

- **Functionality:** This principle refers to the practical aspect of a building's design. The design should effectively serve the purpose for which it was intended, whether it's a home, office, or public space.

The Pompidou Centre in Paris, France has a radical design that places the structural and mechanical building systems on the exterior allowing more interior space to be used for exhibitions. This Postmodernism Style was designed by Architects Renzo Piano, Richard Rogers, and Gianfranco Franchini, and completed in 1977. Wikipedia.

- **Materiality:** The choice of materials can significantly influence a building's character, aesthetic appeal, and durability. Materiality involves considering the tactile experience, the visual appeal, and the longevity and sustainability of materials used.

The Heydar Aliyev Center in Baku, Azerbaijan (Glass Fibre Reinforced Polyester (GFRP) used to create an almost seamless flowing exterior). Architect: Zaha Hadid. Wikipedia.

- **Symbolism:** Symbolism in architecture involves using design elements to convey certain ideas or beliefs. Buildings often symbolize values such as power, prestige, or community. In the context of segregation, architectural symbolism can be used to denote and reinforce societal divisions.

Falling Water designed by Frank Lloyd Wright, symbolizing the harmony between people and nature. Source: Wikipedia.

These principles guide the design process and influence how spaces are perceived and experienced. By understanding these ideals, architects can create spaces that are functional and aesthetically pleasing and mindful of the broader societal context and its implications. With a strong set of principles, what could possibly go wrong?

04

"I did then what I knew how to do. Now that I know better, I do better."

Maya Angelou

"WHO...ME?"

ARCHITECT AS COLLABORATOR

A. Historical Examples of Segregated Architectural Designs

Throughout history, architecture has played a significant role in facilitating and reinforcing segregation. Whether intended or unintentionally, the built environment often reflects and shapes the social, racial, and economic divisions in society. Here are a few historical examples, some of which have been briefly mentioned in the preceding chapters:

- **Ancient Rome:** The Roman Colosseum, built in the first century AD, was designed with a clear hierarchy. Senators had their designated marble benches in the lower rows while slaves and women were only allowed in the upper sections, physically illustrating the social hierarchy of Roman society.

Interior of the Colosseum by late nineteenth-century photographer Francis Frith. Wikipedia.

- **American Slave Cabins:** In the antebellum South of the United States, the layout of plantations often mirrored the harsh social hierarchy. Slave cabins were typically small, rudimentary, and located farther from the main house, starkly contrasting the grandeur and proximity of the owners' residences. This architectural layout served to reinforce the racial and social divide.

Early 20th-century view of the slave quarters when used to house paid laborers and their families. Hampton, Maryland. National Park Service.

- **Apartheid South Africa:** In the mid-20th century, South Africa's apartheid regime utilized architecture and urban planning as tools for segregation. Black South Africans were forced to live in separate townships on the outskirts of cities, typically far from economic opportunities and amenities. The architecture of these townships reflected the government's intention to isolate and control the black population.[1]

Khayelitsha township, Cape Town, where blacks were sent during apartheid. Folha De S.Paulo.

- **Redlining in the United States:** During the 20th century, redlining—a discriminatory practice where services (such as loans and insurance) were denied to residents of certain areas based on racial or ethnic composition—shaped the built environment in many American cities. Minority neighborhoods, marked in red on maps by lenders, were often deprived of investment and development opportunities. Over time, these areas became physically distinguishable due to their poorer quality of housing and infrastructure.

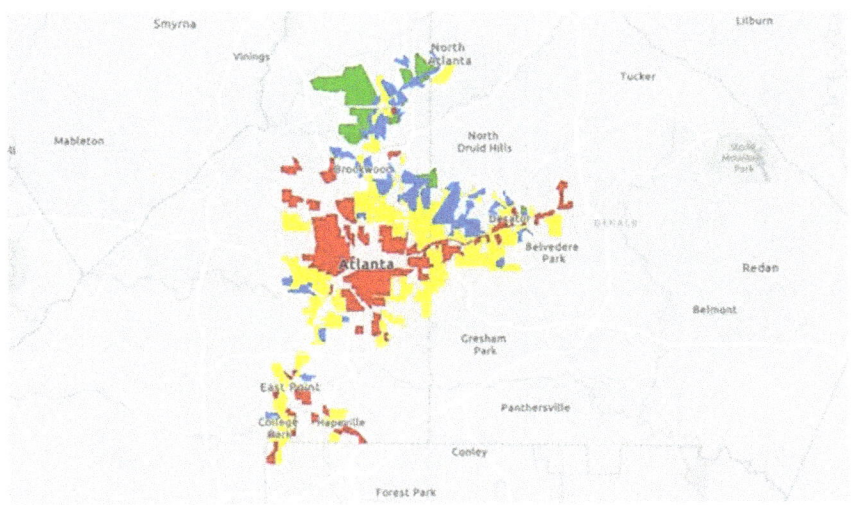

This map layer depicts the government classification of neighborhoods which impacted available government-insured financing. Map by National Geographic.

Green – Best • Blue – Desirable • Yellow – Declining • Red – Hazardous

- **Gated Communities:** In recent years, the rise of gated communities worldwide can be seen as a modern form of architectural segregation. These "fortress-like" residential areas are designed to separate their inhabitants from the rest of the urban fabric, creating a physical and symbolic barrier based on class and, often, racial lines.

Entrance to a guarded gated community in Saskatoon, Saskatchewan, Canada. Wikipedia.

- **The Jewish Ghettos of Europe:** The ghettos established in European cities during the Middle Ages and later during the Holocaust are tragic examples of forced segregation. These were neighborhoods where Jews were compelled to live, separated from the rest of society by walls or other physical barriers. The ghettos were often cramped, with poor living conditions and a lack of basic amenities. They serve as potent reminders of how architecture and urban planning can be manipulated to marginalize and persecute minority communities.

Jewish ghettos established in Riga, Latvia after Soviet Union annexed in 1940. UShmm.org

- **Colonial Architecture in India:** British colonial rule in India led to the creation of "White Towns" and "Black Towns" in many Indian cities. The "White Towns" were well-planned, had better infrastructure, and were reserved for British officials and citizens. The "Black Towns," where the local Indian population lived, were often characterized by overcrowding and inferior infrastructure. These spatial divisions accentuated and perpetuated the social and racial segregation imposed by the colonial regime.[2]

Black town, Madras, India in 1851. Wikimedia.

George Town, Madras. Author: Herman Moll. Wikimedia.

- **Segregation Walls in Northern Ireland:** Often known as "peace walls," these barriers were built to separate Catholic and Protestant neighborhoods in Belfast and other cities during the period known as The Troubles.[3] Despite their intended purpose to reduce violence, these walls have reinforced sectarian divides and continue to shape the urban landscape.

5.5-metre-high (18-foot) peace line along Springmartin Road in Belfast, with a fortified police station at one end. Author: Ross. Wikimedia.

- **Internment Camps during World War II:** In the United States, internment camps were established during World War II for Japanese-Americans, most of whom were U.S. citizens. The camps were often located in remote, desolate areas and were surrounded by barbed wire and guard towers, signifying a clear intention to segregate and confine.

Internment Camp in Crystal City. Courtesy of the Texas Historical Commission.

- **Favelas in Brazil:** The favelas in Brazilian cities like Rio de Janeiro are another example of spatial segregation, although not enforced by law. These informal settlements, often lacking proper infrastructure and services, house a significant portion of the city's poor population, separated from the wealthier neighborhoods that are better planned and equipped.

Inside Rocinha favela, Rio de Janeiro, Brazil, 2010. Author: Chensiyuan. Wikimedia.

These examples illustrate how architecture and urban planning have been used as tools to segregate and marginalize certain groups. It's important to understand these historical contexts as they continue to shape our built environments and influence our approach to inclusive, equitable design.

B. Impact of Architecture on Social Hierarchies and Power Dynamics

In any society, architecture and urban planning play a significant role in defining social hierarchies and power dynamics. The design and layout of buildings, neighborhoods, and cities can amplify or diminish social inequalities, influencing how people interact with each other and perceive their places in society.

Architectural Exclusion and Control

Architecture can enforce social hierarchies through exclusion and control. Physical barriers such as walls, gates, highways, or lack of public transportation can restrict access to certain areas. For example, gated communities or luxury condominiums reinforce economic disparities by physically separating the wealthy from the poor. On a larger scale, the location and design of neighborhoods can limit access to quality schools, healthcare, and job opportunities, further entrenching social hierarchies.

The way public spaces are designed can also control how people use them. For instance, park benches with dividers prevent people from lying down, targeting homeless individuals. This phenomenon, often termed "hostile architecture," [4] subtly enforces societal norms and hierarchies.

A homeless man tries to sleep on a hostile designed bench in downtown LA. Photo by Tyler Nix on Unsplash. Realchangenews.org

Symbolism and Status

Architecture is a powerful symbol of status and power. Grand edifices like palaces, government buildings, or corporate headquarters are designed to impress and even intimidate, reinforcing the power of the rulers, the state, or the corporate world. Even residential architecture, from the size and opulence of one's home to the neighborhood one resides in, serves as a status symbol and a reflection of one's position in the social hierarchy.

Segregation and Alienation

As discussed in previous examples, architecture can segregate communities along racial, economic, or social lines, fostering an environment of "us versus them." This segregation can breed alienation and mistrust between different groups, exacerbating social tensions.

Standardization and Erasure of Identity

Large-scale, uniform architectural developments, such as public housing projects or suburban developments, can erase local identities and cultures, imposing a top-down power dynamic. This standardization often fails to consider the needs and lifestyles of the communities who live there, creating spaces that are physically inhabitable but psychologically distressing and culturally alienating.

Resistance and Empowerment

On a positive note, architecture can also challenge social hierarchies and empower communities. Participatory design processes that engage community members in planning and designing their environments can democratize architectural practice. Architecture can also celebrate local cultures and identities, promote community cohesion, and provide spaces for social interaction and public discourse.[5]

C. Spatial Segregation in Urban Planning and Design

Spatial segregation in urban planning and design refers to the spatial distribution of population groups, often divided along lines of income, race, ethnicity, or religion within a city or urban area. This segregation has tangible impacts on the built environment, access to services, quality of life, and social mobility of residents.

Historical Development of Spatial Segregation

The advent of industrialization led to the increased growth and complexity of cities. With the rise of factories and industries, cities started to segregate residential areas from commercial and industrial ones for health and safety reasons. Over time, this separation took on a more socioeconomic character. Wealthy individuals tended to cluster in more desirable areas, often removed from the noise and pollution of the industrial sectors, while the working class lived closer to their places of work. The introduction of zoning laws in many cities institutionalized these divisions.

Impact on the Built Environment

Spatial segregation has significant effects on the built environment. In segregated cities, you may see clear differences between neighborhoods in terms of housing quality, density, infrastructure, and access to green spaces. High-income neighborhoods often have larger, high-quality houses, wider streets, more green spaces, and better infrastructure. In contrast, low-income neighborhoods may suffer from overcrowding, poor-quality housing, inadequate infrastructure, and lack of green spaces. These physical manifestations of segregation can exacerbate social and economic disparities.

Access to Services and Opportunities

Spatial segregation often results in unequal access to essential services and opportunities. For example, in many cities, schools are funded through local property taxes, meaning that schools in wealthier neighborhoods have more resources than those in poorer ones. This inequality in educational resources can reinforce and perpetuate socioeconomic disproportion. Similarly, low-income neighborhoods often have fewer healthcare facilities, grocery stores with fresh produce, and recreational amenities.

Mobility and Connectivity

The layout and design of a city can either reinforce or reduce spatial segregation. A well-connected city with good public transportation allows residents from all areas to access jobs, services, and amenities throughout the city. On the other hand, a city with poor public transportation and physical barriers like highways or walls can isolate neighborhoods, limiting their residents' opportunities and reinforcing segregation.

Socio-Political Implications

Spatial segregation can have socio-political implications. It can create a sense of isolation and "otherness" among segregated communities, reduce social cohesion, and lead to political polarization. However, it can also foster a strong sense of identity and community in certain areas, particularly in ethnic or cultural enclaves.

Contemporary Approaches to Spatial Segregation

Contemporary urban planning and design aim to address spatial segregation through various strategies. These include mixed-use development to integrate different functions within neighborhoods, inclusionary zoning policies to encourage affordable housing in all parts of a city, investment in public transportation to improve connectivity, and participatory planning processes to ensure that the needs and voices of all communities are considered.

D. Symbolic Representation of Segregation through Architecture

Architecture, as a medium of human expression, conveys a wide array of messages. The buildings and structures we inhabit are not merely functional entities but also bear symbolic significance. Through form, function, and location, architecture can subtly or explicitly reflect societal dynamics and hierarchies, including those of racial segregation.

Architecture as a Tool for Reinforcing Segregation

Beyond the functional division of space, architecture often plays a symbolic role in reinforcing segregation. For instance, walls, fences, gates, and other physical barriers serve not just to keep people out but also as potent symbols of division and separation. The design and planning of buildings can subtly send messages about who belongs where and reinforce divisions between different social groups.

An example of this can be seen in the residential architecture of the American South during the Jim Crow era. "Shotgun houses," so named because one could theoretically fire a shotgun through the front door and the pellets would exit through the back door without hitting any walls, were a common feature in African American neighborhoods. These houses, which were narrow, small, and packed closely together, were a stark contrast to the spacious, detached houses in white neighborhoods. This difference in architectural styles was a potent symbol of the racial and socioeconomic divides of the era.

Battleground Baptist Church and neighboring shotgun-style houses, Fazendeville, Louisiana, 1960. Wikipedia.

Architects' Involvement in Designing and Implementing Racially Segregated Spaces

Architects, often unwittingly, have been implicated in the creation and perpetuation of segregated spaces. During periods of explicit racial segregation, architects were called upon to design separate, often unequal, facilities for different racial groups. For instance, during apartheid in South Africa, architects designed townships on the periphery of cities where the non-white population was relocated. These townships were designed with minimal amenities and were physically separated from the white-dominated city centers by buffer zones, creating a distinct spatial and symbolic division.

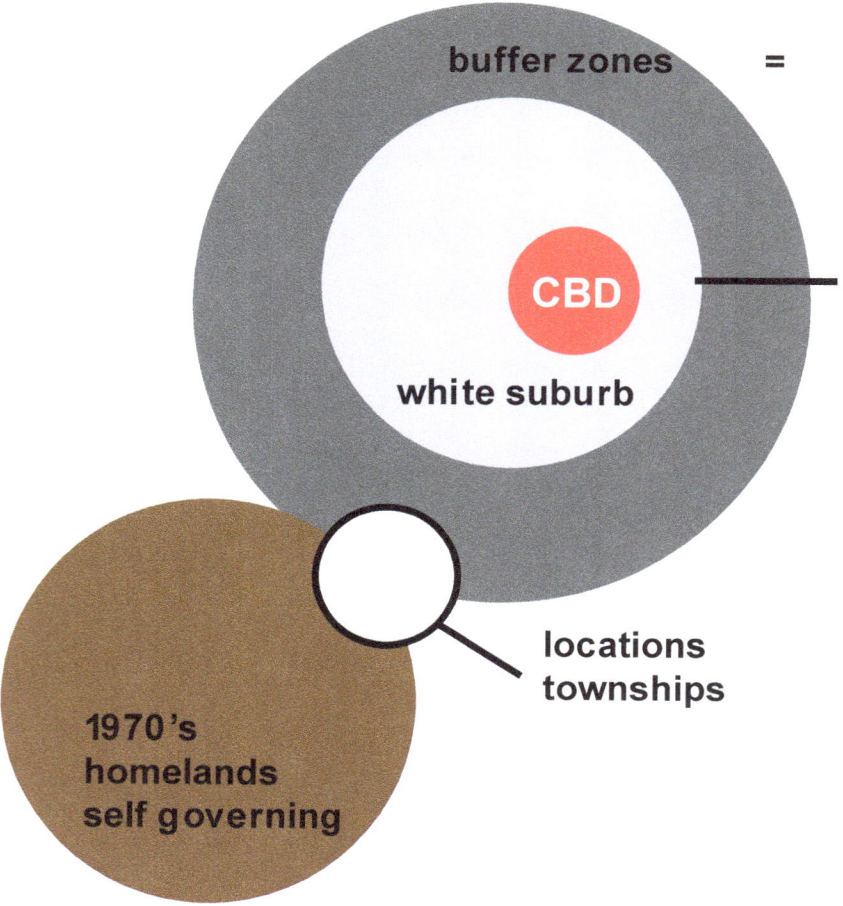

The structure of South African cities inherited from the Apartheid Era. ResearchGate.net

The neighborhoods of Strand and Nomzamo in Cape Town. (Johnny Miller/ Millefoto)

Even in the absence of explicit segregation policies, architects may inadvertently contribute to segregation through design decisions influenced by prevailing societal biases and norms. For instance, the design of public spaces can either encourage or discourage their use by certain groups, depending on factors such as accessibility, safety, comfort, and cultural appropriateness.

In recent years, architects have become more conscious of their role in shaping socially inclusive or exclusive spaces. Many are now committed to "socially conscious" architecture, seeking to design spaces that promote integration, accessibility, and social justice.[6] Nonetheless, the challenge of overcoming historical and ongoing patterns of segregation remains a complex task.

E. Examples of Architectural Projects that Perpetuated Institutionalized Racism

In the landscape of architectural history, several notorious examples underscore how design and planning have been employed to perpetuate institutionalized racism. Buildings, urban layouts, and infrastructure have at times been specifically engineered to reinforce racial segregation and discrimination.

1. Pruitt-Igoe, St. Louis, USA (1954)

Pruitt-Igoe was a large urban housing project first occupied in 1954 in St. Louis, Missouri. It's an infamous example of how architectural planning directly contributed to institutionalized racism. Named after two prominent St. Louisans (Wendell O. Pruitt, an African-American fighter pilot in World War II, and William L. Igoe, a former U.S. Congressman), the project was initially designed to provide modern, affordable housing to low-income families.

Housing for thousands, Pruitt-Igoe Development next to slums in the 1950's. wsws.org

However, Pruitt-Igoe became a significant manifestation of racial segregation, with thirty-three 11-story high-rises in a 57-acre compound housing exclusively African-American families, despite the initial promise of integration. The complex suffered from shoddy construction and poor maintenance. Its remote location, away from the city center and isolated from social amenities, further marginalized the residents. The building's design, with its long, anonymous corridors and limited communal spaces, led to safety concerns and social dislocation. The failure of Pruitt-Igoe, culminating in its demolition less than 20 years after its construction, demonstrated the harmful impacts of neglectful architectural planning on marginalized communities.

2. District Six, Cape Town, South Africa (1867)

The District Six neighborhood in Cape Town, South Africa, provides a chilling example of how architecture and urban planning were exploited during apartheid. Established in 1867, District Six was a vibrant multicultural district, home to a close-knit community of freed slaves, merchants, artisans, immigrants, and laborers.

However, in 1966, District Six was declared a "white" area under the Group Areas Act, leading to the forced eviction of more than 60,000 residents.[7] Homes, shops, and churches were razed to the ground, replaced by sterile apartment buildings and office spaces for the white population. Despite resistance, District Six was entirely remodeled, erasing its rich cultural heritage and scattering its close-knit community.

The vacant land stood as a stark reminder of apartheid's architectural legacy. Post-apartheid, efforts to rebuild District Six and repatriate its former inhabitants have been slow and fraught with challenges, demonstrating the lasting impact of architectural disenfranchisement.

District Six after the removals. Photographer: Jimi Matthews, undated. Saha.org

3. Racist Zoning Laws, USA

The institution of racist zoning laws across the United States in the early 20th century is another example of how architecture and city planning have been weaponized for racial segregation. This practice involved rating neighborhoods according to their "credit risk," leading to the denial of home loans or insurance to households in "riskier" areas, predominantly black neighborhoods. These neighborhoods were literally outlined in red on maps used by banks and other lending institutions.

The legacy of redlining is still evident today, with formerly redlined neighborhoods suffering from significant disparities in wealth, education, and health outcomes. The infrastructure in these areas often lacks investment, contributing to a cycle of poverty and neglect that can be hard to break.

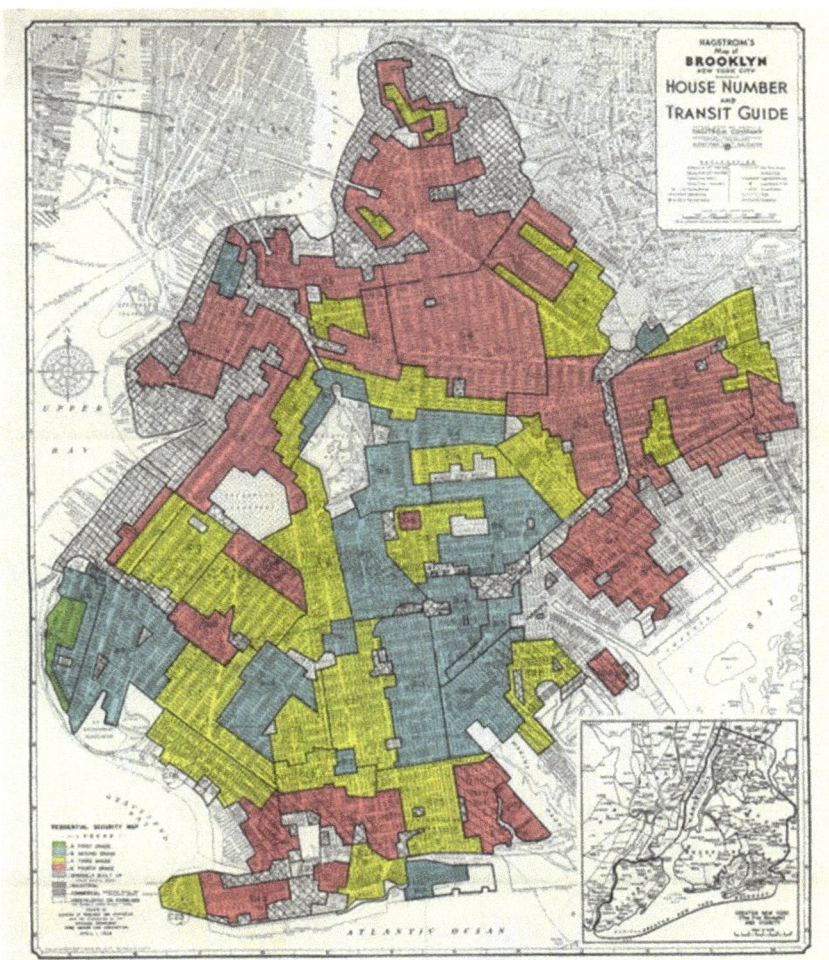
A redlined map of Brooklyn, New York, 1938. Wikimedia.

These examples offer sobering reminders of how architectural planning can reinforce institutionalized racism. While they're a part of our architectural history, it's essential to learn from these past mistakes and strive to create spaces that break down barriers rather than erect them.

Here are some case studies of architectural design perpetuating psychological divisions:

Case Study: West Bank Barrier, Israel-Palestine

The West Bank Barrier, often referred to as the "Apartheid Wall" or "Separation Wall,"[8] presents a notable case study of how architectural design can physically enforce segregation and perpetuate psychological divisions.

Israeli West Bank barrier near Mount Zion in 2009. Author: Kyle Taylor. Wikimedia.

1. Historical Context and Physical Characteristics

The West Bank Barrier's construction began in 2002 during the Second Intifada, with Israel declaring it a necessary security measure against Palestinian attacks. Conversely, Palestinians and their advocates argue that the barrier infringes on their freedom of movement, cuts off communities from essential resources, and facilitates further Israeli territorial annexation.

The structure itself is a complex combination of trenches, electronic fences, vehicle-barrier trenches, and 8-meter (26-foot) high concrete walls. As of now, the barrier's planned 712 km route cuts deep into the West Bank territory, often deviating from the internationally recognized Green Line.[9]

2. Psychological and Socioeconomic Impacts

The imposing architecture of the barrier presents a constant, unavoidable reminder of the Israeli-Palestinian conflict for those living in its shadow. Similar to other barrier walls in the World, such as the U.S.-Mexico Wall, The Berlin Wall, and The Great Wall of China, its physical presence ingrains the concept of "us verses them," fostering animosity, fear, and despair on both sides.

For Palestinians, the wall often separates them from their agricultural lands, jobs, schools, hospitals, and family members. This physical division has severe socioeconomic consequences, including increasing unemployment and poverty rates. The feeling of being "caged in" also exerts significant psychological pressure, leading to heightened stress and reduced community cohesion.

A Palestinian man climbs the ladders to cross the separation wall to reach Jerusalem on May 25, 2018. [Issam Rimawi/Anadolu Agency]. Middleeastmonitor.com

3. Symbolic Power of Architecture

The West Bank Barrier's architecture is replete with symbolism. The towering concrete walls are not just physical barriers; they're visual representations of power dynamics and dominance. The watchtowers, looming over Palestinian towns, are an architectural manifestation of surveillance and control.

The Separation Barrier Guard Tower, Aida Refugee Camp. Twice as tall as the Berlin Wall. Palestinians call it the "Apartheid Wall." CMEP.org

4. Global Reactions and Activism

The wall has sparked international outcry and activism. Artists like Banksy have used the wall as a canvas for politically charged artwork, transforming the symbol of segregation into a platform for resistance and dialogue.[10] Despite these efforts, the wall remains a contentious and divisive structure, underlining the profound impact that architecture can have on societies and individuals.

Banksy's "Dove of Peace" can be seen next to a "Welcome to Palestine" sign. Author: Davide Mauro. Wikipedia.

While the West Bank Barrier stands as an architectural symbol of division and conflict, it also offers essential lessons. It underscores the power of architecture as a tool not only in creating physical spaces, but also in shaping socio-political landscapes and individual psychologies. It stands as a stark reminder of the responsibility that architects and urban planners hold in creating built environments that foster unity rather than division.

Case Study: Cabrini-Green Housing Project, Chicago, USA

The Cabrini-Green Housing Project in Chicago stands as validation of the role of architecture in reinforcing societal divides, institutional racism, and creating psychological barriers. It showcases how public housing projects, originally envisioned as solutions to urban poverty, can become spaces of entrapment and marginalization.

1. Historical Context and Design

The Cabrini-Green Homes, located on the near North Side of Chicago, consisted of a combination of mid and high-rise apartment buildings. The project was initially seen as a beacon of modernist design, with its promise of affordable, clean, and safe living conditions. The design featured open spaces and playgrounds, a stark contrast to the crowded, unhygienic tenements they replaced.

A 1999 photograph looking northeast at the William Green Homes of the Cabrini–Green Housing Project, with visible former right-of-way of Ogden Avenue. Wikimedia.

2. Rise of Crime and Deterioration

However, by the late 1960s, Cabrini-Green had become synonymous with crime, poverty, and racial segregation. The architectural design—common corridors, multiple entries/exits, and a lack of private spaces—unwittingly facilitated criminal activities. The open spaces designed for community interactions became contested territories for gang activities. The poor maintenance of the buildings led to dilapidation, and the promised sense of community never materialized.

3. Psychological Impacts

Living in Cabrini-Green became a stigmatizing experience. The architecture reinforced an "us verses them" dichotomy between residents and the rest of the city, creating a psychological barrier that furthered their sense of isolation and marginalization. The perception of danger and criminality around the project not only impacted the mental health of residents but also their opportunities, as employers were often reluctant to hire residents from the notorious project.

4. Redevelopment and Gentrification

In the 1990s, the City of Chicago embarked on an ambitious plan to demolish Cabrini-Green and other similar projects and replace them with mixed-income housing as part of the "Plan for Transformation." [11] However, this initiative has been fraught with issues. While some original residents have been able to return, many have been displaced due to insufficient affordable units. The redevelopment has also been criticized for making the neighborhood more affluent and less racially diverse.

One of the last towers at Cabrini-Green. Photographed by Richie Diesterheft. Flickr.

5. Lessons and Reflections

Cabrini-Green exemplifies the social and psychological consequences of architectural design and urban planning decisions. While its initial intention was to provide a solution to housing inequality, its implementation ended up perpetuating divisions, reinforcing stigma, and undermining residents' quality of life. It serves as a critical lesson for architects and urban planners, underscoring the importance of considering social dynamics, community input, and long-term sustainability when designing built environments.

Case Study: Pruitt-Igoe Housing Complex, St. Louis, USA

The final case study is that of the Pruitt-Igoe housing complex, briefly discussed above. Pruitt-Igoe, once hailed as a hallmark of modernist architecture and a panacea for housing issues faced by the poor in St. Louis, stands today as a symbol of the failure of public housing policy and the far-reaching impact of design decisions on the quality of life and social dynamics.

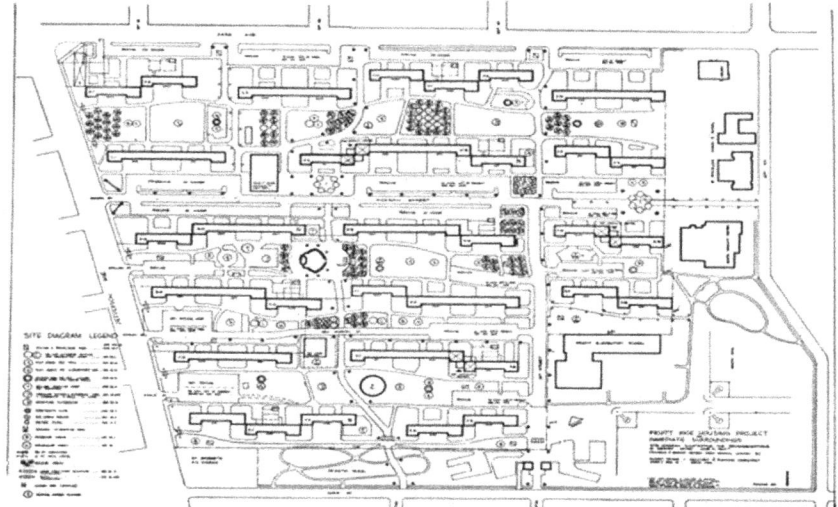

Blueprint of Pruitt-Igoe Development. Opened as "the jewel of modern housing." Weebly.com

1. Design and Vision

Built in 1954, the Pruitt-Igoe project was designed by architect Minoru Yamasaki (who later designed the World Trade Center). The project was conceived as a solution to the overcrowded slums, and was seen as a promising move towards modern, clean-living spaces for the city's poor. The buildings featured skip-stop elevators (which stopped only at certain floors) and communal corridors, reflecting the architects' intention to foster community interactions.

2. Decay and Crime

However, Pruitt-Igoe soon became plagued with maintenance issues, crime, and declining occupancy rates. The communal corridors, instead of promoting socialization, became crime hotspots due to lack of oversight. The skip-stop elevators meant that residents often had to use the stairs, making them vulnerable to crimes. The intended open spaces between the buildings turned into no man's land where law enforcement was difficult.

Abandoned dwellings in the Pruitt-Igoe housing development became the target of vandals. Wikimedia.

3. Psychological Impacts

Like Cabrini-Green, living in Pruitt-Igoe became stigmatized. The architecture and the resulting crime levels created an environment of fear, which took a toll on the residents' mental well-being. The high-rise buildings, disconnected from the street level, fostered a sense of isolation. Furthermore, the decay of the buildings served as a constant reminder to the residents of their socioeconomic status, furthering their sense of marginalization.

4. Demolition and Aftermath

By the late 1960s, most residents had left, and Pruitt-Igoe had become a symbol of failed public housing policy. In 1972, the first of the Pruitt-Igoe buildings was demolished, an event that signaled the end of the modernist public housing era. The site remained vacant for many years and became a haunting reminder of the project's failure.

April 1972. The second, widely televised demolition of a Pruitt–Igoe building that followed the March 16th demolition. Wikipedia.

5. Lessons and Reflections

The story of Pruitt-Igoe offers vital lessons about the connection between architecture, segregation, and social dynamics. It illustrates the importance of understanding the needs and lifestyles of intended residents and the crucial role of ongoing maintenance and management. More importantly, Pruitt-Igoe serves as a stark reminder that architecture alone cannot solve deeply entrenched social and economic issues.

Has this need to separate communities been present since the beginning of structures created by human hands? Let's examine early civilizations and how some of the first humans created societies.

05

"A nation's culture resides in the hearts and in the soul of its people."

Mahatma Gandhi

ARCHITECT AS DECIDER

ARCHITECTURE'S ROLE IN THE DEVELOPMENT OF CIVILIZATIONS

A. Creation of Permanent Structures

Architecture plays an essential role in the advancement of civilizations. The development of permanent structures signals a significant turning point in human history, shifting societies from nomadic lifestyles to settled communities.

1. Neolithic Revolution and the Rise of Permanent Structures

The creation of permanent structures coincided with the Neolithic Revolution, which occurred around 10,000 BCE. This was a period when humans started to abandon the nomadic hunting and gathering lifestyle in favor of agriculture and settlement. With the establishment of farming communities came the need for permanent shelters that could house families, store harvested crops, and offer protection from both the elements and potential adversaries.[1]

House Three at the Neolithic Village of Barnhouse Settlement, Orkney, Scotland. Constructed and occupied 3300-2600 BCE. Photo by Martin McCarthy. Wikipedia.

Knap of Howar Farmstead occupied from 3700 BC to 2800 BC. Orkney, Scotland. Wikipedia.

2. Architectural Development and Societal Growth

The earliest permanent structures were modest and utilitarian, often comprising simple mud-brick homes.

Vernacular buildings in Siwa Oasis, Egypt with small apertures. M.Sc. Thesis - Ain Shams University, Egypt 2013. ResearchGate.net

As societies developed, so did their architecture. Societies began to construct larger, more complex buildings, reflecting not only their growing technical capabilities but also their increasing social complexity. These structures were often indicative of a community's social hierarchy, with larger and more elaborate homes housing wealthier or more influential community members.

The creation of specialized buildings like granaries, temples, and palaces signified a complex societal structure where labor was divided and certain individuals or groups held power. In ancient Egypt, for example, the construction of grand pyramids as tombs for the pharaohs demonstrated both the architectural prowess and the rigid social hierarchy of the civilization.

A view of the Giza Pyramid complex from the plateau to the south of the complex. From left to right, the three largest are: the Pyramid of Menkaure, the Pyramid of Khafre, and the Great Pyramid of Giza. The three smaller pyramids in the foreground are subsidiary structures associated with Menkaure's Pyramid. Author: KennyOMG. Wikimedia.

3. Urbanization and the Expansion of Architecture

As communities grew and formed city-states, architectural endeavors became larger in scale. The planning and creation of cities required significant coordination and resources, and cities' layout and architecture often reflected the prevailing power dynamics. Walls were constructed around cities for defense, and streets were laid out to facilitate trade and transportation.[2]

Public buildings and monuments became prevalent, serving various civic functions and symbolizing the city's wealth and power. Ancient Rome, for instance, was renowned for its advanced urban planning and grand architecture, including the Colosseum, the Pantheon, and an extensive system of roads and aqueducts.

A bird's eye view of the Colosseum showing the 14 aedicules of the Station of the Cross around the arena, 1776, by Piranesi, etching. 53.7cm x 78cm. Bridgeman Images.

View of the Pantheon and the Fontana del Pantheon, Rome, Italy. Author: Rabax63. Wikimedia.

Architect as Decider

These structures not only fulfilled practical needs but also embodied the Roman Empire's ideals and aspirations.

4. Architecture as a Reflection of Cultural Identity

The architecture of a civilization is often a reflection of its cultural values and artistic expressions. From the intricate carvings of temples or "wats" in far east Asia to the geometric designs of Islamic architecture, each civilization has its unique architectural language that communicates its identity.

Carved stonework on the Khmer Empire's Bayon temple located within the Angkor Thom, Cambodia. Built in the late 12th century. Photo by Jerel McCants in 2018.

Fine architectural detail at the Alhambra Palace in Southern Spain. Archway at the Palace. Built in 1238 AD under Muhammad I Ibn al-Ahmar. Author: Yves Remedios. Wikimedia.

These structures serve as indisputable evidence of a civilization's achievements and provide indelible insights into its historical and cultural context.

The creation of permanent structures has been pivotal in human societal development. These structures serve practical purposes, reflect social hierarchies, demonstrate technological advancements, and encapsulate cultural identities. The study of these architectural developments allows us to better understand the progression of civilizations and the human capacity for innovation and creativity.[3]

B. Reflecting Cultural Values and Identity

As aforementioned, architecture is a powerful medium through which a civilization's cultural values, identity, and societal norms are expressed. It demonstrates the way people perceive and interact with their environment, beliefs, aspirations, and societal structure. Each civilization throughout history has left its unique architectural imprint, narrating stories of its cultural fabric and societal evolution.

1. Architectural Language as Cultural Reflection

A civilization's architectural language is more than just the materials used or the structures built; it is an artistic expression of its originality and identity. This language speaks volumes about the civilization's understanding of the world, their technological advancement, religious beliefs, and political power structures.[4]

For instance, the pyramids of Egypt are not only architectural marvels but also expressions of the ancient Egyptians' complex belief systems about death and the afterlife. The grandeur of these structures underlines the power and divinity of the pharaohs, reflecting a society where the pharaoh was at the pinnacle of the social and political hierarchy.

Scrapbook page containing a photograph of a man standing in front of the Pyramids of Giza complex. The page also includes several quotes, drawings of cartouches, and information about the Egyptian dynasties; William Vaughn TupperFlickr uploader BPL, Public domain, via Wikimedia Commons.

2. Architecture and Religion

Architecture has often served as a conduit for expressing religious beliefs. This is evident in the gothic cathedrals of Europe, with their high spires reaching towards the heavens, representing the Christian aspiration for divine connection. Similarly, the intricate geometric patterns and calligraphy in Islamic architecture serve both an aesthetic function and a religious one. They not only beautify the structures but also symbolize the Islamic emphasis on unity, order, and the infinite nature of God.[5]

*Cathédrale Saint-Gatien in Tours, Indre-et-Loire, France.
Author: Rungbachduong. Wikipedia*

The Shah Nematollah Vali Shrine, Mahan, Iran, 1431. Author: Anaareh Saaveh. Wikimedia.

3. Architecture and Social Structure

The architecture of a civilization often mimics its social structure and power dynamics. Castles and fortified structures, common in medieval Europe, highlight a period characterized by Feudalism and frequent warfare. On the other hand, the open courtyards and public baths in Roman architecture demonstrate a society that valued public life and civic engagement.

Bodiam Castle in East Sussex, England. Built in 1392 AD. Established to defend attacks from the French. Author: Antony McCallum. Wikipedia

Remains of the Baths of Trajan, Rome, which was laid over the palace area of Nero. Author: Rabax63. Wikimedia.

4. Adapting to Environment

The architecture of a civilization also exhibits its interaction with and adaptation to its environment. This is clearly seen in the cliff dwellings of the Ancestral Puebloans in the southwestern United States. They demonstrate a harmonious blend with the natural landscape. The stilt houses in Southeast Asia were designed to cope with frequent flooding.

A four-story house built by the Sinagua Tribe about 1,400 BC. Arizona. Author: Phillip Capper. Wikimedia.

City of Yawnghwe in the Inle Lake, Heho, Burma. Author: 3coma14. Wikimedia.

5. Expressing National Identity

In more recent history, architecture has been used to express national identity and inspire unity. For instance, after achieving independence from British rule, India embarked on constructing new architectural projects that merged modern design with traditional Indian elements. This resulted in iconic structures like Le Corbusier's city of Chandigarh, which symbolizes India's progressive vision post-independence.

Palace of Assembly at the Capitol Complex in Chandigarh, India. Author: Duncid. Wikipedia.

Architecture serves as a mirror to a civilization's soul, encapsulating its cultural values and identity. Whether expressing religious beliefs, demonstrating supremacy, or showcasing adaptation to the environment, architecture provides a physical manifestation to understand and appreciate the rich tapestry of human culture and societal evolution.

C. Facilitating Social Organization and Cohesion

Architecture's role extends far beyond mere physical construction. It has the capacity to shape and transform societal structures and bring about social cohesion. It is a potent tool in facilitating social organization, fostering a sense of belonging and shared identity, and cultivating an environment conducive to social interaction and community building.

1. The Architectural Layout and Social Hierarchy

In many ancient civilizations, the architectural layout of settlements was a direct reflection of the society's organization and hierarchy. For instance, in the Indus Valley civilization, the uniformity in urban planning and house sizes suggests an egalitarian society with little wealth differentiation.

Excavated ruins of Mohenjo-daro, Sindh Province, Pakistan, showing the Great Bath in the foreground. Built around 2,500 B.C. Photo by Saqib Qayyum. Kduptonauthor.com

In contrast, the palaces, temples, and public buildings dominating the landscape in ancient Greece, Rome, or Maya civilizations denote a society with well-established social and political hierarchies.

The Erechtheum, western side, Acropolis, Athens, Greece. Author: Jebulon. Wikimedia.

The central plaza of Tikal, Guatemala. By Chensiyuan taken in 2014. Worldhistory.org

2. Architecture and Social Interaction

The way spaces are designed profoundly impacts social interactions. Plazas, parks, and public buildings have long been a part of urban planning, serving as spaces for public gatherings, markets, political debates, or religious ceremonies. These shared spaces cultivate social interaction, community engagement, and a sense of belonging. They also facilitate societal rituals and customs, strengthening the social fabric.[6]

For example, the agora in ancient Greek city-states was a central public space that facilitated open debate, political discourse, and community interaction, integral to their democratic way of life.

What the Athenian Agora looks like today with Acropolis in the background. Author: Mpd01605. Wikimedia.

Remains of the Roman Agora built in Athens during the Roman period. Author: Robert Freeman. Taken in 2010. Wikimedia.

3. Residential Structures and Social Cohesion

Residential structures also play a vital role in fostering social cohesion. Traditional housing structures, such as the longhouses in Borneo or the communal houses of Native American tribes, were designed to accommodate multiple families, promoting cooperation, shared responsibility, and a strong sense of belonging and togetherness.

A modern timber 'Uma Daro' longhouse at Sungai Asap, Belaga District, Sarawak, Malaysia. Many families live in this type of housing. Author: Yukari Fukui. Flickr.com

An "Uma," the traditional communal house of the Mentawai. Located off the coast of Sumatra, Indonesia. Photo by Alex Lapuerta. Wikimedia.

The reconstructed longhouse by Viking Ring Circle. "Trelleborg." Langhus. Norway. Photo by Jens Cederskjold. Wikimedia.

In contrast, modern urban residential designs often aim to balance community interaction with the privacy of individual households. For instance, communal courtyards in Japanese apartment blocks or shared facilities in contemporary co-housing projects encourage social interaction while preserving private spaces.

*Hotakubo housing project in Kumamoto, Japan by Architect Riken Yamamoto. Wikidata
"It challenges traditional notions of community and individuality." Archeyes.com*

4. Architectural Symbols of Shared Identity

Architecture often serves as a potent symbol of shared identity, whether a religious building like a church, mosque, or temple, a national monument, or a local community center. These structures carry deep emotional resonance, becoming focal points for communal solidarity and shared cultural heritage.

5. Healing Architecture

Architecture can also play a role in societal healing, especially post-conflict or disaster. Memorials and monuments can offer spaces for collective mourning and remembrance, aiding in social recovery. Conversely, redesigning public spaces to be inclusive and engaging can help heal societal divisions and positively influence the community.

Architecture, by shaping our environment, significantly influences our social organization and cohesion. From reflecting societal structures to facilitating social interactions, from fostering a sense of shared identity to aiding in societal healing, architecture plays a crucial role in our social lives. It is an indispensable tool in creating sustainable, inclusive, and cohesive societies.

D. Advancing Technological and Engineering Advancements

Architecture has always been at the forefront of technological and engineering advancements, often pushing the boundaries of what is possible and paving the way for societal betterment. As civilizations evolved, so did their architectural practices, reflecting a continuous dialogue between design, technology, and society. This section will explore the central role architecture has played in advancing technological and engineering innovations.

1. Early Architectural Engineering Innovations

Early civilizations demonstrated exceptional engineering prowess in their architecture. The ancient Egyptians, for instance, developed sophisticated construction techniques to build their pyramids, which still attest to their technological abilities. They used principles of geometry, lever systems for lifting heavy stones, and innovative construction processes that are studied and admired to this day.

Average core blocks of the Great Pyramid weigh about 1.5 tons each, and the granite blocks used to roof the burial chambers are estimated to weigh up to 80 tons each. Source: Wikipedia.

Similarly, the Romans were renowned for their architectural innovations, including the arch, the dome, and the use of concrete. The Roman aqueducts and the Pantheon stand as eternal symbols of their engineering ingenuity, enabling the creation of expansive, open interior spaces that had not been possible before.

Pont du Gard seen from the river Gardon. Source: Wikipedia.

2. Influence of Material Innovations

The discovery and exploitation of new materials often led to significant advancements in architecture. The Industrial Revolution, with its innovations in steel and glass manufacturing, revolutionized architectural design. The invention of the Bessemer process in the mid-19th century, for example, allowed for the mass production of steel, leading to the construction of skyscrapers and suspension bridges.[7]

The development of reinforced concrete in the 20th century further transformed architecture, enabling the creation of structures with unprecedented forms and scales, such as Le Corbusier's Villa Savoye or Oscar Niemeyer's Cathedral of Brasília.

3. Modern Technological Advances

In the modern era, technology continues to shape architecture in exceptional ways. The advent of digital design tools, including CAD (Computer-Aided Design) and BIM (Building Information Modeling), has fundamentally changed the architectural design process, allowing for more complex and precise designs. Moreover, the development of sustainable technologies, such as solar panels, green roofs, and energy-efficient materials, is driving the trend towards an environmentally friendly style of architecture.

4. The Future of Architectural Technology

Looking forward, advancements in AI, virtual reality, and 3D printing are set to push architectural possibilities even further. Artificial Intelligence can aid in optimizing design processes, making them more efficient and less error-prone. Virtual Reality can offer immersive design experiences, helping architects and clients visualize spaces before they are built. 3D printing technology holds the promise of revolutionizing construction methods, potentially enabling the rapid and cost-effective creation of complex, custom-designed structures.

Architecture has always been an arena for technological and engineering innovation. It acts as a crucible where design ideas, engineering principles, and technological innovations interact and evolve. This interplay not only influences the built environment but also shapes societal evolution, as new architectural breakthroughs often herald broader changes in the way we live, work, and interact. The continuing technological advancements promise an exciting future for architecture, opening up possibilities that we as designers can only begin to imagine.

E. Fostering Economic Growth and Trade

Architecture has a noteworthy role in facilitating economic growth and trade within civilizations. The built environment is a powerful economic engine, providing infrastructure for commerce, attracting investments, and creating jobs. Moreover, architecture contributes to the economic vitality of a city or region by enhancing its aesthetic beauty and making it more desirable for businesses, tourists, and residents. This section will delve into how architecture and the built environment foster economic growth and trade.

1. Infrastructure and Commerce

The built environment provides the necessary infrastructure for economic activities to take place. Roads, bridges, ports, markets, and more recently, airports and train stations have been central to the growth and development of trade within and between civilizations. For instance, the ancient Roman road network, consisting of over 250,000 miles of roads and bridges, facilitated trade and commerce across the vast Roman Empire, connecting various cities and regions.[8] In contemporary society, architecture continues to provide vital commercial infrastructure, from the high-tech industrial parks of Silicon Valley to the bustling retail hubs of New York City.

The Roman Empire in the time of Hadrian (r. 117–138), showing the network of main Roman roads. Wikiwand.

2. Attracting Investment

Architecture plays a significant role in attracting both domestic and foreign investment. Iconic architectural designs often serve as landmarks, attracting companies and sightseers alike. For example, cities like Paris, Dubai, and Sydney are instantly recognizable by their iconic structures - the Eiffel Tower, the Burj Khalifa, and the Sydney Opera House, respectively. These landmarks not only enhance the cities' global image but also stimulate economic activity through tourism.

Moreover, well-designed urban environments can attract businesses by offering attractive spaces for offices, factories, and shops. Businesses are often willing to invest more in areas with good infrastructure, safe and attractive public spaces, and well-planned transport links.

3. Job Creation

Architecture and construction are significant sources of employment. The process of planning, designing, and constructing buildings requires a wide range of professionals, including architects, engineers, construction workers, and real estate agents. Moreover, the maintenance and renovation of existing buildings also provide ongoing employment opportunities. In addition, architecture indirectly creates jobs through the businesses it facilitates. For instance, a well-designed shopping center can stimulate retail activity, leading to job creation in the retail sector.

4. Enhancing Aesthetic Appeal

Architecture enhances the aesthetic appeal of cities and regions, which can bolster its economic ambitions. Beautiful and distinctive architecture can make a place more attractive for residents, businesses, and tourists, increasing its economic vitality. Studies have shown that cities with high-quality architecture and design often have higher property values, attract more tourists, and experience economic growth.

5. Sustainable Architecture and Economic Growth

In recent years, sustainable architecture has been recognized as a driver of economic growth. Green building technologies, such as energy-efficient designs and renewable energy installations, can reduce energy costs and create new jobs in the green technology sector. Furthermore, sustainable architecture can improve public health and productivity, leading to economic benefits. For instance, buildings designed with natural light and ventilation can improve occupants' well-being, potentially reducing healthcare costs and improving productivity.

Architecture is an effective driver of economic growth and trade. By providing the necessary infrastructure, attracting investment, creating jobs, enhancing aesthetic charm, and promoting sustainability, architecture plays an imperative role in economic development. As such, the importance of architecture in economic planning and development cannot be understated.

In summary, these five topics showcase the importance of building cultural legacies and empires. They highlight the formation of civilizations and how architecture defines identity and evokes a brand for many cultures and ethnic groups throughout the development of human society:

- A. Creation of Permanent Structures – Man vs. Nature in the establishment of permanent societies and fostering of developing culture.
- B. Reflecting Cultural Values and Identity – Building beyond culture to formulate traditions and rules of governance that is symbolized in its Architecture.

C. Facilitating Social Organization and Cohesion – Man's achievement is not monolithic by nature.
D. Advancing Technological and Engineering Advancements – Architecture incorporates the latest and greatest technological and scientific achievements.
E. Fostering Economic Growth and Trade – Infrastructure has provided interconnectedness, further extending the impact of thriving civilizations having greater influence in the known world.

06

"Faith is not contrary to reason."

Sherwood Eddy

ON EARTH AS IT IS IN HEAVEN

SEGREGATION IN BIBLICAL TIMES

A. Ethnic Groups in the Bible and Their Customs

The Bible is a rich tapestry that encompasses diverse ethnic groups, each having distinct cultures and customs. The first five books of the Bible, known as the Torah, serve as a historical record detailing these myriad cultures, making it a precious resource in understanding societal organization and segregation in biblical times.

Among the numerous ethnic groups mentioned in the Torah, the Israelites, Canaanites, Egyptians, Assyrians, and Babylonians hold prominence. Each had distinctive societal norms, governance, and, most importantly, unique architectural structures that served not only as dwelling places but also symbols of their culture and societal organization.[1]

The Israelites, for instance, are known for their nomadic lifestyle in the early biblical period. They lived in tents known as "succoth," which were not only easy to set up and disassemble but also facilitated their wandering way of life. However, with time, they transitioned into a sedentary lifestyle, building permanent structures often characterized by a four-room house design that was common throughout Israel during the Iron Age.[2]

Sukka in the Desert, Hut made of dry palm leaf. Photo by Aspargos. Wikimedia.

The Canaanites, meanwhile, had walled cities like Jericho, which was famed for its massive defensive walls. These were perhaps an architectural response to the turbulent times and a testament to their advanced construction techniques. Similarly, the Egyptians showcased their societal hierarchy and religious beliefs through their architectural marvels. The iconic pyramids, temples, and palaces served not only as burial sites or residences for the Pharaohs, but also represented an undeniable symbol of the socio-political landscape of Egyptian society.[3]

The Assyrians and Babylonians, known for their militaristic cultures, built imposing city walls, palaces, and ziggurats that reached for the heavens. These structures were a demonstration to their engineering prowess and reflected their societal values.[4]

The city walls of Babylon, surrounding the Hanging Gardens and the Tower of Babel. By Ioanna Viskou. Top.io.es.

An understanding of these ethnic groups and their architectural choices presents a fascinating lens to view the role of architecture in societal segregation. The construction of city walls, the design of dwelling places, and the segregation of sacred and secular spaces all contributed to a physical manifestation of societal hierarchies and segregation.

As we dive deeper into this chapter, we will trace the development of segregation based on tribal origins, the role of indentured servitude, the influence of architectural design on societal organization, and how these factors came to a head in the case of King Solomon's architectural segregation. Through this exploration, we'll uncover the intricate ways in which architecture in biblical times was not merely about creating spaces for shelter but also a potent tool for reinforcing societal norms and segregations.

B. Formation of Hierarchies and Segregation Based on Tribal Origins

In the Biblical Era, the emergence of hierarchies and segregation was closely tied to the structure and organization of tribal communities. Each tribe, as mentioned in the Torah, was distinct in its customs, culture, and governance. Over time, these tribal origins became markers of identity, giving rise to hierarchies and forming the basis for segregation in society.[5]

The formation of these hierarchies was often a result of interactions between different tribes. Usually, the tribe that triumphed in conflicts could impose its laws on the vanquished, thereby establishing a system of dominance and subordination. These interactions led to the establishment of a social hierarchy that was deeply embedded in tribal origins.

In the formation of hierarchies and segregation based on tribal origins, a significant example can be seen in the Israelites, who were the descendants of the patriarch Jacob. The Israelites were organized into twelve tribes, each tracing its lineage back to one of Jacob's sons.

The story of the Israelites and their tribal origins can be found in the biblical narrative, specifically in the book of Genesis. According to the biblical account, Jacob, also known as Israel, had twelve sons: Reuben, Simeon, Levi, Judah, Issachar, Zebulun, Joseph, Benjamin, Dan, Naphtali, Gad, and Asher. These twelve sons became the eponymous founders of the twelve tribes of Israel.[6]

Each tribe had its own distinct identity, history, and territory within the Promised Land. This tribal organization was essential in shaping the social, political, and religious life of the Israelite community. It provided a framework for the distribution of land, resources, and responsibilities among the tribes.

The tribal system also had implications for the social hierarchy and segregation within the Israelite society. Certain tribes held positions of prominence and leadership, while others had different roles and responsibilities. For example, the tribe of Levi was designated as the priestly tribe and was responsible for the religious rituals and ceremonies. They were not given a specific territorial inheritance but were allocated cities and scattered throughout the land to serve as religious leaders and teachers.

The tribe of Judah held a significant position among the tribes and eventually became the dominant tribe. It produced a line of kings, including King David and King Solomon. The Davidic dynasty, based in Jerusalem, became the ruling power over the United Kingdom of Israel.

Other tribes had their own unique characteristics and roles within the community. For instance, the tribe of Benjamin was known for its skilled warriors, while the tribe of Issachar was known for its expertise in agriculture and understanding of the times.

The tribal system also established boundaries and divisions among the tribes, creating a sense of identity and solidarity within each tribe. While the tribes maintained their individual distinctiveness, they were also expected to come together as a united people, particularly during times of war, celebration, and the observance of religious festivals.

The tribal origins and hierarchies within the Israelite community provided a sense of order, structure, and identity. However, these divisions also had the potential to create tensions and conflicts. Throughout the biblical narrative, we see instances of rivalries and power struggles between the tribes, highlighting the complex dynamics that emerged within this tribal framework.

For instance, following the reign of King Solomon, the United Kingdom of Israel was divided into two separate kingdoms: the northern kingdom of Israel and the southern kingdom of Judah. This division occurred due to political and tribal rivalries between the ten northern tribes and the two southern tribes (Judah and Benjamin). The two kingdoms often engaged in conflicts and maintained separate political entities, leading to a divided Israelite community.

Jeroboam, a member of the tribe of Ephraim, led a rebellion against King Solomon's successor, Rehoboam, from the tribe of Judah. This revolt resulted in the establishment of the northern kingdom of Israel, which consisted of ten tribes. Jeroboam strategically created alternative places of worship in his territory to prevent his people from traveling to Jerusalem, the religious center in the southern kingdom. This action fostered a sense of division and segregation between the tribes of the northern and southern kingdoms.

Throughout the history of the divided kingdom, there was often animosity and conflict between the northern kingdom of Israel and the southern kingdom of Judah. This included wars, territorial disputes, and struggles for dominance. The tribes of Israel, located in the northern kingdom, often viewed the tribe of Judah as a rival and competitor for power and resources.

In 722 BCE, the Assyrians conquered the northern kingdom of Israel, resulting in the exile and dispersion of many of the northern tribes. This event further deepened the divisions and segregation among the Israelites, as the tribes were scattered and assimilated into other cultures.[1]

Similarly, the Babylonians under King Hammurabi developed one of the earliest known legal codes. Hammurabi's Code laid out distinct laws for different social classes, institutionalizing a form of segregation and hierarchy within their society.[7]

Interestingly, tribal affiliations and the ensuing hierarchies were not merely abstract social concepts but were embodied in the very architecture and spatial organization of these societies. For instance, within a city or a settlement, different tribes or social classes often had distinct dwelling places, reflecting their standing within the societal hierarchy.

Indentured servitude, a common practice across different tribes, further contributed to these hierarchies. The dwelling places of servants were separate from those of their masters, creating a physical manifestation of societal divisions.

This architectural segregation was a powerful symbol of the entrenched hierarchies and was fundamental in maintaining societal order.

Perhaps one of the most telling examples of such segregation based on tribal origins and societal hierarchy is found in the kingdom of King Solomon. His architectural designs were emblematic of the societal structures of the time and provided valuable insights into the dynamics of hierarchy and segregation in biblical times. As we will explore in the following sections, the spaces Solomon created for his servants, concubines, and family members were a clear reflection of societal roles and divisions.

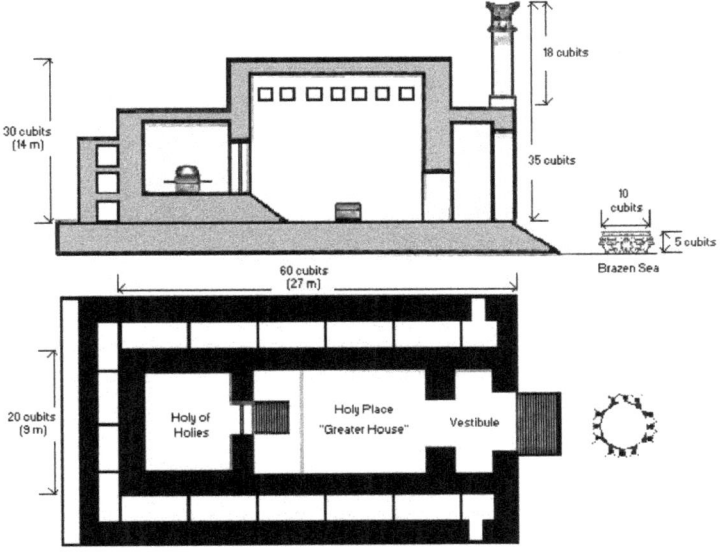

A sketch of Solomon's Temple, based on descriptions in the Scriptures. Wikipedia.

C. Indentured Servitude and Its Role in Segregation

Certainly, indentured servitude played a significant role in the segregation and stratification of societies during biblical times. This system, under which individuals would serve a master for a predetermined period to pay off a debt or as a result of defeat in war, was not uncommon among ancient civilizations. However, in the Bible, it takes on a unique, nuanced dimension.

One such unique instance can be found in the story of Jacob and Laban in the book of Genesis (Genesis 29:15-30). Jacob, fled from his brother Esau, arrived in Haran and began working for his uncle Laban. He fell in love with Laban's younger daughter, Rachel, and offered to work seven years as an indentured servant to earn her hand in marriage. However, Laban tricked Jacob into marrying his older daughter, Leah, first, leading to another seven years of servitude for Rachel. Here, indentured servitude is seen as a means to secure a better future, but it also underscores the power imbalance between Laban and Jacob, which translates into familial segregation.[8]

Another narrative involved the Prophet Elisha and the Shunammite woman in the book of Kings (2 Kings 4:1-7). In this account, a widow, burdened by the debts left by her deceased husband, was at risk of losing her two sons to indentured servitude. Elisha, moved by her plight, performed a miracle that allowed her to sell enough oil to pay off her debts, sparing her sons from servitude. This narrative depicts the potential of indentured servitude to create divisions within families and accentuate social hierarchies, further contributing to segregation.

The story of Joseph, also in the book of Genesis (Genesis 37, 39-45), presents yet another perspective on servitude and segregation. Sold into slavery by his jealous brothers, Joseph ended up in Egypt, where he rose through the ranks from being a slave in Potiphar's house to the Pharaoh's second-in-command. Despite his rise in status, Joseph remained separate from Egyptian society; he was always a Hebrew, an outsider. His story underscores how even when indentured servitude could lead to upward mobility, it might not necessarily break down the barriers of segregation.

One of the clearest depictions of indentured servitude, however, is in the book of Exodus. The Israelites, enslaved by the Egyptians, were subjected to hard labor and brutal treatment. This represents a form of racial and ethnic segregation, with the Israelites clearly identified as a subordinate group.

According to the narrative, the Israelites initially came to Egypt during a time of famine, seeking refuge and sustenance. However, as the years went by, their numbers multiplied, and they became a threat in the eyes of the Egyptian Pharaoh.

In Exodus 1:8-14, it is described how the Pharaoh enslaved the Israelites, subjecting them to hard labor and treating them as a captive workforce. This forced servitude was a form of indentured servitude where the Israelites were bound to work for the Egyptians against their will. They were subjected to harsh conditions, toiling in fields, constructing buildings, and engaging in various forms of labor.

The portrayal of indentured servitude in Exodus highlights the oppressive nature of the system and the dynamics of power. The Israelites were segregated from the Egyptian society, confined to their designated tasks and locations. They lived separately in their own communities within Egypt, further reinforcing the divisions between the Israelites and the Egyptians.

The story of Moses, one of the central figures in the book of Exodus, also sheds light on the dynamics of indentured servitude. Moses, an Israelite by birth, was raised as an Egyptian prince in Pharaoh's palace. However, when he witnessed an Egyptian overseer mistreating an Israelite slave, he intervened and killed the overseer (Exodus 2:11-12).

This act forced Moses to flee Egypt and live in exile, ultimately leading to his encounter with God at the burning bush.

The story of Moses highlights the tension and conflict arising from the hierarchical and segregated nature of indentured servitude. Moses, having grown up in privilege, became acutely aware of the injustice and suffering experienced by his fellow Israelites. This realization became a driving force in his later role as the liberator and leader of the Israelites, leading them out of slavery and towards the Promised Land.

The depiction of indentured servitude in the book of Exodus serves as a powerful reminder of the consequences of segregation and the struggles faced by those who are subjected to such oppressive systems. It showcases the resilience and determination of the Israelites to overcome their bondage and seek freedom, ultimately challenging the societal norms that perpetuated segregation and injustice.

However, it's important to note that after their emancipation from Egypt, the Israelites themselves maintained a system of indentured servitude, as laid out in Leviticus 25:39-55. This demonstrates how the institution of servitude could be embedded into the very laws and customs of a society, thereby creating clear lines of segregation.

In contrast to the oppressive servitude under the Egyptians, the Israelite version was more humane and bound by religious law. An Israelite who had fallen into debt could sell himself into service, but his treatment was regulated. They were not to be treated as slaves but as hired workers, and their service was limited to six years, after which they would be set free in the year of Jubilee.[9]

Nevertheless, this practice still led to societal segregation, as those in servitude lived separately from their masters and were restricted in their rights and freedoms. Their status was also visible in their living quarters, which were more modest compared to those of their masters, reflecting their lower position in the societal hierarchy.

The book of Ruth provides another perspective on servitude and segregation. Ruth, a Moabite widow, became a servant in the fields of Boaz, an Israelite. Here, segregation was apparent not only in terms of societal status but also in terms of ethnicity and gender. Despite this, Ruth's story was also one of integration and social mobility, as she eventually married Boaz and became an ancestor of King David, demonstrating that while servitude created divisions, it did not always result in permanent segregation.

To say the least, indentured servitude in biblical times was a dominant force for societal segregation, shaping not only social relations but also the physical landscapes of communities. However, it was also an adaptable system, and its role in societal segregation was indeed complex and multifaceted.

D. Layout of Housing Quarters and Segregation of Master and Servants

In the biblical context, the layout of housing quarters and the segregation of masters and servants was a determining factor in reflecting social hierarchies and maintaining distinct social positions. The arrangement of living spaces served as a physical representation of the social order within ancient Israelite society. Here is an exploration of the layout of housing quarters and the segregation of masters and servants in the Bible.

The Household Structure

In ancient Israelite society, the household formed the core social unit. The patriarch, often the head of the family, held authority over the household and its members. The layout of the housing quarters was designed to reflect the hierarchy within the family, with the patriarch typically occupying a central living space or an area of prominence.

Understanding the household structure provides insights into the organization and dynamics of the Israelite society during biblical times.

The village of Samaria, c. 1915. Modern representative of the city where Elijah delivered his flaming messages, where Elisha dwelt, and Herod the Great held his court. Wikimedia Commons

- **Patriarchal Authority:** The household was typically headed by a patriarch who held significant authority and served as the primary decision-maker. The patriarch, often the oldest male in the family, exercised control over the family's assets, resources, and members. His role extended beyond the immediate family and included responsibility for extended family members and even servants or slaves.

This is a reconstruction of the central courtyard of a two-story house in ancient Israel. Womaninthebible.net

- **Multi-Generational Family Units:** The Israelite household consisted of multiple generations living together under one roof. It encompassed not only the patriarch and his wife but also their children, grandchildren, and other relatives. This extended family structure fostered a sense of communal living and interdependence.

Another typical home in ancient Israel. By Msgr. Charles Pope. Archdiocese of Washington.

- **Core Family Unit:** At the heart of the household structure was the core family unit comprising the patriarch, his wife, and their immediate children. This nucleus formed the foundation of the household and represented the continuity of the family lineage.

- **Roles and Responsibilities:** Each member of the household had specific roles and responsibilities based on their age, gender, and social status. The patriarch was responsible for providing leadership, guidance, and protection to the family. The wife, often referred to as the matriarch, played a significant role in managing the domestic affairs, raising children, and preserving the family's heritage.
- **Inheritance and Succession:** The household structure was emphasized in determining inheritance and succession within the family. The patriarch had the authority to allocate property, assets, and responsibilities among his sons based on birthright and seniority. This ensured the continuation of the family line and maintained the stability of the household.
- **Kinship Ties:** The household structure also encompassed broader kinship ties beyond the immediate family. Relatives such as grandparents, aunts, uncles, and cousins often resided within the household or in close proximity. These extended family connections strengthened social bonds, provided support networks, and contributed to the overall functioning of the household.
- **Economic Functions:** The household served as an economic unit, engaging in various agricultural, trade, and craft activities. Different family members would contribute their skills and labor to sustain the household's economic well-being. For instance, sons might assist in farming or herding, while daughters could be involved in textile production or household management.

The Main Dwelling

The main dwelling within the household was typically the residence of the master or the head of the family. It was usually larger and more spacious compared to the quarters of other family members or servants. This dwelling often consisted of several rooms and was equipped with amenities and comforts that reflected the status and wealth of the master.[10]

An ancient Israelite Home. Posted by Abrahamus. Guildofbezalel.blogspot.com

- **Size and Spaciousness:** The main dwelling was typically larger and more spacious compared to the quarters of other family members or servants. It represented the prominence and importance of the master within the household. The size of the dwelling could vary depending on the social standing and wealth of the family.
- **Architecture and Design:** The main dwelling was designed to accommodate the needs of the master, and often showcased architectural elements that reflected the prevailing styles and craftsmanship of the time. It could include multiple rooms arranged in a specific layout, with attention given to aesthetics, functionality, and comfort.

- **Amenities and Comforts:** The main dwelling offered a range of amenities and comforts to ensure the well-being and convenience of the master. It could feature private sleeping quarters, a designated study or workspace, and a gathering area for hosting guests or conducting family affairs. The dwelling might have had access to natural light through windows or openings to provide illumination and ventilation.
- **Decor and Furnishings:** The interior of the main dwelling was adorned with decor and furnishings that showcased the taste, preferences, and wealth of the master. Fine craftsmanship, decorative motifs, and luxurious materials might be employed to create an ambiance of elegance and refinement. Furniture, including seating arrangements, tables, and storage units, would be present to enhance functionality and provide comfort.
- **Symbolic Significance:** The main dwelling symbolized the authority and centrality of the master within the household. It served as a representation of his status, power, and control over the family. The size, design, and quality of the dwelling communicated the social standing and influence of the master to both family members and visitors.
- **Privacy and Exclusivity:** The main dwelling provided a sense of privacy and exclusivity for the master. It served as a sanctuary where he could retreat from the demands and responsibilities of daily life. This separation of space between the master's dwelling and other areas of the household reinforced the hierarchical structure and emphasized the distinction between the master and other family members or servants

Separate Quarters for Servants

Within the household, servants or slaves were allocated separate living quarters. These quarters were usually situated in separate areas or designated spaces within the premises. The servants' quarters were often smaller and less well-appointed compared to the main dwelling, emphasizing the social divide between the master and the servants.[11]

- **Purpose and Function:** The separate quarters for servants were designated spaces within the household that served as living areas for the servants and other subordinate members of the household. These quarters were distinct from the main dwelling of the master and provided a specific space for the servants to reside and fulfill their responsibilities.

- **Physical Separation:** The separate quarters for servants were physically separated from the main dwelling of the master. This physical segregation helped maintain a clear distinction between the roles, status, and living conditions of the master and the servants. It emphasized the hierarchy within the household.

- **Location and Layout:** The location of the servants' quarters varied depending on the size and layout of the household. In larger households, the servants' quarters might be situated in a separate wing or annex of the main dwelling, while in smaller households, they could be located in a separate area within the compound.

- **Living Conditions:** The living conditions in the servants' quarters were often more modest compared to the main dwelling. The size of the quarters, the number of rooms, and the amenities provided were generally less luxurious. The servants' quarters could consist of shared spaces or individual rooms, depending on the social standing of the servant and the preferences of the master.

- **Privacy and Proximity:** The servants' quarters provided a degree of privacy for the servants, allowing them to have their own space separate from the main household. However, they were still in close proximity to the main dwelling to ensure accessibility for performing their duties and tasks. This arrangement facilitated the efficient functioning of the household.
- **Social and Cultural Dynamics:** The separation of the servants' quarters from the main dwelling reinforced the social and cultural norms of the time. It reflected the societal belief in hierarchical divisions and the distinction between the master and the servant class. The physical separation served as a reminder of the different roles and responsibilities within the household.
- **Duties and Responsibilities:** The separate quarters for servants were not just living spaces but also areas where servants could rest, prepare for their duties, and store their belongings. It provided a place for them to gather, receive instructions from the master or other household members, and coordinate their tasks.
- **Supervision and Control:** The physical separation of the servants' quarters facilitated the supervision and control of the servants by the master or other higher-ranking members of the household. It allowed for a clear delineation of authority and facilitated efficient management of the household operations.

Division of Spaces

The physical division of spaces between the master and the servants contributed to the segregation and social hierarchy. Servants' quarters were intentionally kept separate from the main dwelling to maintain boundaries and reinforce the distinction between the master and the servants. This spatial division reflected the power balance and social hierarchy prevalent in ancient Israelite society.

Symbolic Significance

The layout of housing quarters and the segregation of masters and servants symbolically represented the social order and the roles assigned to each individual within the household. It reinforced the perception of social stratification, with the master positioned as the authority figure and the servants occupying subordinate positions.

Here is a deeper exploration of the symbolic significance:

- **Status and Hierarchy:** The existence of separate quarters for servants symbolized the social hierarchy and the distinction between the master and the servants. It visually represented the dynamics at play and the differing levels of status within the household. The separation emphasized the privileged position of the master and the subordinate position of the servants.

- **Symbol of Authority:** The separate quarters served as a symbol of the master's authority and control over the household. By providing designated living spaces for the servants, the master asserted their position as the head of the household and their role as the one who provides housing and provisions for those under their authority.

- **Boundaries and Bound Duties:** The physical separation between the main dwelling and the servants' quarters established clear boundaries and demarcated the areas of responsibility for each individual within the household. It emphasized the division of labor and the specific roles that each member was expected to fulfill. The symbolic significance of these boundaries reinforced the hierarchical structure and maintained order within the household.

- **Social Order and Stability:** The separate quarters for servants served as a visual representation of the social order and stability of the Israelite society. It conveyed the idea that each individual had a designated place and role within the household, ensuring that everyone knew their position and responsibilities. This symbolic arrangement contributed to the overall functioning and harmony of the household.
- **Reinforcement of Norms and Values:** The existence of separate quarters for servants communicated and reinforced the societal norms and values regarding social divisions and hierarchy. It reflected the cultural understanding of the Israelite society at that time, where distinctions based on social class and status were deeply ingrained. The symbolic significance of the separate quarters helped perpetuate these norms and values from one generation to another.
- **Identity and Belonging:** The separate quarters shaped the identity and sense of belonging for both the master and the servants. For the master, it affirmed their position of authority and reinforced their identity as the head of the household. For the servants, the separate quarters established their role and identity within the household as individuals who served the master and contributed to the functioning of the household.
- **Preservation of Order and Discipline:** The symbolic significance of the separate quarters for servants contributed to the preservation of order and discipline within the household. By visually representing the social divisions and maintaining a clear distinction between the master and the servants, it reinforced the importance of hierarchy and respect for authority. It instilled a sense of discipline and obedience among the servants, ensuring that they adhered to their assigned roles and responsibilities.

Examples From the Bible

Several biblical narratives illustrate the layout of housing quarters and the segregation of masters and servants.

- **Abraham and His Servants:** In Genesis 14:14, we see Abraham assembling 318 of his trained servants to pursue and rescue his nephew, Lot. This incident suggests that Abraham had a sizable household with a considerable number of servants. While the specific details of their living quarters are not mentioned, it is reasonable to assume that Abraham had separate lodging for his servants within his household. The number of servants mentioned indicates that they were likely accommodated in separate quarters that were designated for their residence and activities.
- **Uriah and David:** In 2 Samuel 11:11, we encounter the account of Uriah the Hittite, who was a loyal servant in King David's army. When David attempted to cover up his affair with Bathsheba by summoning Uriah to sleep with his wife, Uriah chose to sleep with the servants of his lord instead and did not go to his own house. This incident highlights the segregation of living quarters between the servants and the master. Uriah's decision to stay with the servants rather than going to his own home indicates that there were separate quarters for the servants within the royal residence.
- **Joseph and Potiphar's House:** In Genesis 39, we find the story of Joseph, who was sold into slavery in Egypt and ended up serving in the household of Potiphar, an Egyptian official. As a trusted servant, Joseph was given responsibilities within Potiphar's house. The narrative suggests that Joseph had his own living quarters within Potiphar's household, separate from the living quarters of Potiphar and his family. This separation

reinforces the social hierarchy and the distinction between the master and the servant.
- **Nehemiah's Reforms:** In the book of Nehemiah, when the Israelites returned from exile and began to rebuild Jerusalem, Nehemiah addresses issues of social injustice and economic exploitation. In Nehemiah 5:1-13, he confronts the nobles and officials who were taking advantage of their fellow Israelites. Part of Nehemiah's reforms involved restoring the rightful ownership of land and property to those who had been exploited. This implies that there were separate quarters for the nobles and officials, distinct from the common people and servants, reinforcing the social divisions within the community.

E. The Case of King Solomon and His Hierarchical Segregation

The case of King Solomon provides an intriguing example of hierarchical segregation within the biblical narrative. Solomon, renowned for his wisdom and wealth, ruled over the United Kingdom of Israel at its pinnacle of power and prosperity. However, his reign was not without its challenges, particularly when it came to issues of social hierarchy and segregation.

Solomon's hierarchical segregation can be seen in various aspects of his rule, including his administration, personal life, and architectural projects. Let's explore these in more detail.

- **Administration:** Solomon implemented a hierarchical structure within his administration, which was organized according to different roles and responsibilities. He appointed high officials, governors, and chiefs to oversee different regions and sectors of his kingdom. These officials held positions of authority and power, further reinforcing the hierarchical nature of the society.

The administrative divisions and the clear hierarchy of positions reflected the social order and segregation present in Solomon's kingdom.

- **Personal Life:** Solomon's personal life exemplified hierarchical segregation through his extensive harem and the distinction between his wives and concubines. According to biblical accounts, Solomon had a vast number of wives, often from foreign nations, as a means of forming political alliances. These wives were not only symbols of his wealth and power, but also represented the segregation and hierarchy within his personal life. The wives had their own quarters and were part of a carefully structured system, with the queen mother occupying a position of prominence. This hierarchical arrangement reflected Solomon's desire to maintain his status and the cultural norms of the time.
- **Architectural Projects:** In the architectural projects of King Solomon, including the construction of the First Temple, there was a clear hierarchical segregation based on the types of workers employed and the tasks assigned to them. The biblical account in 2 Chronicles 2:17-18, KJV, sheds light on this aspect. "And Solomon numbered all the strangers that were in the land of Israel, after the numbering wherewith David his father had numbered them; and they were found an hundred and fifty thousand and three thousand and six hundred. And he set threescore and ten thousand of them to be bearers of burdens, and fourscore thousand to be hewers in the mountain, and three thousand and six hundred overseers to set the people a work."

The Second Jewish Temple. Model in the Israel Museum. Photo by Ariely. Wikimedia.

According to this passage, Solomon identified and numbered the "strangers" or non-Israelites living in the land of Israel. These individuals were then assigned specific roles based on their skills and abilities. The roles mentioned in the passage are the bearers of burdens, hewers in the mountain, and overseers.

- **Bearers of Burdens:** The bearers of burdens were tasked with the labor-intensive work of transporting materials and supplies required for the construction of the temple. They were responsible for carrying heavy loads, such as stones, timber, and other construction materials, to the construction site. This role involved physical labor and required strength and endurance.
- **Hewers in the Mountain:** The hewers in the mountain were skilled workers who were involved in quarrying and shaping the stones used in the construction of the temple. They were responsible for extracting the stones from the mountains and

shaping them according to the architectural requirements. This role required expertise in stone masonry and craftsmanship.

- **Overseers:** The passage also mentions the appointment of three thousand six hundred overseers. These overseers were responsible for supervising and organizing the work of the bearers of burdens and hewers in the mountain. They ensured that the construction tasks were carried out efficiently and according to the plans and specifications.[12]

The hierarchical segregation within the workforce of the temple construction is evident in the division of labor and the allocation of tasks based on skills and capabilities. The bearers of burdens and hewers in the mountain performed the manual and physically demanding tasks, while the overseers held positions of authority and were responsible for managing and coordinating the labor force.

This hierarchical division of labor reflects the social structure of the time, where individuals were assigned roles and responsibilities based on their skills, abilities, and social standing. It also highlights the complex organization required for such monumental construction projects, with a clear chain of command and supervision.

It is important to note that the biblical account focuses on the roles of the workers in the construction project and does not provide explicit details regarding their social or ethnic backgrounds. However, the reference to the "strangers" suggests that some of these workers may have been non-Israelites, further illustrating the diverse composition of the labor force involved in the temple's construction.

This chapter highlights a deep dive into biblical accounts to reinforce the need for physical and hierarchical structures to further advance mankind.

> A. Ethnic Groups in the Bible and Their Customs – Introduction to biblical ethnicities.

B. Formation of Hierarchies and Segregation Based on Tribal Origins – Understanding the importance of ethnic heritage and the formulation of new nations based on cross-cultural integration.
C. Indentured Servitude and Its Role in Segregation – Identifying critical roles performed by indentured servants and how different ethnic groups established laws and codes of conduct that must be maintained by servants. Although some examples exhibit triumphs of individuals to overcome their position or 'lot' in life and achieve a greater legacy than those that were born into a higher class.
D. Layout of Housing Quarters and Segregation of Master and Servants – Exhibits the hierarchy of living and examines the homelife of persons based on social status.
E. The Case of King Solomon and His Hierarchical Segregation – The exceptional and extraordinary hierarchy reflected in King Solomon's projects along with the internal power structure as it relates to delegation of authority is worthy of a chapter in itself.

07

"Seek to perform your duties to your highest ability, this way your actions will be blameless."

Egyptian Proverb

WHEN WE WERE GODS

ARCHITECT'S ROYAL POSITION IN ANCIENT TIMES

ANCIENT EGYPT

Ancient Egypt, one of the most fascinating and iconic civilizations in history, offers us a glimpse into a society that thrived along the banks of the Nile River for thousands of years. The ancient Egyptians built magnificent structures, created breathtaking art, and left behind a rich cultural legacy that continues to captivate our imagination to this day. Architecture played a pivotal role in shaping the lives of the Egyptians, reflecting their values, social structure, and unique way of life.

Residing in a desert landscape with extreme temperature swings and relying on the annual flooding of the Nile for sustenance, the ancient Egyptians developed an agrarian society where the occupation defined a person's social status. The social hierarchy was divided into three main categories: slaves, free citizens, and royalty, each with distinct roles and responsibilities.[1]

One distinctive aspect of ancient Egyptian society was the absence of money as a means of exchange. Instead, the value of goods and services was measured by bartering. Farmers toiled the fertile Nile delta, tilling the soil to yield crops such as wheat, barley, and vegetables. The produce they grew, along with other resources like weeds, served as a form of currency. During the off-season, when farming was not possible, the Egyptians directed their energies toward monumental construction projects, including the construction of pyramids and temples.[2]

Life for the average Egyptian was challenging, and the average life expectancy was around 40 years old. Young Egyptians were considered adults and would often marry around that time. The societal structure was built upon the principle of occupation, where individuals were respected and valued for their contribution to society.[3]

Within the framework of ancient Egyptian society, there existed a system of servitude that encompassed three sub-typologies: chattel, bonded, and forced labor. Chattel slaves were often prisoners of war who were used as directed by the royals and Pharaohs. The Egyptians did not practice racial discrimination, and there is no direct evidence suggesting that individuals bought and sold as slaves were of any particular race. Bonded laborers would sell themselves or family members to pay off debts, with the creditor acquiring the individual and their family until the debt was settled. Some slaves were obtained through foreign markets or captured as war prisoners. While foreign servants had the possibility of returning to their homelands, those brought from regions like Nubia and Libya were forced to remain in Egypt.[4]

The Egyptian government had the authority to draft forced laborers from the general population for state projects. These individuals, who were conscripted into part-time labor systems, worked on various endeavors such as military expeditions, mining, quarrying, and state construction projects. Although these forced laborers were paid a wage depending on their skill level and social status, they still endured arduous working conditions.

The architectural landscape of ancient Egypt reflected the social and economic disparities that existed within the society. Modest houses made of thick mud-brick walls were prevalent among the majority of Egyptians. These dwellings featured a four-chamber interior progression of rooms, including a receiving chamber, kitchen, storeroom, and bedroom. Families typically slept together in the same room, often on the floor, as furniture was considered a luxury in this predominantly wood-deprived desert region.

A recreation of an Ancient Egyptian mud house. By Institute for the Study of the Ancient World – CC BY 2.0 on Flickr.

In contrast, the homes of the wealthy and elite showcased their elevated status. These houses were constructed using more durable and long-lasting materials like stone, and some even had two stories. Open courtyards adorned with flowers, fruits, and vegetables provided a tranquil and aesthetically pleasing environment. Wealthy families enjoyed the luxury of bathrooms, indoor toilets, and private wells for fresh water. Furniture, although rare, consisted of items like stools and beds with mattresses.[5]

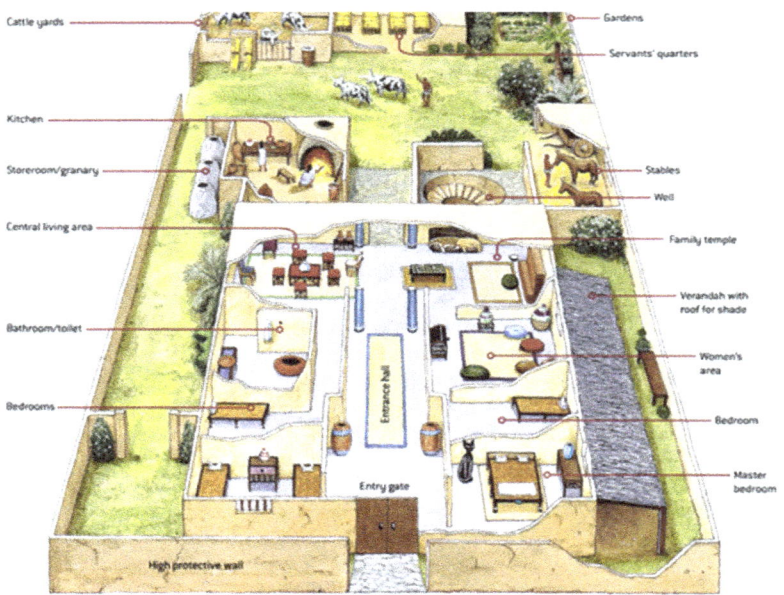

Ancient Egyptian homes for the elite. Diagram Ancient Egyptian Homes. Hotcore.info

Pharaonic homes, belonging to the royal elite, occupied central positions within grand complexes, surrounded by temples and attended to by a retinue of servants. These structures were self-sustaining, with each room serving essential purposes such as gardens, kitchens, event spaces, and separate royal apartments for Pharaohs, Queens, and harems.

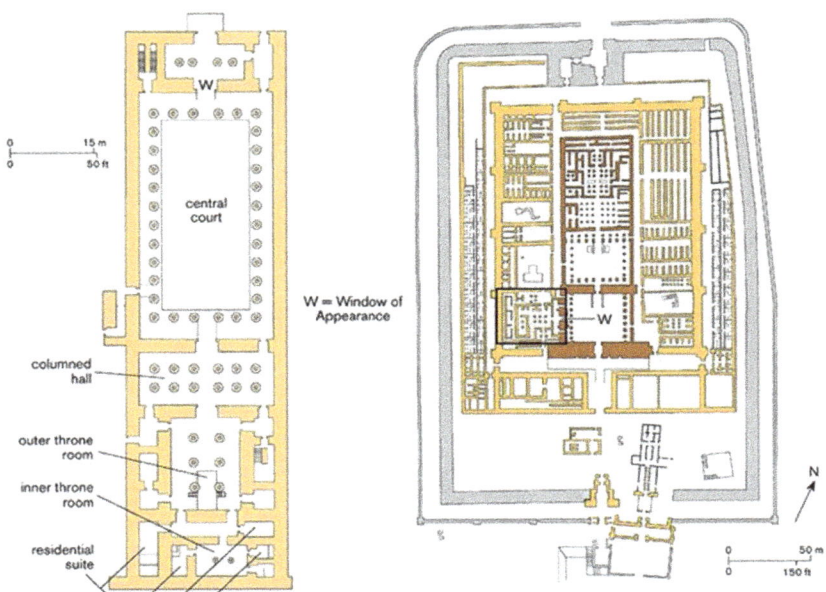

The left side shows King Merenptah's palace at Memphis, mainly designed for royal audiences with basic living quarters. The right side shows a small palace at Ramesses III's mortuary temple, possibly used as a royal residence in the Third Intermediate Period. Both observations are by Steven Snape. Erenow.org

The stark contrast in furnishings between common households and royal residences was evident, with royal floors finished with ceramic tiles and walls adorned with murals reminiscent of the grandeur seen in burial tombs. Furniture was embellished with gold leaf, and oil lamps provided a warm glow.[6]

The architectural ingenuity of ancient Egypt extended to the design of rooftops, which were flat due to the lack of rainfall and the arid climate. This construction style also facilitated easier access for various activities. Rooftops often served as versatile spaces for lounging, dining, and even sleeping under the vast expanse of the Egyptian sky.

When We Were Gods

An ancient rural Egyptian house (20th century) showed the practice of typical storing over the roof and the illustrated house plan. (Photo by authors: Ibrahim A. Touman and Farraj F. Al-Ajmi.) ResearchGate.net

Ancient Egypt's architectural achievements were intertwined with its societal structure, reflecting the values, customs, and daily realities of its people. The diverse range of housing styles, from humble mud-brick dwellings to opulent royal complexes, mirrored the socioeconomic disparities that existed within this ancient civilization. The ancient Egyptians' ability to create magnificent structures that stood the test of time continues to inspire admiration, serving as a testimonial to their remarkable architectural adeptness and their timeless contribution to mankind.

A. Architect Royal as a Prestigious Position

In the grandeur of ancient Egypt, one position stood out as a symbol of prestige, intellect, and artistic genius—the Architect Royal. This esteemed role held immense importance in the realm of Egyptian society, as architects were responsible for designing and overseeing the construction of monumental structures, temples, tombs, and royal complexes. The Architect Royal was integral in shaping the architectural landscape and capturing the essence of Egyptian culture and beliefs.

The position of Architect Royal was held in high regard, and those who assumed this role were revered for their exceptional skills, knowledge, and ability to bring the visions of the pharaohs to life. These architects were considered master craftsmen and were highly valued for their expertise in engineering, design, and construction techniques. Their abilities extended beyond architectural prowess; they possessed a deep understanding of mathematics, astronomy, and religious rituals, which were all integral to the architectural projects they undertook.

The Architect Royal worked closely with the pharaohs, priests, and other high-ranking officials to translate their visions into an organized system made by human hands that would serve various purposes, such as religious worship, funerary rituals, and administrative functions. They were involved in every phase of the building process, from conceptualization and design to superintending construction and ensuring the structures adhered to precise specifications.[7]

One of the notable roles of the Architect Royal was overseeing the construction of temples, which held immense religious significance in ancient Egyptian culture. These magnificent structures were not only places of worship but also served as the dwelling places for the gods and the centers of religious and social life. The Architect Royal created magnificent temples that embodied the spiritual beliefs and rituals of the Egyptians.

The Architect Royal's responsibilities also extended to the construction of royal tombs and complexes. These monumental structures were built to ensure the eternal existence of the pharaohs in the afterlife and were considered sacred spaces. The architects meticulously designed and constructed elaborate tombs, including the iconic pyramids, which served as eternal resting places for the pharaohs.

The Architect Royal's influence extended beyond individual projects; they also played a crucial role in urban planning and the overall architectural development of ancient Egyptian cities. They were responsible for ensuring the harmony and coherence of the architectural landscape, incorporating elements that reflected the social, religious, and cultural values of the society.

The prestige associated with the position of Architect Royal was not solely based on their technical expertise and artistic abilities. They held a privileged status within Egyptian society, often interacting with the pharaoh and other members of the royal court. Their knowledge and skills were highly sought after, and they were held in high esteem by their peers and the general populace.

The Architect Royal in ancient Egypt was not just a master builder but a visionary and a custodian of the cultural heritage of the civilization. Through their innovative designs, they immortalized the glory of the pharaohs, shaped a unique architectural spectacle, and bequeathed a legacy that has been unmatched to this day.[8]

B. The Relationship Between the Architect Royal and the Pharaoh in Ancient Egypt

In the grandeur of ancient Egypt, the relationship between the Architect Royal and the pharaoh was one of utmost significance. The Architect Royal held a distinguished position within the royal court, and worked in close association with the pharaoh to translate their visions into architectural masterpieces that embodied the pharaoh's divine authority and immortalized their reigns.

The pharaoh, considered the earthly embodiment of the gods, held immense power and authority in ancient Egypt. As the supreme ruler, they had the final say in all matters, including the construction of monumental structures and the architectural context of the kingdom.

Throughout the construction process, the Architect Royal maintained constant communication with the pharaoh, providing updates on the progress and seeking their guidance and approval at every phase. This connection allowed the pharaoh to exercise their authority and make decisions that aligned with their vision and the desired outcome.

The Architect Royal's ability to transform the pharaoh's visions into reality was highly regarded and earned them great respect and admiration. Their work was seen as a direct reflection of the pharaoh's power and divine authority, and their successes were celebrated as triumphs for the entire kingdom.

The pharaoh, in turn, appreciated the skill and dedication of the Architect Royal. They recognized the architect's ability to bring their dreams to fruition and understood the profound impact that monumental structures could have on the perception of their reigns by future generations. The collaboration between the Architect Royal and the pharaoh extended beyond individual projects. Their guidance ensured the harmony and coherence of the kingdom's architectural heritage, incorporating elements that reflected the pharaoh's grandeur and the cultural values of the society.

Together, the Architect Royal and the Pharaoh created a legacy that has withstood the test of time as a testament to the unparalleled achievements of the pharaohs and their architectural visionaries.

C. Responsibilities of the Architect Royal in Temple and Pyramid Construction

In ancient Egypt, the Architect Royal's position came with significant responsibilities, particularly in the construction of temples and pyramids. As the chief architect and overseer of these monumental projects, their expertise and knowledge were crucial in ensuring the successful realization of these grand structures.

Responsibilities in Temple Construction

- **Planning and Design:** The Architect Royal was responsible for the planning and design of the temple, coordinating with religious authorities and the pharaoh. They had to understand the religious significance and symbolism associated with the temple and translate these concepts into architectural form. This involved considering the layout, dimensions, orientation, and arrangement of the various sections of the temple, such as the sanctuary, hypostyle halls, courtyards, and pylons.
- **Incorporating Religious Beliefs:** Temples in ancient Egypt were not just architectural structures but also spiritual sanctuaries where the divine was believed to reside. The Architect Royal had the responsibility of incorporating religious beliefs and rituals into the temple design. The Architect Royal, priests, and religious authorities ensured that the layout and architectural elements of the temple facilitated the proper execution of rituals, the display of sacred objects, and the interaction between worshipers and deities.
- **Structural Engineering:** The Architect Royal had to possess a deep understanding of engineering principles to ensure the structural integrity and stability of the temple. They were responsible for designing the foundation, walls, columns, roofs, and other structural elements. The architect had to consider the weight and size of the stones used in construction and develop innovative methods to distribute and support the loads, ensuring the long-term stability of the temple.

- **Artistic and Aesthetic Considerations:** The Architect Royal collaborated with skilled artisans and craftsmen to incorporate artistic and aesthetic elements into the temple design. This included decorative carvings, intricate reliefs, colorful murals, and symbolic hieroglyphs. The architect had to ensure that these artistic elements harmonized with the overall architectural design and conveyed the desired religious and cultural messages.
- **Spatial Organization:** The temple had to be organized in a way that facilitated the religious rituals and ceremonies that took place within it. The Architect Royal carefully planned the layout of different areas, such as the sanctuaries, offering halls, and processional routes, to create a seamless flow and allow for the proper sequence of rituals. They also considered factors such as lighting, acoustics, and ventilation to enhance the spiritual experience within the temple.
- **Material Selection and Procurement:** The architect was responsible for selecting the appropriate building materials for the temple construction. They had to consider factors such as durability, aesthetics, availability, and the symbolism associated with specific materials. The Architect Royal supervised the procurement of stones, such as limestone or granite, for the construction of the temple, ensuring their quality and suitability for the intended purpose.
- **Construction Supervision:** The Architect Royal was instrumental in overseeing the construction process. They managed the workforce, including skilled craftsmen, laborers, and artisans, ensuring that each aspect of the construction adhered to the architectural plans and met the required standards of craftsmanship. The architect also had to coordinate

the logistics of the construction site, ensuring the timely delivery of materials and the smooth progress of the project.
- **Preservation and Restoration:** The Architect Royal had a long-term interest in the preservation and maintenance of the temple. They implemented construction techniques and employed materials that would withstand the test of time. Additionally, they established protocols for regular maintenance and restoration to ensure the temple's longevity and to protect it from natural elements and decay.

The responsibilities of the Architect Royal in temple construction were extensive and required a deep understanding of architecture, engineering, religious beliefs, and artistic expression. Their vision, technical expertise, and attention to detail contributed to the creation of visually striking temples that embodied the ancient Egyptian civilization's devotion to the gods and their belief in the divine presence on Earth.

Responsibilities in Pyramid Construction

The construction of the pyramids stands as one of the most iconic achievements in the history of the World. The pyramids served as monumental tombs for pharaohs, symbolizing their divine power and eternal afterlife. The Architect Royal held a significant role in overseeing the construction of these architectural wonders. Let's explore the responsibilities of the Architect Royal in pyramid construction.
- **Planning and Design:** The Architect Royal was responsible for the planning and design of the pyramid complex. To determine the pyramid's size, shape, and orientation, the architect meticulously calculated the dimensions, angles, and ratios to ensure precise alignment with celestial bodies and religious symbolism.

- **Site Selection:** The architect, in consultation with priests and astronomers, chose the most suitable location for the pyramid. The site had to adhere to specific religious and astronomical criteria, aligning with cosmic principles and the pharaoh's divine connections. Factors such as geographic features, prevailing winds, and visual prominence were considered in the site selection process.
- **Construction Techniques and Engineering:** The Architect Royal was responsible for devising innovative construction techniques and engineering methods. They supervised the quarrying of stone blocks, overseeing the transportation and assembly of these massive stones to create the pyramid's core structure. The architect employed advanced techniques, such as inclined ramps, pulleys, and levers to lift and position the heavy stones in place.
- **Internal Structure and Chambers:** The architect designed the internal structure of the pyramid, including the corridors, chambers, and burial chamber. They ensured the chambers were architecturally sound, incorporating features like corbelled ceilings and relieving chambers to distribute the weight of the stones and prevent collapses. The architect also coordinated the placement of sarcophagi and funerary furniture within the burial chamber.
- **Pyramid Facades:** The Architect Royal oversaw the construction of the pyramid's external facades. They designed and supervised the precise placement of the outer casing stones, creating smooth, polished surfaces that reflected the pyramid's grandeur. The architect ensured the alignment of the casing stones, resulting in a visually stunning structure that shimmered in the sunlight.

- **Pyramid Complex Design:** The architect was responsible for the overall design of the pyramid complex, which included the mortuary temple, causeway, valley temple, and associated structures. They ensured the integration of these components into a cohesive and harmonious architectural ensemble. The architect paid attention to the placement of statues, obelisks, and inscriptions, imbuing the complex with religious symbolism and the pharaoh's divine authority.
- **Symbolic Elements and Decorations:** The Architect Royal coordinated with skilled artisans to incorporate symbolic elements and decorative features into the pyramid complex. They commissioned intricate reliefs, hieroglyphic inscriptions, and sculptures that conveyed religious and mythological narratives. These artistic elements celebrated the pharaoh's achievements, emphasized their divine status, and ensured their eternal legacy.
- **Security and Concealment:** The architect implemented security measures to protect the pyramid and its burial chamber from theft and desecration. They designed secret passages, hidden doors, and intricate false chambers to confuse potential tomb raiders. The architect employed architectural strategies to safeguard the pharaoh's treasures and ensure the secrecy of the burial location.[9]
- **Legacy and Longevity:** The Architect Royal was responsible for creating structures that would endure for eternity. They incorporated architectural elements and construction techniques to ensure the structural stability and longevity of the pyramid. The architect employed geometric precision, precise stone-cutting, and careful planning to ensure that the pyramid would stand as a lasting testament to the pharaoh's power and divine connection.

The responsibilities of the Architect Royal in pyramid construction were immense. They combined architectural expertise, engineering skills, and religious symbolism to create monumental structures that continue to be of interest and fascination in modern times.

Notable Architect Royals in Ancient Egypt

Ancient Egypt was home to many talented architects who held the esteemed position of Architect Royal. These skilled individuals played a crucial role in shaping the architectural landscape of the civilization. Let's explore some of the notable Architect Royals in ancient Egypt:

- **Imhotep:** Imhotep was one of the most renowned Architect Royals in ancient Egypt. He served under Pharaoh Djoser during the Third Dynasty and was best known for his design of the Step Pyramid at Saqqara.

Statuette of Imhotep, 664–30 BC. Theodore M. Davis Collection, Bequest of Theodore M. Davis, 1915. Wikimedia.

The Step Pyramid of Djoser. Photography by Ulrich Hollmann via Getty Images.

Imhotep's innovative architectural approach transformed the traditional mastaba tomb into a monumental structure composed of multiple layers, setting the precedent for future pyramid construction. Imhotep's genius extended beyond architecture, as he was also a skilled physician, high priest, and scholar.

- **Amenhotep, son of Hapu:** Amenhotep, son of Hapu was a prominent architect and official who lived during the reign of Pharaoh Amenhotep III in the 18th Dynasty. He was renowned for his architectural designs, including the Temple of Amenhotep III at Luxor, which featured colossal statues known as the Colossi of Memnon. Amenhotep, son of Hapu was not only an architect but also a statesman, serving in various administrative roles and revered as a sage and prophet.

Double row of columns with papyrus bundle capitals – The Court of Amenhotep III, Luxor Temple. Photographed by Jorge Lascar, Wikipedia

Amenhotep, son of Hapu, as an elderly man. Egyptian Museum, Cairo. Wikimedia.

- **Senenmut:** Senenmut was a prominent architect during the reign of Pharaoh Hatshepsut in the 18th Dynasty. He was responsible for designing many monumental structures, including the famous mortuary Temple of Hatshepsut at Deir el-Bahari.

Temple of Hatshepsut, Luxor, Egypt. Aerial View. Wikimedia.

Senenmut's architectural achievements were remarkable, and he enjoyed a high position in Hatshepsut's court. His association with the queen raised speculation about the nature of their relationship, with some suggesting a romantic involvement.

Statue of a kneeling Senenmut from the Brooklyn Museum. Wikimedia.

- **Khaemwaset:** Khaemwaset was a prominent architect and priest who lived during the reign of Ramses II in the 19th Dynasty. He was a son of Ramses II and held several important positions, including that of the High Priest of Ptah. Khaemwaset was an avid restorer of ancient monuments and temples, and he was credited with the preservation and restoration of the Pyramid of Unas at Saqqara.

Pyramid of Unas in Saqqara, Egypt. Wikipedia.

His passion for the preservation of Egypt's architectural heritage earned him the title "The First Egyptologist."

Statue of Khaemweset from the British Museum. Wikipedia.

- **Ineni:** Ineni was an Architect Royal and high-ranking official during the reign of Pharaoh Amenhotep II in the 18th Dynasty. He was involved in the construction of numerous temples and monuments, including the Karnak Temple Complex at Thebes.

Karnak Temple Complex at Thebes. From Megalithic Builders.

Ineni also served as a military commander and was depicted in various reliefs and inscriptions, showcasing his dual roles as an architect and warrior.[9]

Ineni (upper left, partly destroyed) in a hunting scene from his tomb. Wikipedia.

These are just a few examples of the notable Architect Royals in ancient Egypt. Their contributions to Egyptian architecture were significant, and their designs continue to captivate and inspire admiration in modern times. The skills and expertise of these Architect Royals played a momentous role in creating the wonderful structures that define ancient Egypt's architectural heritage.

Ancient Greece

Ancient Greece is renowned for its remarkable contributions to art, culture, philosophy, and architecture. This magnificent civilization, which thrived from the 8th century CE to the 6th century BCE, left a permanent impression on the world with its innovative architectural designs, iconic structures, and ageless principles of aesthetics. From the towering temples dedicated to the gods to the grand theaters that showcased dramatic performances, ancient Greece's architectural achievements are still of great interest and intrigue.

The Greeks had a deep appreciation for beauty, balance, and harmony, which is reflected in their architectural masterpieces. Their structures were not only functional but also embodied their reverence for the gods and their pursuit of artistic perfection. The architectural offerings of ancient Greece not only influenced subsequent civilizations but also laid the foundation for the development of architectural principles that still resonate today.

The city-states of ancient Greece were each known for their distinctive architectural styles, which evolved over time. From the Doric order, characterized by its simplicity and strength, to the Ionic order, with its graceful and ornate features, Greek architecture displayed a rich diversity of forms and expressions.[11]

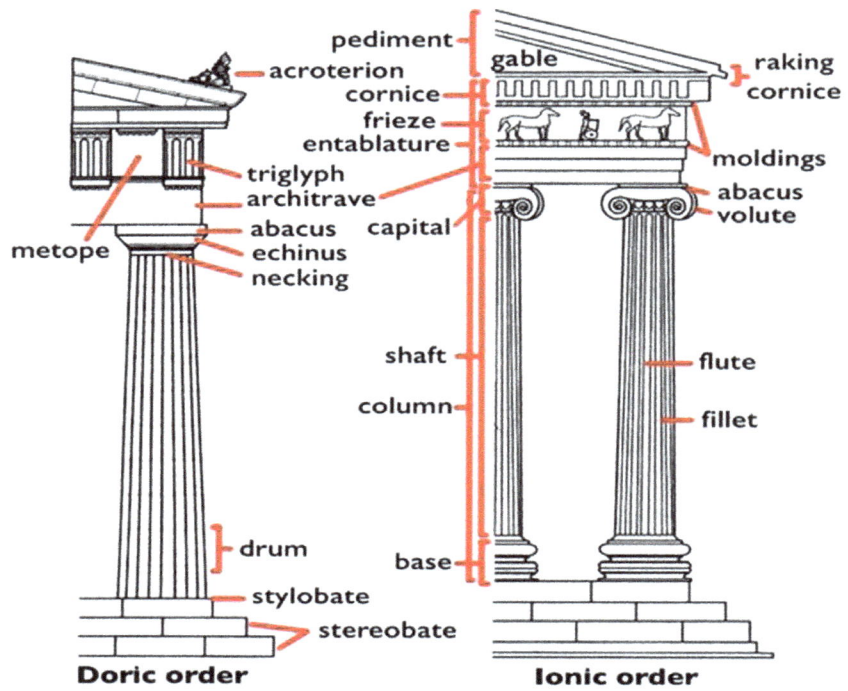

The Greek Architectural Orders by Dr. Jeffrey A. Becker. Khan Academy.org

The Greeks sought to create structures that not only served practical purposes but also conveyed a sense of grandeur, elegance, and transcendence.

Temples held a central place in Greek architecture, serving as sacred spaces dedicated to various deities. The most famous example is the Parthenon temple set atop the Acropolis in Athens.

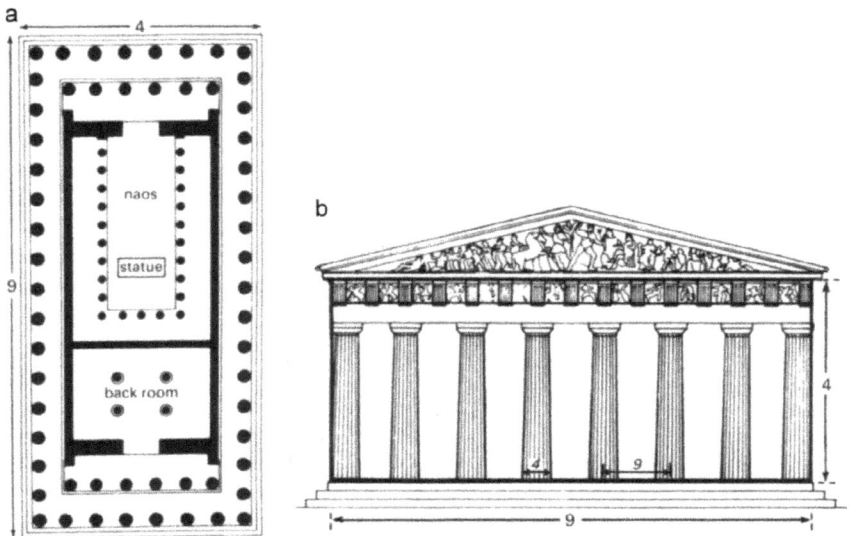

Iktinos and Kallikrates, (a) Plan of the Parthenon showing the 9:4 ratio of width to height; (b) Elevation of the Parthenon showing the 9:4 ratio of interaxial to diameter of columns (Source: Woodford, 1981, p. 17). ResearchGate.com

It is an exemplification to the ingenuity and skill of the ancient Greek architects who carefully calculated every proportion and detail to create a structure that exudes balance and harmony. The Parthenon's ionic columns, pediments, and friezes adorned with sculptures have become eternal symbols of Greek civilization.

In addition to temples, the Greeks also constructed theaters, stadiums, and public buildings that was an essential part of cultural and civic life. The Theater of Epidaurus, with its remarkable acoustics and seating design, allowed for immersive and captivating theatrical performances. The Olympic Stadium in Olympia, where the ancient Olympic Games were held, stands as an attestation to the Greeks' celebration of athletic prowess and communal unity.

Ancient Greece was also known for its urban planning, with cities like Athens and Corinth featuring well-organized street layouts and public spaces.

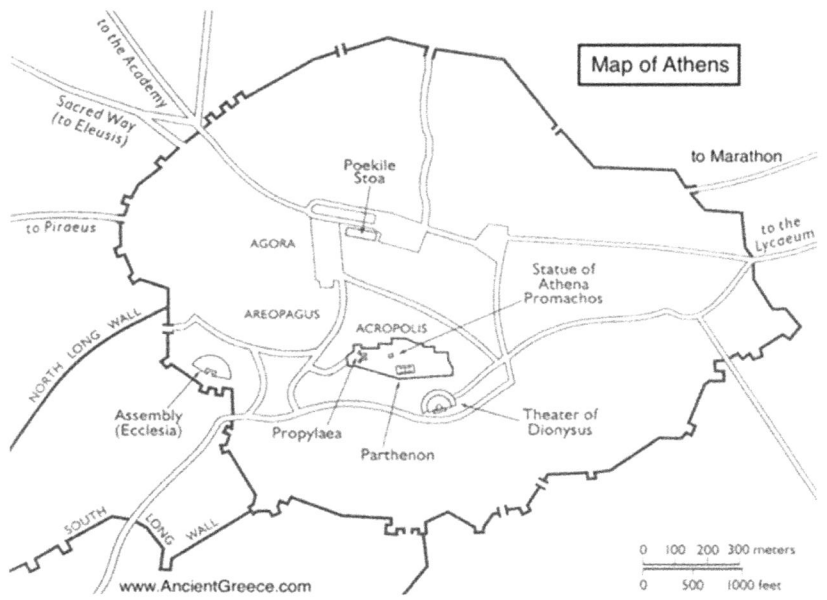

Athenian Agora located at the base of Acropolis with a size of 200m to 250m. By Asyabuyukerk.

The agora, or marketplace, served as the heart of the city, where people gathered for trade, socializing, and political discussions. These urban spaces reflected the Greeks' commitment to creating environments that fostered community interaction and democratic ideals.

In ancient Greece, the concept of segregation was not as prevalent as it was in some other civilizations. Greek society was organized in city-states, each with its own unique characteristics and social structures. While there were distinctions among social classes, such as citizens, foreigners, and slaves, the architectural design of Greek cities and buildings did not specifically enforce segregation based on these distinctions.

Greek architecture, instead, aimed to create spaces that cultivated community and unity. Public spaces, such as marketplaces, theaters, and religious sanctuaries, were designed to accommodate gatherings and interactions among people from different backgrounds. Temples, another prominent architectural feature in ancient Greece, were not segregated spaces but rather places of worship open to all believers. Although certain areas within temples were reserved for priests and initiates, the main sanctuaries were accessible to worshipers from various social backgrounds. People from different social classes would gather together during religious festivals and rituals, reinforcing identity and community.[12]

However, it is worth noting that there were some distinctions in the use of certain buildings or areas within cities. For instance, there might have been specific areas designated for the training of soldiers, the housing of certain groups like foreigners or slaves, or the accommodation of dignitaries. But these divisions were more functional in nature, serving practical purposes rather than strictly segregating different social groups.

It is important to understand that the ancient Greek concept of citizenship played a notable role in shaping their architectural practices. Citizenship in ancient Greece was closely tied to one's rights and participation in the political and social life of the city-state. While citizenship was primarily limited to free-born male individuals, the concept of civic identity emphasized the collective responsibility and shared values of the citizens. This emphasis on citizenship prompted closeness and solidarity rather than strict segregation.

The Role of Architect Royal in City Planning and Public Buildings

The Architect Royal in ancient Greece held a principal part in city planning and the design of public buildings. These highly skilled individuals were responsible for shaping the physical and aesthetic aspects of the city, ensuring that it functioned harmoniously and reflected the values and aspirations of the community.

- **City Planning**

The Architect Royal was crucial in the overall layout and organization of Greek cities. They considered factors such as topography, natural resources, and the needs of the inhabitants when designing the city's infrastructure. The goal was to create a functional and aesthetically pleasing urban environment.

The Architect Royal collaborated with city officials, surveyors, and engineers to determine the most suitable locations for important structures, such as marketplaces, government buildings, and religious sites. With their oversight, these key buildings were strategically positioned to facilitate ease of access and enhance the city's overall efficiency.

- **Public Buildings**

The Architect Royal oversaw the design and construction of significant public buildings that served as cultural, political, and social centers within the city. These structures were meant to inspire civic pride, showcase the achievements of the community, and provide spaces for communal gatherings and activities.

a. Temples: Temples were one of the most iconic types of public buildings in ancient Greece. They were dedicated to various gods and goddesses, and served as places of worship and religious ceremonies. The Architect Royal worked closely with priests and religious authorities to create stunning temples that harmonized with the surrounding landscape and embodied the religious beliefs and rituals of the community.

b. Theaters: The Architect Royal orchestrated the design of theaters, which were integral to Greek culture and served as venues for theatrical performances, festivals, and civic events. The theaters were carefully planned to optimize acoustics and sightlines, allowing large audiences to enjoy performances. These structures often incorporated semicircular seating areas, an orchestra space, and a stage area where actors performed.

c. Stadia and Gymnasiums: As physical fitness and sports were highly valued in ancient Greece, the Architect Royal was responsible for designing stadia and gymnasiums. Stadia were large structures used for athletic contests, especially the Olympic Games, while gymnasiums provided spaces for exercise, training, and intellectual pursuits. These buildings were designed to accommodate large crowds and promote physical well-being.

d. Assembly Halls and Government Buildings: The Architect Royal also contributed to the design of assembly halls and government buildings, where democratic processes and administrative functions took place. These structures were designed to reflect the importance of civic engagement and the democratic principles cherished by the Greeks.

In addition to these specific buildings, the Architect Royal influenced the design and aesthetics of various other public structures such as baths, libraries, monuments, and fountains. Their expertise extended to the selection of materials, proportions, and decorative elements, ensuring that the buildings were not only functional but also visually striking.

The Architect Royal collaborated closely with skilled craftsmen, including masons, carpenters, sculptors, and painters, to bring their designs to life. Their role extended beyond the initial design phase, as they supervised the construction process to ensure that the buildings met their specifications and maintained the desired architectural integrity.

Influence of Architect Royals in Designing Temples and Monuments

In the previous section, we briefly discussed the role of Architect Royals in city planning and public buildings in ancient Greece, including the temple buildings. Now, let's delve deeper into their specific influence in designing these temples and monuments, which left a far-reaching impact on Greek architecture. The Architect's extraordinary ability in shaping the religious and cultural landscape of ancient Greece through their innovative designs and construction methods was immense.

Temple architecture held great significance in ancient Greece, serving as sacred spaces dedicated to the worship of various gods and goddesses. Architect Royals, with their expertise in geometry, aesthetics, and engineering, manifested the design and construction of these temples. One notable example of their influence can be seen in the iconic Acropolis of Athens, a fortified hilltop that housed several temples and monuments. At the heart of the Acropolis stands the majestic Parthenon, a temple dedicated to the goddess Athena. Designed by the Architect Royal, Ictinus, and sculpted by Phidias, this temple exemplifies the harmonious proportions and refined architectural details that are characteristic of ancient Greek architecture. The Architect Royal's meticulous planning and attention to detail ensured that the Parthenon stood as a timeless masterpiece of architectural beauty.

Current state of the Parthenon on February 13, 2019. Athens, Greece. Wikimedia.

Another significant site influenced by Architect Royals is the Ancient Agora of Athens. The Architect Royals played a central role in designing important structures such as the Stoa of Attalos, a two-story colonnaded building that housed shops and administrative offices. The Stoa of Attalos showcased the Architect Royal's ability to create functional yet aesthetically pleasing spaces that fostered social connectiveness and commerce.

The Temple of Olympian Zeus, located in Athens, is another example of the Architect Royal's influence. This colossal temple, dedicated to Zeus, showcased their mastery in designing grandiose structures that commanded attention and reverence. Although unfinished, the temple's sheer scale and intricate architectural elements, such as the Corinthian columns, exemplify the Architect Royal's commitment to creating monumental works of art.[13]

Temple of Olympian Zeus from Olympieion (Athènes). Wikipedia.

Aside from the temples, Architect Royals also left their mark on various other monuments throughout ancient Greece. The Odeon of Herodes Atticus, a magnificent amphitheater located on the slopes of the Acropolis, stands as proof of their ability to design structures that harmonize with the natural environment. This open-air theater, with its intricate stonework and excellent acoustics, provided a venue for musical and theatrical performances, showcasing the Architect Royal's understanding of both functionality and aesthetics.

The Panathenaic Stadium, situated in Athens, is another notable monument influenced by Architect Royals. Originally built in the 4th century BCE, this stadium underwent significant renovations under the architect Herodes Atticus, who transformed it into a grand marble structure. The Architect Royal's vision and expertise ensured that the stadium became emblematic of Greek athletic heroism and valor for prestigious sporting events.

Beyond Athens, Architect Royals left their mark on the Archaeological Site of Olympia, the birthplace of the Olympic Games. Here, the ancient stadium and various other structures showcased their skill in designing spaces that accommodated large gatherings and celebrated the spirit of competition.

The architectural wonders of Meteora, located in Kalabaka, Greece, also bear the imprint of the Architect Royals. The monasteries perched atop towering rock formations is evidence to their ability to integrate structures seamlessly into challenging natural landscapes, creating spaces that evoke feelings of marvel in awe from visitors.

The Great Meteoron by Bernard Gagnon. Built in 14th century. Wikipedia.

Architect Royals in ancient Greece played were essential in shaping the design and construction of temples and monuments. Their mastery of architectural principles, artistic sensibilities, and engineering techniques allowed them to perfect structures that embodied the ideals and aspirations of the Greek civilization. The Parthenon, Ancient Agora, Temple of Olympian Zeus, and many others, epitomize their undying legacy in Greek architecture.

Famous Architect Royals in Ancient Greece

In ancient Greece, there were several notable Architect Royals who made significant contributions to the field of architecture. These individuals were revered for their artistic vision, technical expertise, and ability to create enduring structures. Let's explore some of the famous Architect Royals of ancient Greece and their remarkable achievements.

1. Ictinus: Ictinus was a renowned architect who was pivotal in the design and construction of the Parthenon on the Acropolis of Athens. His expertise in architectural planning and proportional

harmony helped shape the iconic temple. Ictinus focused on creating a visually balanced and harmonious structure by using mathematical ratios, such as the Golden Ratio, to determine the ideal proportions of the building. His meticulous attention to detail can be seen in the precise alignment of columns and the careful placement of sculptures and decorative elements.

2. Phidias: Phidias was primarily a sculptor, but his artistic vision extended to architecture as well. He collaborated closely with Ictinus and was responsible for the sculptural decoration of the Parthenon. Phidias's skill in creating colossal statues, including the famous statue of Athena Parthenos, brought a sense of grandeur and divine presence to the temple. His sculptures adorned the pediments, metopes, and friezes, depicting mythological narratives and honoring the gods.

3. Callicrates: Callicrates worked alongside Ictinus as one of the architects of the Parthenon. He was responsible for designing the eastern front of the temple, which faced the city of Athens. Callicrates's expertise in architectural composition and proportions contributed to the graceful and imposing appearance of the temple. His design incorporated subtle refinements to create a sense of balance and harmony, emphasizing the visual impact of the structure.

4. Mnesicles: Mnesicles was best known for his design of the Propylaea, the monumental gateway to the Acropolis of Athens. His architectural lingering influence was evident in the complex and sophisticated structure of the Propylaea. Mnesicles skillfully combined elements of the Doric and Ionic orders, seamlessly integrating the two architectural styles. The Propylaea served as

an impressive entrance to the sacred site, with its grand staircase, monumental colonnades, and intricate architectural details.
5. Hippodamus of Miletus: Although not specifically an Architect Royal, Hippodamus was a renowned urban planner and architect who made significant contributions to the field. He introduced the concept of the grid plan, or Hippodamian plan, which organized cities into rectangular blocks and straight streets.

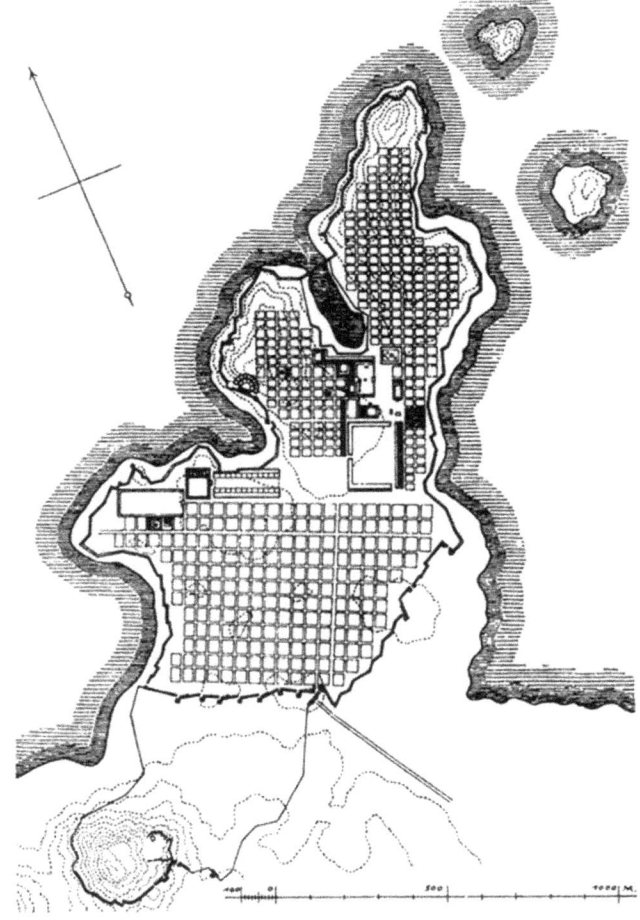

The grid plan of Miletus in the Classical period. By Hippodamos - Den svenska staden, Public Domain. Wikipedia.

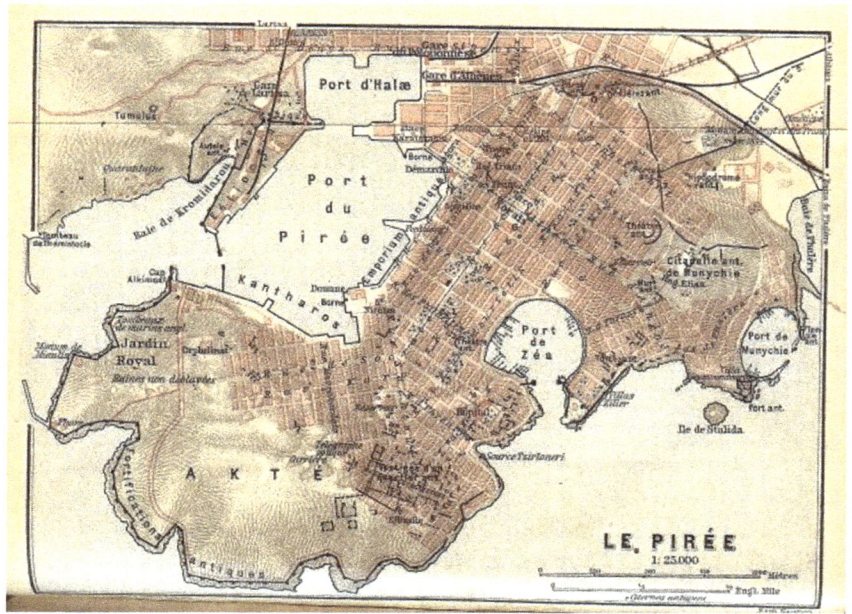

Map of Piraeus, showing the grid plan of the city. By Baedeker. Wikipedia.

Hippodamus believed that a well-structured city would nurture social order and harmony. His innovative ideas influenced the layout of many Greek cities, promoting efficient urban planning and facilitating easier navigation.

6. Pythius of Priene: Pythius was a celebrated architect who worked on various monumental projects, including the Temple of Artemis in Ephesus, one of the Seven Wonders of the Ancient World.

This model of the Temple of Artemis, at Miniatürk Park, Istanbul, Turkey, attempts to recreate the probable appearance of the third temple. Wikipedia.

The site of the temple of Artemis, Ephesus, Turkey in 2017. By FDV. Wikipedia.

His architectural skill and imaginative designs contributed to the magnificence of this temple. Pythius incorporated intricate decorative elements, such as ornate friezes and elaborate sculptures, enhancing the visual impact of the structure and reflecting the importance of the deity it honored.

7. Dinocrates: Dinocrates was an ambitious architect and urban planner known for his grand projects. He proposed carving a colossal statue of Alexander the Great on Mount Athos, envisioning a monument that would pay homage to the great conqueror. Additionally, Dinocrates designed an elaborate city plan for Alexandria, Egypt, showcasing his visionary approach to urban design. His concepts reflected a harmonious integration of architectural and natural elements, emphasizing the interconnectedness between the built environment and the surrounding landscape.[14]

These famous Architect Royals of ancient Greece left a permanent mark on the architectural heritage of the civilization. Their innovative designs, meticulous craftsmanship, and artistic sensibilities not only shaped the physical landscape of ancient Greece, but also influenced architectural principles and aesthetics for many centuries. Their works continue to inspire and captivate modern-day architects, historians, and art enthusiasts, reflecting the remarkable achievements of ancient Greek architecture.

Ancient Rome

Ancient Rome, one of the most influential civilizations in history, set a precedent in the world through its sophisticated engineering, political power, and cultural achievements. The Roman Empire, founded around 750 BCE, spanned vast territories and incorporated diverse cultures and customs under its control. Lasting for over a thousand years, this civilization showcased remarkable longevity and adaptability.

At the heart of the Roman Empire's success was its advanced engineering, which allowed for the construction of impressive infrastructure and architectural wonders. The Romans built an extensive network of roads, including the famous Appian Way, to facilitate communication, trade, and military movements.[15]

Via Appia within the ancient city of Minturno. Wikimedia.

Map of the Appian Way, and the later and shorter Via Appia Traiana. Wikimedia.

This intricate road system connected various regions within the empire and enabled the efficient administration and control of its vast territories.

The Romans also developed a strong political platform that ensured stability and governance. The empire was divided into two territories, the Western Roman Empire and the Eastern Roman Empire, with Rome serving as the epicenter of power. The emperors held significant authority and were responsible for maintaining law and order, overseeing public works, and promoting the welfare of the citizens. The empire's strength was further bolstered by its well-organized military, which stood as the largest and most powerful force of its time.

One intriguing aspect of Roman society was its approach to slavery. Slavery was a prevalent institution, with slaves constituting at least a fifth of the population. However, unlike the American system of slavery, Roman slavery was not determined by race. Slaves could occupy various roles, including teaching and other professional positions, as well as working in agrarian industries. The Romans had complex rules and terminology regarding slavery, allowing some slaves to earn wages (peculium) and eventually gain their freedom (manumission) through various means. The granting of freedom to slaves, known as Libertini, came with certain restrictions, such as restrictions on marriage with the upper class.[16] Nonetheless, exceptions to these rules existed, showcasing the nuances of Roman society.

The wealthy Romans resided in impressive homes known as "domus" or "villas." These dwellings, which were typically country homes for the affluent, demonstrated the grandeur and sophistication of Roman architecture. The villas spanned approximately 9,000 square feet and featured a well-thought-out layout. The main entrance led to an atrium, a central space with a skylight and smaller rooms for entertaining and accommodating guests. Behind the atrium was the "back of the house," which included a peristyle, an open-air garden surrounded by columns. The peristyle area housed the dining room, kitchen, bathrooms, and bedrooms. At the end of the villa was the "exedra," a space for private conversations. The wealthy Romans employed numerous slaves, sometimes reaching up to 50, to manage and maintain these opulent residences.[17]

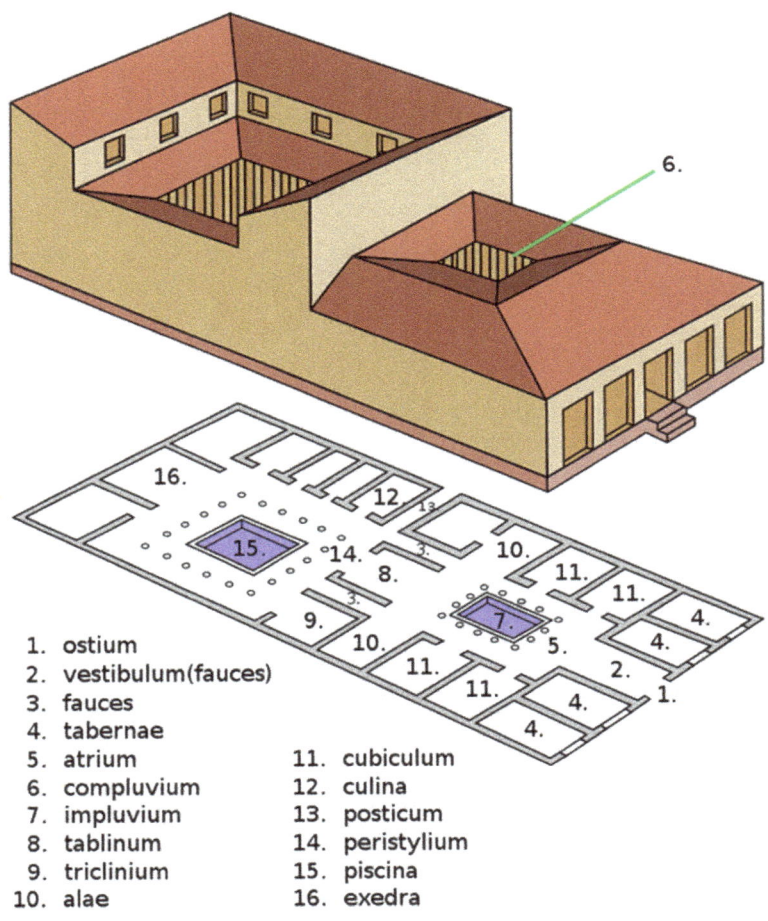

1. ostium
2. vestibulum (fauces)
3. fauces
4. tabernae
5. atrium
6. compluvium
7. impluvium
8. tablinum
9. triclinium
10. alae
11. cubiculum
12. culina
13. posticum
14. peristylium
15. piscina
16. exedra

Schematic of a domus. By Domus_romana. Wikipedia.

However, Roman society was not solely characterized by wealth and luxury. Working-class neighborhoods and slums also existed, showcasing a stark contrast in living conditions. The city of Rome was organized into districts, and public areas were designated for temples, the Colosseum, the Campus Martius, bath complexes, and gardens. Gentrification was also evident, as slum areas were demolished to make room for expanded wealthy villas. The poor inhabited apartment-style buildings called "insulae," with six to eight apartment blocks surrounding a central courtyard and staircase. These Insulae were primarily constructed of concrete, wood, and mud-brick. Living conditions in these crowded and often dangerous buildings were challenging, with the streets housing gangs, thieves, and even assassins.[17] Landlords would rent out the ground floors for retail spaces, further reflecting the dynamic nature of Roman urban life.

Ruins of an Insulae built in ancient Rome. Britannica.com

The city of Rome itself was encompassed by the Aurelian Walls, marking the edge of the city. The Old Republican Walls, an inner wall system, were also integrated into the city's defense. Immigrant districts, such as Trastevere, emerged, serving as working-class neighborhoods situated across the Tiber River on the western side of the city.[18]

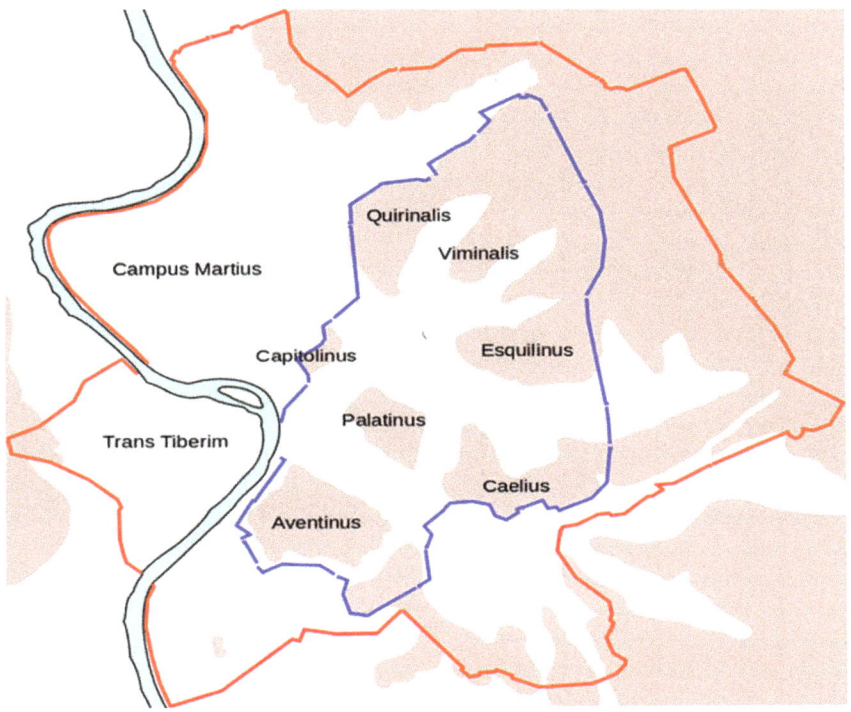

Map of ancient Rome, showing the Servian wall with a blue line, and the Aurelian wall with a red line. Highlands are shown in pink (including the Seven Hills of Rome, with names) and lowlands are shown in white. Wikipedia.

An interior view of the Aurelian walls near Porta San Sebastiano. Built between 271 – 275 AD. Wikipedia.

A preserved section of Servian Wall next to the Termini Railway Station. Photo by Salvatore Falco, June 2005. Wikimedia.

Ancient Rome, with its intricate social structures, impressive architectural achievements, and diverse urban landscapes, continues to captivate and intrigue modern-day scholars and enthusiasts. The remnants of this once-great civilization offer valuable insights into the complexities of Roman society and the tremendous legacy it imparted.

Architect Royal as a High-Ranking Position in the Roman Society

In the hierarchical society of ancient Rome, the role of the Architect Royal held significant prestige and influence. As a high-ranking position, the Architect Royal was responsible for overseeing the design, construction, and maintenance of public buildings, infrastructure, and monumental structures. This esteemed position required not only technical skills but also a deep understanding of Roman aesthetics, engineering principles, and the political landscape.

The Architect Royal served as a trusted advisor to the emperor, playing a crucial role in shaping the architectural landscape of the city and the empire at large. They were tasked with executing the grand visions of the ruling elite, translating their ambitions into magnificent structures that showcased the wealth, power, and the greatness of Rome.

One notable example of the Architect Royal's influence can be seen in the construction of temples. Temples held immense religious and symbolic significance in Roman society, serving as sacred spaces dedicated to various gods and goddesses. The Architect Royal collaborated frequently with the priesthood, ensuring that the temples adhered to religious conventions and rituals while also embodying the architectural splendor expected by the ruling elite.

The Architect Royal not only supervised the construction process but also was essential in the planning and design stages. They worked alongside skilled craftsmen, engineers, and artisans to create structures that were not only visually stunning but also structurally sound and functional. The Architect Royal's expertise in architectural principles, proportions, and aesthetics assured that each temple harmoniously blended with its surroundings, creating a remarkable presence within the cityscape.

Monuments also occupied a significant place in Roman architecture, serving as visible symbols of triumph, power, and the legacy of emperors and important figures. The Architect Royal's experience designing and overseeing the construction of these monumental structures ensured that they conveyed the desired message and left an unchanging impression on the Roman people.

One of the most iconic architectural achievements of ancient Rome, the Colosseum, stands as validation to the mastery and vision of the Architect Royal. This colossal amphitheater, with its intricate network of arches and vaults, showcased the engineering ingenuity of the time. The Architect Royal, along with a team of skilled architects and engineers, meticulously planned and executed this grand structure, which hosted thrilling gladiatorial contests, spectacles, and other public events.

The Baths of Caracalla provide another remarkable example of the Architect Royal's influence in creating monumental public buildings. These vast bathing complexes, characterized by their sophisticated heating systems, ornate decorations, and vast open spaces, served as social hubs and exemplified Roman innovation and luxury. The Architect Royal's role in designing these complex structures involved considerations of aesthetics, functionality, and engineering.

Ruins of the Baths of Caracalla, Rome. Britannica.com

The architectural achievements under the Architect Royal's guidance were not limited to Rome alone. Throughout the vast Roman Empire, cities and colonies showcased their allegiance to Rome and the emperor through the construction of public buildings and monuments. The Architect Royal heavily influenced these projects, ensuring that the architectural styles and designs reflected the influence of Roman culture while accommodating local customs and traditions.

The position of the Architect Royal in ancient Rome held immense prestige and responsibility. Architects who held this esteemed role were not only skilled professionals but also visionaries who contributed to the shaping of the Roman architectural landscape. Their creations are still admired today, serving as an indication to the ingenuity and creativity of the Architect Royal in ancient Roman society.

Architectural Achievements Under the Guidance of Architect Royals

The architectural achievements under the guidance of Architect Royals in ancient Rome involved inventiveness, skill, and artistic vision from these esteemed professionals. Their contributions left a significant mark on the cityscape and the Roman Empire as a whole. Let's explore some of the notable architectural achievements that emerged under their guidance.

One of the most iconic architectural accomplishments is the Colosseum, also known as the Flavian Amphitheater. This grand structure, commissioned by Emperor Vespasian and completed under the supervision of the Architect Royal, stands as a remarkable example of Roman engineering and design. The Colosseum's elliptical shape, towering arches, and tiered seating system allowed it to accommodate tens of thousands of spectators who gathered to witness gladiatorial contests, animal hunts, and other spectacles. Its innovative construction techniques, including the use of concrete, made it possible to create such colossal and immortal structures.

The Pantheon is another architectural marvel that showcases the genius of the Architect Royals. This temple, originally dedicated to the Roman gods, was rebuilt by Emperor Hadrian in the 2nd century CE.

The Architect Royal responsible for its design created a perfect blend of artistic expression and structural innovation. The Pantheon's iconic dome, with its oculus at the top, exemplifies the mastery of concrete construction and the use of natural light as a design element. Its harmonious proportions and intricate details make it one of the best-preserved ancient Roman buildings, demonstrating the architectural excellence of that time period.

The Pantheon dome. The coffered dome has a central oculus as the main source of natural light. Ceiling of Pantheon, Rome, Italy. Wikimedia.

Roman aqueducts, such as the Aqua Claudia and the Pont du Gard, stand as astounding feats of engineering under the guidance of Architect Royals. These monumental structures were designed to transport water from distant sources to the cities, providing a reliable water supply for public baths, fountains, and private households. The precise alignment, ingenious use of arches, and the ability to overcome natural obstacles showcase the engineering prowess and meticulous planning involved in these aqueducts.

View of the Aqua Claudia near Vecchia Roma in Rome. On top of the Aqua Claudia is the Anio Novus channel. Wikipedia.

Pont du Gard, built in 1st century A.D. Wikimedia.

The Forum Romanum, the political and social hub of ancient Rome, was transformed under the direction of Architect Royals. This sprawling complex of temples, basilicas, and public spaces served as the center of political, commercial, and social activities in the city. The Architect Royals were essential in the design and development of the Forum, creating a visually striking and functional space that reflected the magnificence of Rome.

Roman villas, such as the Villa of Hadrian in Tivoli, are another testament to the architectural achievements under the guidance of Architect Royals. These luxurious residences, owned by the elite class, exemplified Roman lifestyle and design sensibilities. Architect Royals incorporated elements such as peristyles, gardens, and intricate frescoes to create elegant and comfortable living spaces that epitomized the ideals of Roman aesthetics.

Villa of Hadrian in Tivoli. Wikipedia.

Beyond the city of Rome, Architect Royals left their mark on various provinces of the Roman Empire. The city of Pompeii, preserved by the volcanic eruption of Mount Vesuvius, provides a glimpse into Roman urban planning and architectural sophistication. The Architect Royals contributed to the layout of the city, the design of public buildings, and the construction of elegant houses adorned with intricate mosaics and frescoes.

The architectural achievements under the guidance of Architect Royals in ancient Rome were not limited to a single style or structure. They encompassed a wide range of building types, from temples and amphitheaters to baths and villas. These structures personified the values and aspirations of Roman society, which included temperance, courage, justice, and prudence. These were listed within the "mos maiorum" that means "customs of the ancestors." [19]

The influence of the Architect Royals extended far and wide, shaping the architectural landscape not only in Rome but throughout the vast Roman Empire. Their vision, technical expertise, and artistic brilliance

When We Were Gods

provided impeccable grandness that continues to captivate and inspire admiration to this day.

Notable Architect Royals in Ancient Rome

Ancient Rome was home to many notable Architect Royals who left an unquestionable relevance on the city's architectural landscape. These talented individuals contributed to shaping the opulence and magnificence of Rome through their innovative designs and engineering expertise. Let's delve into the lives and contributions of some of the most renowned Architect Royals of ancient Rome.

- **Marcus Vitruvius Pollio:** Marcus Vitruvius Pollio, commonly known as Vitruvius, was one of the most influential figures in Roman architecture. He served as an Architect Royal and was best known for his treatise "De Architectura," a comprehensive guide on architecture and engineering. Vitruvius emphasized the importance of functionality, durability, and aesthetic harmony in architectural design. His work laid the foundation for architectural principles that influenced generations of architects in ancient Rome and beyond.
- **Apollodorus of Damascus:** Apollodorus of Damascus was a prominent Architect Royal during the reign of Emperor Trajan. He is celebrated for his contributions to various monumental structures, including Trajan's Forum and Trajan's Column.[20]

Trajan's Column and Forum around 1896. Wikimedia.

Apollodorus demonstrated exceptional engineering skills in designing structures that blended functionality, grandeur, and artistic expression. His innovative use of concrete and mastery of large-scale construction projects solidified his reputation as one of the greatest architects of ancient Rome.

- **Lucius Septimius Flavianus:** Lucius Septimius Flavianus, commonly known as Severus, was a skilled Architect Royal who served during the reign of Emperor Septimius Severus. He played a pivotal role in the construction of the impressive Arch of Septimius Severus in the Roman Forum. This triumphal arch commemorated the military victories of Emperor Septimius Severus and showcased intricate reliefs and ornamental details. The arch stands as a testament to Severus' skill in designing monumental structures that exude strength and authority.

- **Gaius Julius Lacer:** Gaius Julius Lacer was an esteemed Architect Royal known for his contributions to the magnificent Baths of Caracalla. These colossal public baths, built during the reign of Emperor Caracalla, epitomized Roman engineering and luxury. Lacer's expertise in designing complex heating and plumbing systems assured comfort and functionality of the baths. The prominence and scale of the Baths of Caracalla showcased Lacer's architectural prowess and his ability to create breathtaking spaces for public use.

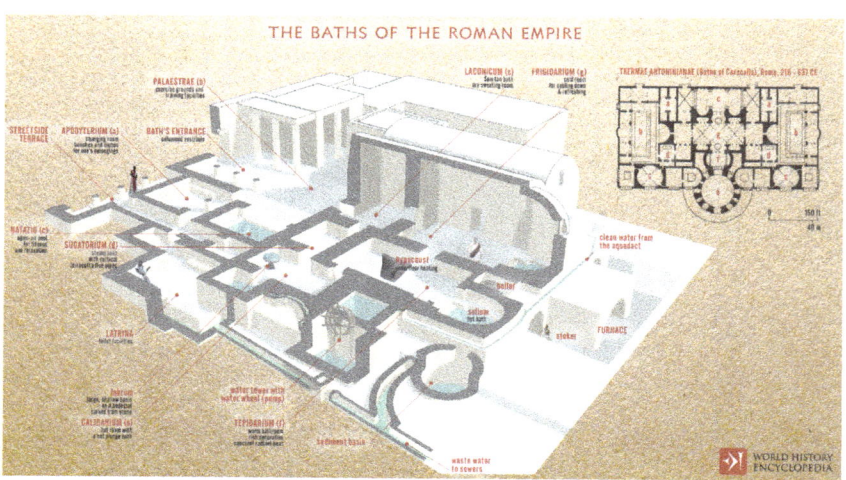

Diagram of the Baths of Caracalla. Illustration by Simeon Netchev. WorldHistory.org

- **Apollonius of Tyana:** Apollonius of Tyana, a philosopher and Architect Royal, was renowned for his architectural and urban planning projects. He was appointed by Emperor Vespasian to oversee the rebuilding of the city of Antioch after a devastating earthquake. Apollonius introduced innovative design elements and utilized advanced engineering techniques to reconstruct the city with greater resilience. His work in Antioch exemplified his commitment to urban planning and his skill in creating functional and aesthetically pleasing urban environments.

- **Hadrian:** The Emperor Hadrian is considered by many to have been an accomplished architect.[21]
- **Vitruvius:** Also known as Marcus Vitruvius Pollio, he was a Roman author, architect, and engineer in the 1st century BC. His book *De Architectura* introduced the idea of stability, utility, and beauty. Architecture students still use this book today.[22]

These notable Architect Royals, among many others, contributed significantly to the architectural permanence of ancient Rome. Through their vision, technical expertise, and creative brilliance, they shaped the city's skyline and built structures that are critically-acclaimed, even in this modern period. Their significant contributions stand as exceptional achievements of ancient Roman architecture and the indispensable role of Architect Royals in shaping the city's majesty.

08

"May the city build like me! May the Land live like me!"

Sumerian Proverb

SEGREGATION IN EARLY CIVILIZATIONS

A. Overview of Civilizations: Crete, Assyria, and Mesopotamia

In this chapter, we will explore the early civilizations of Crete, Assyria, and Mesopotamia, focusing on their societal structures, power dynamics, and the presence of segregation within these ancient cultures.

1. Crete:

Crete, a prosperous island in the Mediterranean Sea, flourished around 7000 BCE. The Minoan civilization, named after the legendary King Minos of Crete, was a Bronze Age civilization that flourished on the island of Crete in the Mediterranean Sea. Spanning roughly from 3000 BCE to 1100 BCE, the Minoans left behind a rich and fascinating culture that continues to captivate historians and archaeologists.[1]

The Minoans were known for their advanced culture and impressive achievements in various fields, including architecture, art, trade, and governance. Their civilization thrived during the height of the Bronze Age, and they developed a sophisticated society characterized by prosperity, maritime trade, and technological advancements.

One of the notable features of the Minoan civilization was their considerable architectural achievements. They built magnificent palaces, such as the famous Palace of Knossos, which served as centers of administration, trade, and culture. These palaces were grand multi-story structures with intricate designs, colorful frescoes, and advanced infrastructure, showcasing the Minoans' architectural skill.

The Minoans also developed a unique artistic style characterized by vibrant frescoes, pottery, and sculptures. Their artwork often depicted scenes of nature, animals, and religious rituals, reflecting their close connection with the natural world and their rich religious beliefs. The Minoans were skilled craftsmen, creating exquisite pottery vessels and intricate jewelry using precious metals and gemstones.

Trade was a catalyst to the Minoan civilization's success, as they established extensive networks throughout the Aegean Sea and beyond. They were seafaring people who built a powerful navy, enabling them to engage in long-distance trade with other civilizations, such as Egypt, Anatolia, and the Levant. This trade brought wealth, exotic goods, and cultural influences to Crete, contributing to the cosmopolitan nature of their society.

The Minoans also had a unique social structure that reflected a relatively egalitarian society. Women held significant roles in Minoan society, participating in religious ceremonies and often depicted in positions of authority and power. The absence of defensive fortifications in their palace complexes suggests a relatively peaceful existence, with emphasis placed on art, culture, and trade rather than warfare.

However, the Minoan civilization faced challenges and eventual decline. Around 1450 BCE, a catastrophic event, possibly a volcanic eruption on the nearby island of Thera (Santorini), and subsequent earthquakes, severely impacted Crete. The damage caused by these natural disasters, along with potential political instability and invasions, led to the eventual collapse of the Minoan civilization.

Despite its decline, the Minoan civilization left its mark on history. Its advanced architecture, artistry, and cultural achievements continue to inspire and fascinate scholars and visitors alike. It's evident that the Minoans influenced other cultures through their ingenuity and creativity, showcasing the heights that a human civilization can achieve.

2. Assyria:

The Assyrian civilization was an ancient empire that emerged in Mesopotamia, present-day Iraq, and flourished from the 25th century BCE to the 7th century BCE. Known for their military might, efficient administration, and cultural achievements, the Assyrians left a meaningful impact on the ancient world.

The Assyrians were highly skilled warriors and established one of the most powerful and formidable empires of the time. Under the leadership of ambitious rulers, they expanded their territories through military conquests, conquering vast regions of Mesopotamia, including Babylon, Egypt, and parts of Anatolia.[2]

The Assyrians developed advanced military strategies and techniques, utilizing a well-disciplined army equipped with iron weapons and chariots. Their military dominance allowed them to establish control over diverse and distant territories, effectively ruling over a vast empire with efficient administrative systems.

The Assyrian empire was organized into a centralized administration, with a highly structured bureaucracy that ensured effective governance. They developed an extensive network of provinces, each governed by appointed officials who reported to the central authority. This administrative system enabled the Assyrians to efficiently manage their vast territories and extract resources to support the empire.

In addition to their military and administrative expertise, the Assyrians made significant cultural and architectural contributions. They built magnificent cities and palaces adorned with intricate stone carvings and reliefs. One of the most famous examples of Assyrian architecture is the city of Nineveh, which served as their capital. The palaces of Nineveh, particularly the grand palace of King Ashurbanipal, showcased their architectural sophistication and artistic achievements.

Artist's impression of Assyrian Palaces. The Monuments of Nineveh. Wikimedia.

The Assyrians also excelled in the arts, literature, and science. They developed an impressive library in Nineveh, containing thousands of clay tablets that preserved valuable works of literature, historical records, and scientific texts. This library, discovered in modern times, provided invaluable insights into the knowledge and cultural achievements of the ancient Assyrians.[3]

Religion played a significant role in Assyrian society, and they worshiped a pantheon of deities, with the supreme god, Ashur, at the helm. They built grand temples dedicated to their gods and engaged in elaborate religious rituals and ceremonies. The Assyrians believed that their empire was divinely sanctioned, with the king serving as the intermediary between the gods and the people.

However, the Assyrian empire faced internal rebellions and external invasions over the centuries. In the 7th century BCE, the combined forces of the Medes, Babylonians, and others successfully invaded and destroyed Nineveh, bringing an end to the mighty Assyrian empire.

The Assyrian civilization's legacy lives on through their military strategies, administrative systems, architectural achievements, and the preservation of knowledge in their libraries. Despite their reputation as fierce conquerors, they made notable contributions to ancient civilization and left an indelible mark on history.

3. Mesopotamia:

Mesopotamia, often referred to as the "Cradle of Civilization," was one of the earliest and most influential civilizations in human history. Located between the Tigris and Euphrates rivers, in present-day Iraq, Mesopotamia witnessed the rise of several remarkable civilizations that made extensive contributions to various fields, including agriculture, governance, law, writing, literature, art, and architecture.

The history of Mesopotamia spans several millennia, but its earliest known civilization is that of the Sumerians. The Sumerians developed a complex urban society in the southern region of Mesopotamia around 4000 BCE. They built city-states with monumental structures, such as ziggurats, which served as religious and administrative centers. The Sumerians also invented one of the earliest known writing systems, cuneiform, which allowed them to record their laws, literature, and historical accounts.[4]

In the 24th century BCE, the Akkadians, led by Sargon the Great, conquered the Sumerian city-states and established the Akkadian Empire. The Akkadians adopted many aspects of Sumerian culture and contributed to the development of Mesopotamian civilization through their administrative reforms and military achievements. One of their most significant contributions was the spread of the Akkadian language, which became the lingua franca of the region.

Following the decline of the Akkadian Empire, Mesopotamia experienced a series of power shifts and the emergence of various empires and city-states. The Babylonians, led by Hammurabi in the 18th century BCE, established the Babylonian Empire and created one of the most famous legal codes in history, Hammurabi's Code. This set of laws regulated various aspects of Mesopotamian life, including social hierarchy, trade, and family matters.[5]

As stated previously, the Assyrians, who rose to power in the northern region of the territory. Known for their military might and administrative efficiency, the Assyrians built a vast empire that extended its influence over much of the Near East. They developed advanced warfare techniques, including siege warfare and the use of cavalry, which allowed them to conquer and control vast territories.

Throughout its history, Mesopotamia witnessed the rise and fall of various civilizations, including the Neo-Babylonians, the Achaemenid Persians, and the Hellenistic Seleucids. Each of these civilizations left its impression on the region, contributing to its cultural diversity and intellectual heritage.[6]

In addition to its political and military achievements, Mesopotamia made significant advancements in various fields. It pioneered the development of agriculture through the invention of irrigation systems, allowing for the cultivation of crops on a large scale. Mesopotamians also developed complex trade networks, facilitating the exchange of goods and ideas across vast distances.

In the realm of intellectual and cultural achievements, Mesopotamia gave birth to some of the earliest known works of literature, such as the *Epic of Gilgamesh*, which tells the story of a hero's quest for immortality. It also saw the construction of magnificent temples, palaces, and ziggurats, showcasing the architectural dominance of its civilizations.

The effect of Mesopotamian civilization extends far beyond its geographic boundaries. Its contributions to writing, law, mathematics, astronomy, and literature have influenced subsequent civilizations throughout history. The knowledge and innovations developed in Mesopotamia laid the foundation for future civilizations and helped shape the course of human development henceforth.

In these early civilizations, segregation was a prevalent social phenomenon, resulting from hierarchical structures, power differentials, and access to resources. The architectural landscape of these civilizations embodied and reinforced these divisions, with palaces, temples, and other grand structures serving as symbols of power and social segregation. By examining the societal structures and architectural achievements of Crete, Assyria, and Mesopotamia, we gain insights into the complexities of ancient civilizations and the impact of segregation on their development and organization.

B. Babylonian Codified Laws and Organized Servitude

The Babylonians, one of the major civilizations of ancient Mesopotamia, are renowned for their contribution to the development of written laws and the organization of servitude. Under the rule of Hammurabi in the 18th century BCE, the Babylonian Empire reached its peak and established one of the most famous legal codes in history, known as Hammurabi's Code.

Hammurabi's Code was a comprehensive set of laws that aimed to regulate various aspects of Babylonian society. The code consisted of 282 laws inscribed on a large stone monument called the Code of Hammurabi, which was displayed publicly for all to see. The laws covered a wide range of subjects, including family law, property rights, trade, labor, and criminal offenses.

One of the significant aspects of Hammurabi's Code was its focus on social hierarchy and the establishment of a just system of servitude. The code recognized different classes of individuals within Babylonian society and assigned specific rights and responsibilities to each.

At the top of the social hierarchy were the nobles and the free citizens, who enjoyed certain privileges and had more extensive legal protections. They were expected to fulfill their civic duties and contribute to the well-being of the empire.

Below the free citizens were the dependent classes, which included the peasants, artisans, and laborers. These individuals formed the backbone of the Babylonian economy and were responsible for providing goods and services to the society. They were subject to various regulations and obligations, including payment of taxes and compulsory labor for public projects.

The code also recognized the existence of slaves within Babylonian society. Slavery in Babylon was different from the racialized slavery seen in later periods of history, as slaves were not necessarily of a particular race or ethnic group. Slaves were often individuals who were captured during wars or acquired through debt bondage. They were considered property and lacked personal freedom and legal rights.

However, Hammurabi's Code included provisions that sought to protect the rights of slaves and ensure their fair treatment. It set limits on the power of slave owners, forbidding extreme physical abuse and granting slaves the right to own property and engage in business activities. The code also allowed slaves the possibility of attaining freedom through various means, such as self-purchase or release by their masters.[7]

In addition to laws related to servitude, Hammurabi's Code addressed matters of commerce, trade, and contractual obligations. It provided regulations for transactions, loans, and debt repayment, aiming to ensure fairness and stability in economic activities. The code emphasized the importance of honoring contracts and prescribed penalties for those who breached their agreements.

The significance of Hammurabi's Code extends beyond its immediate legal impact. It represented a major step forward in the codification of laws and the establishment of a centralized legal system. By enforcing standardized laws across the empire, Hammurabi aimed to promote order, justice, and social harmony.

The organized system of servitude, as outlined in Hammurabi's Code, played a crucial role in the Babylonian economy and societal structure. It provided a framework for the functioning of various sectors, including agriculture, craftsmanship, and construction. The labor of the dependent classes, including slaves, contributed to the overall prosperity and development of the empire.

The codification of laws and the organization of servitude in Babylonian society demonstrated the civilization's commitment to maintaining social order and ensuring the smooth operation of its institutions. Hammurabi's Code stands as an attestation to the Babylonians' sophisticated understanding of governance and their efforts to establish a just and regulated society.

C. Egyptian Society and Its Social Structure

Ancient Egyptian society was structured hierarchically, with distinct social classes and a well-defined social structure. As mentioned in chapter seven, occupation played a significant role in determining a person's social status in Egyptian society.

At the top of the social hierarchy were the pharaohs, who held absolute power and were considered divine rulers. They were seen as the intermediaries between the gods and the people, and held immense authority over religious, political, and administrative matters.

Below the pharaohs were the upper classes, consisting of the nobility and the elite. This group included high-ranking officials, priests, and members of the royal family. They enjoyed privileges such as land ownership, wealth, and access to education and prestigious positions within the government and religious institutions.

The middle class of ancient Egypt comprised skilled craftsmen, merchants, scribes, and some lower-ranking officials. They formed a significant portion of the population and played essential roles in the economic and administrative systems of the civilization. Skilled craftsmen, such as stonemasons, metalworkers, and carpenters, were highly respected for their specialized skills.

Below the middle class were the lower classes, which encompassed a diverse range of occupations and social groups. Farmers and agricultural workers constituted a significant portion of the population and were vital to the sustenance of the empire. They cultivated the land and produced food and other essential resources. Artisans and laborers who worked on construction projects, such as temple and monument construction, also belonged to the lower classes.

Slavery was present in ancient Egypt, but it differed from later forms of racialized slavery seen in other societies. Slaves were individuals who were captured in wars, born into slavery, or acquired through various means. They were considered the property of their owners and were primarily used for domestic service, agricultural labor, or as attendants to the nobility and the wealthy. It's important to note that slaves in ancient Egypt were not solely determined by race or ethnicity but were of various backgrounds.

The lowest social class in ancient Egypt was made up of the poor, including beggars and homeless individuals. They often struggled to meet their basic needs and relied on charity or occasional employment for survival.[8]

Ancient Egyptian society was characterized by a certain degree of social mobility, as individuals could move up or down the social ladder through various means. Achieving a higher social status was possible through marriage into higher classes, acquiring wealth, or displaying exceptional talent and skill in a particular field.

The social structure of ancient Egypt was reinforced by a well-defined set of customs, traditions, and religious beliefs. The concept of ma'at, which encompassed notions of truth, justice, and balance, played a crucial role in maintaining social order and harmony. Adhering to societal norms and fulfilling one's roles and responsibilities were highly valued in Egyptian society.[9]

It's important to recognize that the social structure of ancient Egypt was not solely based on occupation or social class but also had strong ties to the religious beliefs and concepts of the civilization. The Pharaoh, as the embodiment of divine authority, maintained the order and harmony of the society by upholding the principles of ma'at.

Overall, the social structure of ancient Egypt was complex and deeply intertwined with the religious and cultural beliefs of the civilization. It allowed for different roles and contributions within society and played a pivotal role in maintaining stability and prosperity.

D. Different Types of Servitude in Ancient Egypt

In ancient Egypt, there were various types of servitude that existed within the society. These forms of servitude were distinct from the later racialized slavery seen in other societies and were based on specific circumstances, obligations, or debts. Let's explore the different types of servitude in ancient Egypt in greater detail.

- **Chattel Slavery:** Chattel slaves in ancient Egypt were individuals who were captured in wars or obtained through other means, such as trade or as gifts. They were considered the property of their owners and had limited rights and freedoms. Chattel slaves were predominantly used for labor-intensive tasks, such as agricultural work, construction, or serving in households. It's important to note that there is no direct evidence to suggest that the ownership of slaves in ancient Egypt was determined by race or that the Egyptians practiced racial discrimination. Slavery in ancient Egypt was primarily a result of circumstances such as war or economic factors rather than racial or ethnic distinctions.

- **Bonded Labor:** Bonded laborers in ancient Egypt were individuals who voluntarily sold themselves or their family members into servitude to pay off debts or financial obligations. The creditor would acquire the debtor and their family, and the debtor would have to give up all their possessions. Bonded laborers worked for their creditors until the debt was fully repaid. While in servitude, they would perform various tasks or services as agreed upon in the agreement. It's worth noting that bonded laborers had the opportunity to integrate into society and become free citizens once their debt was settled.
- **Forced Labor:** Forced labor was another form of servitude in ancient Egypt. The government had the authority to draft laborers from the general population for state projects, such as military expeditions, mining, quarrying, or construction. These forced laborers were conscripted on a part-time basis and were compensated with wages based on their skill level and social status. Although their work was compulsory, they received payment for their services. Forced laborers were vital in carrying out large-scale projects that contributed to the development and infrastructure of ancient Egypt.
- **Servants and Household Workers:** Within the societal structure, there were individuals who worked as servants and household

workers. They were employed by the nobility, aristocracy, or wealthier families to perform various domestic tasks, including cleaning, cooking, childcare, and personal assistance. Servants were considered part of the household and often lived within the premises, occupying separate quarters. Their status and treatment varied depending on the household they served, with some being treated with dignity and respect while others faced harsher conditions.[10]

It's important to emphasize that the status of being a servant or laborer in ancient Egypt was not necessarily permanent. Some individuals voluntarily entered servitude to improve their circumstances or repay debts, while others were born into servitude. The ancient Egyptian society had provisions for the eventual liberation of slaves or the integration of servants into the dominant society. Slaves who earned wages (peculium) or rendered valuable services could justify their freedom (manumission) and become free citizens. Additionally, temple service or marriage could also provide pathways for servants to gain citizenship.[11]

The existence of different forms of servitude in ancient Egypt served various economic, social, and cultural purposes. While servitude involves limitations on personal freedoms and rights, it's important to note that the experiences and treatment of individuals varied across households and contexts. Ancient Egyptian society, with its complex social structure, acknowledged the existence of servitude while also providing opportunities for upward mobility and integration into the broader society.

E. Influence of Architecture on Social Divisions and Segregation in Other Cultures

Architecture was a determining factor in shaping social divisions and segregation in the early civilizations of Crete, Assyria, Mesopotamia, and Ancient Egypt. Let's explore the influence of architecture in each of these civilizations further.

1. Crete:

In the Minoan civilization of Crete, architecture was central in social divisions and segregation. The palaces, such as the famous Palace of Knossos, were not only grand structures but also served as administrative and ceremonial centers. The layout of these palaces showcased a clear distinction between public and private spaces. The central courtyards, throne rooms, and ceremonial areas were accessible only to the ruling elite, priests, and selected individuals. These areas were designed to emphasize the power and authority of the ruling class.

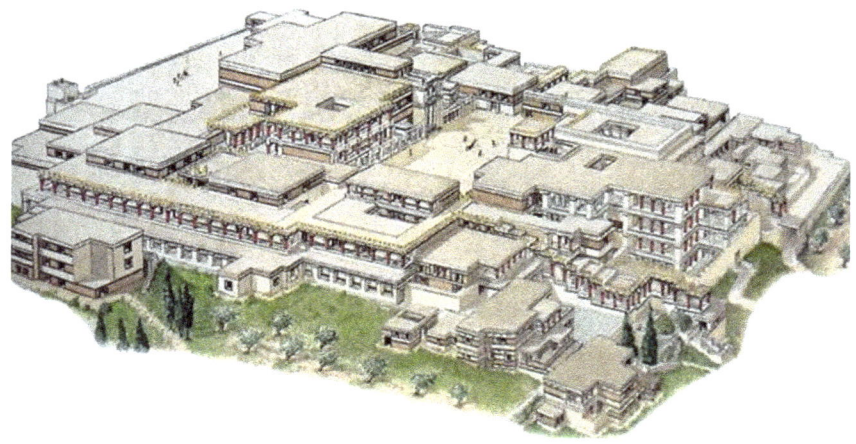

Reconstructed drawing of Palace of Knossos: The Stronghold of the Minoans. (United Kingdom: David and Charles, 2007.)

Furthermore, the Minoan palaces often featured complex labyrinthine layouts, with intricate corridors and multiple levels. These architectural designs served not only as a means of defense but also created a sense of mystery and exclusivity. Certain areas were restricted to specific individuals, while others were reserved for communal activities or public gatherings. The physical arrangement of spaces within the palaces contributed to the segregation of different social groups.

2. Assyria:

In the Assyrian civilization, architecture played a significant role in reinforcing social divisions and asserting power. The Assyrians constructed grand palaces, such as the Palace of Ashurnasirpal II and the Palace of Sargon II, which were designed to showcase the might and prominence of the ruling elite. These palaces were sprawling complexes with impressive halls, courtyards, and audience chambers.

City of Nimrud. At the North West Palace of Ashurnasirpal, 2015, before destroyed. Wikipedia.

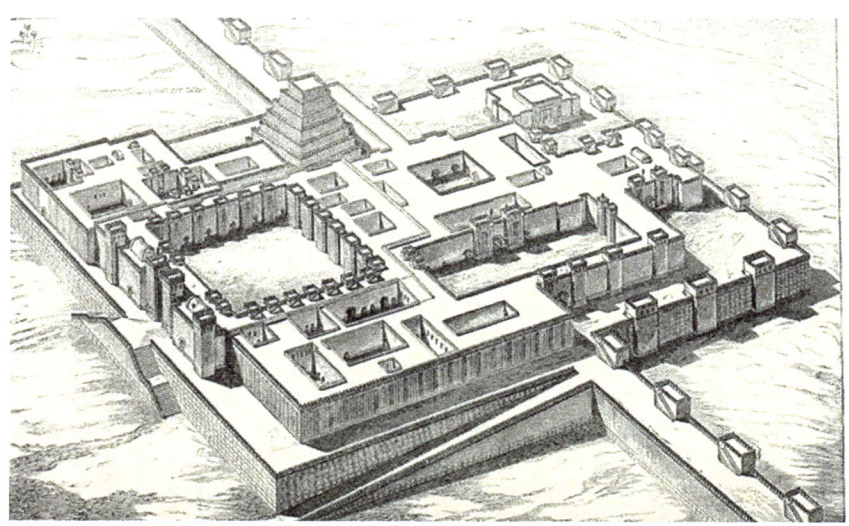

Palace of Sargon II. Reconstructed model of Palace of Sargon at Khosrabad 1905. Wikipedia.

The architectural layout of Assyrian palaces incorporated hierarchical elements, such as elevated platforms, imposing entrances, and elaborate reception halls. These design features symbolized the elevated status of the king and nobility, creating a distinct separation between the ruling class and the general population. The lavish decorations and intricate reliefs on the palace walls further emphasized the wealth and power of the elite, reinforcing social divisions.

3. Mesopotamia:

In Mesopotamia, architecture was instrumental in reinforcing social divisions and segregation, particularly in the city-states of Sumer, Akkad, and Babylonia. The ziggurats, such as the Ziggurat of Ur and the Etemenanki in Babylon, were towering temple complexes that served as religious centers and symbols of authority.

The ruins of the Great Ziggurat of Ur, taken in 2005 CE near Ali Air Base in Iraq. By Hardnfast.

The ziggurats were monumental structures built on multi-tiered platforms, with each tier accessible only to specific individuals, primarily priests and religious elites. The highest tier was reserved for the god or goddess associated with the temple. This architectural design created a clear visual distinction between the divine realm and the human realm, reinforcing the hierarchical nature of Mesopotamian society.

Additionally, city planning in Mesopotamia involved the segregation of different social groups within the urban landscape. The cities were often divided into distinct quarters, with separate areas for the ruling class, priests, merchants, and commoners. The architectural layout of these cities reflected the social stratification and ensured a physical separation between different social groups.

4. Ancient Egypt:

Architecture in Ancient Egypt employed a tiered system in social divisions and segregation. The grand temples, such as the Temple of Luxor and the Temple of Karnak, were monumental structures dedicated to the gods and served as important religious and political centers. These temples were accessible only to the high priests, pharaohs, and the ruling elite, reinforcing their privileged status and separating them from the general population.

Similarly, the royal palaces, such as the Palace of Amenhotep III and the Palace of Ramses II, were imposing structures reserved for the pharaohs and their families. The architectural design of these palaces featured grand halls, audience chambers, and private quarters that emphasized the regal power and exclusivity of the ruling class.

Overall, architecture dominance in shaping social divisions and segregation in the early civilizations of Crete, Assyria, Mesopotamia, and Ancient Egypt is considerable. The design of palaces, temples, and urban spaces reflected the power dynamics, social hierarchies, and religious beliefs of these societies, creating physical boundaries and exclusivity that reinforced social divisions.

GREEK ARCHITECTURE AND SEGREGATION

Power Dynamics and Worship in Ancient Greece

In ancient Greece, architecture shaped the power dynamics and practice of worship. Greek city-states were characterized by a hierarchical social structure, with the gods and goddesses occupying the highest position.

Imagine yourself standing in the heart of Athens, surrounded by majestic temples and structures. Each architectural masterpiece tells a story of power, segregation, and the devotion of the ancient Greeks.

The Acropolis of Athens, perched on a rocky outcrop, rises proudly above the city. At its pinnacle stands the magnificent Parthenon, a temple dedicated to the goddess Athena, the patron deity of Athens. This architectural marvel represents the embodiment of power and the divine presence. The Parthenon's majesty and meticulous design symbolize the excellence and authority of Athens as a city-state.

Parthenon, Athens, Greece taken 1978. Photography by Steve Swayne.

Within the city, the Ancient Agora of Athens served as a central gathering place, where citizens of different social classes would congregate. Here, one could witness the dynamics of power at play. The agora, with its impressive stoa (colonnaded buildings), housed the marketplace, political institutions, and social spaces. It was a hub of activity where citizens engaged in trade, participated in political discussions, and interacted with one another.

Fethiye mosque and roman forum columns in Athens, Greece. Wikimedia.

Temples were not only places of worship but also acted as symbols of segregation and social hierarchy. The Temple of Olympian Zeus, located in Athens, was one of the largest temples in the ancient world. Its colossal size and intricate design conveyed the immense power and grandeur associated with the gods. The temple's construction took several centuries to complete, highlighting the long-standing dedication and devotion to the gods.

SEGREGATION IN THE ROMAN EMPIRE

Slavery in the Roman Empire was a complex institution was fundamental in shaping social divisions and segregation. Let's delve into the details of slavery in the Roman Empire.

1. Nature of Slavery:

Slavery in the Roman Empire differed from other forms of slavery in its characteristics. Slaves were individuals who were considered property and were owned by their masters, known as "dominus." [12] They lacked personal freedom, legal rights, and were considered legal objects rather than individuals. Slaves were acquired through various means, including birth into slavery, capture in warfare, purchase, or as punishment for crimes.

2. Scope and Numbers:

Slavery was widespread in the Roman Empire, and it is estimated that slaves comprised at least one-fifth of the population. They were an integral part of the Roman economy and society, performing a wide range of tasks and roles. Slaves worked in households, mines, fields, workshops, and even held positions as teachers, entertainers, and administrators.[13]

3. Characteristics of Slavery:

a) Lack of Personal Freedom: Slaves had no personal autonomy and were entirely dependent on their masters. They were subject to the will and desires of their owners and had limited control over their own lives.

b) Legal Status: Slaves were considered property under Roman law. They could not enter into legal contracts, own property, or marry freely without the permission of their owners.

c) Treatment and Rights: Slaves varied in their treatment depending on their owners. While some slaves experienced harsh and exploitative conditions, others enjoyed relatively better treatment and opportunities. Slaves could be subjected to physical punishment, sexual exploitation, and even execution, although legal protections were in place to prevent excessive abuse.

d) Social Identity: Slavery in the Roman Empire was not determined by racial or ethnic factors. Slaves came from diverse backgrounds, including conquered peoples, prisoners of war, and individuals born into slavery. Therefore, there was no inherent racial discrimination within the institution of slavery.

e) Opportunities for Freedom: Unlike lifelong servitude, slaves in the Roman Empire had some possibilities for gaining freedom. They could be manumitted by their owners, either as a reward for exceptional service or through the purchase of their freedom using their peculium (wages). Manumitted slaves, known as "liberti," became freedmen and were granted certain legal rights, although they were still required to show respect and loyalty to their former masters.

4. Social Segregation:

Slavery in the Roman Empire also contributed to social segregation. Slaves were segregated from the free population in various ways. They lived in separate quarters or dormitories within households, worked in distinct areas, and were often marked by distinctive clothing or accessories to identify their slave status. This physical separation emphasized their subordinate position and maintained a clear distinction between slaves and the free population.

5. Influence on Society and Economy:

The institution of slavery had a far-reaching impact on Roman society and the economy. Slavery provided a cheap labor force that enabled the expansion of agriculture, mining, construction, and other economic sectors. The wealth generated by slave labor contributed to the prosperity of the Roman Empire and the social status of the elite.

While slavery perpetuated social divisions and segregation, it is important to note that the institution was not monolithic. There were instances of slaves who gained education, skills, and even freedom, and some enjoyed positions of relative privilege within households or other settings.

Certainly, slavery in the Roman Empire was a pervasive institution that shaped social divisions and segregation. The nature of slavery, the treatment of slaves, and the opportunities for freedom varied, but overall, slaves were deprived of personal freedom, legal rights, and social mobility. Slavery contributed significantly to the Roman economy and society, while maintaining a clear distinction between slaves and the free population.

DIFFERENT CLASSES WITHIN ROMAN SOCIETY

Roman society was characterized by a hierarchical structure that divided individuals into different classes, each with its own rights, privileges, and social standing.

- **Patricians:**

At the top of the social hierarchy were the patricians, who belonged to the aristocratic and wealthy elite. They were the original Roman citizens and held the highest positions in government, serving as senators, magistrates, and religious officials. Patricians enjoyed significant political influence, land ownership, and access to education.

- **Plebeians:**

Below the patricians were the plebeians, who constituted the majority of the population. The plebeians were free citizens, but they were not part of the aristocracy. They engaged in various occupations, including farming, trade, and craftsmanship. Plebeians had limited political representation initially but gained greater rights and influence over time through social and political struggles.

- **Equites:**

The equites, also known as the equestrians or knights, formed a class between the patricians and plebeians. They were a wealthy social class associated with business, commerce, and finance. Equites often served as tax collectors, contractors, and held positions in the military. They enjoyed certain privileges, such as special seating at public events and exemption from certain forms of public service.

- **Freedmen:**

Freedmen were former slaves who had gained their freedom. They occupied a distinct class within Roman society and could engage in various occupations. Many freedmen became skilled laborers, merchants, or administrators. Some successful freedmen even accumulated wealth and social status. However, they still faced certain legal and social limitations compared to freeborn citizens.

- **Slaves:**

Slaves constituted a significant portion of the Roman population. They were considered the property of their owners and had no personal freedom or legal rights. Slaves performed various tasks, including domestic work, agricultural labor, and skilled craftsmanship. The social status of slaves was the lowest in Roman society, and they lacked any form of legal or political agency.

It is important to note that these classes were not fixed and rigid, and social mobility was possible within Roman society. Individuals could move between classes through various means such as military service, wealth accumulation, or gaining favor with influential figures.

The social divisions and hierarchy within Roman society led to segregation and distinct privileges for each class. The patricians enjoyed the highest status and wielded significant political power, while the plebeians and equites occupied middle positions with varying degrees of influence. The freedmen experienced a mix of opportunities and limitations, depending on their circumstances and social networks, while slaves had no social standing or personal agency.

The class structure of Roman society influenced access to education, legal rights, political participation, and opportunities for social advancement. It created a system of social segregation and division, with varying degrees of privilege and power among different classes.

CONTRASTING LIFESTYLES AND HOUSING BETWEEN WEALTHY ROMANS AND THE WORKING CLASS

In the Roman Empire, stark contrasts in lifestyles and housing existed between the wealthy Romans and the working class. Let's explore these differences in more detail.

- **Wealthy Romans:**

The wealthy Romans lived in impressive homes known as "domus," which were often situated in urban areas and displayed their wealth and social status. These homes were spacious and designed with luxurious features. They were typically multi-story structures with elaborate architectural designs.

1. Size and Layout: Wealthy Roman homes were expansive, covering a significant area. They often had multiple courtyards, gardens, and fountains, creating a sense of grandeur. The layout of these homes varied but generally included multiple rooms and interconnected spaces.

2. Atrium: The central feature of a wealthy Roman home was the atrium, a large open space with a skylight that allowed natural light to enter the interior. The atrium served as the main reception area and was often adorned with artwork, statues, and decorative elements.

3. Peristyle: Behind the atrium, wealthy Romans had a peristyle, which was a private garden surrounded by columns. The peristyle provided a tranquil outdoor space and often had decorative elements such as sculptures, mosaics, and water features.

4. Lavish Decor: Wealthy Romans adorned their homes with luxurious furnishings, including fine mosaic floors, decorative frescoes, and ornate wall paintings. They displayed artworks, statues, and other decorative objects as a sign of their refined taste and wealth.

5. Private Facilities: Wealthy Romans enjoyed private facilities such as bathrooms with running water, heated floors known as hypocaust for distribution of heat, and elaborate bathing areas. They also had separate dining rooms, kitchens equipped with advanced cooking technologies, and spacious bedrooms with comfortable furnishings.

- **Working Class:**

In contrast, the working-class Romans, including the majority of the population, lived in more modest and compact dwellings. Their housing reflected practicality and functionality rather than extravagance.

1. Insulae: The working class primarily resided in apartment buildings known as "insulae" (meaning "islands"). These buildings were typically made of concrete, wood, and mud-brick and consisted of

multiple floors. Each floor housed several apartments arranged around a central courtyard.

2. Cramped Living Spaces: The insulae apartments were small and often crowded. Families shared limited living space, and individual rooms were compact. They typically lacked private amenities such as bathrooms and kitchens, relying on communal facilities.

3. Street-Level Shops: Insulae buildings also featured street-level shops and businesses, allowing residents to engage in commercial activities. The ground floor of an insulae was often occupied by these shops, providing additional income opportunities for the working class inhabitants.

4. Basic Amenities: Working-class dwellings lacked the lavish decor and amenities of the wealthy. They had simple furnishings and personal belongings were often minimal. Sanitation facilities were communal, with shared public latrines and water sources.

5. Location: Insulae were concentrated in urban areas, especially in densely populated cities like Rome. The working class lived in close proximity to their workplaces, often within walking distance.

The stark contrast in lifestyles and housing between the wealthy Romans and the working class reflected the vast economic and social disparities in Roman society. The wealthy enjoyed spacious and luxurious homes that showcased their wealth and social status, while the working class lived in more modest and utilitarian dwellings that focused on practicality and functionality.

These differences in housing and lifestyles highlights the social divisions and segregation that existed within Roman society. The architectural and housing disparities reinforced the hierarchy and economic disparities prevalent during the Roman Empire.

ETHNIC REGIONS AND CULTURAL DIVISIONS

In the world of ancient Greece, the tapestry of society was woven with a rich diversity of ethnic regions and cultural divisions. From the rugged mountains of Macedonia to the sun-kissed islands of Aegean, Greece encompassed a mosaic of distinct communities, each with its own customs, traditions, and sense of identity. Let's venture through the fascinating ethnic regions of ancient Greece and investigate the cultural divisions that led to its architectural geography.

1. Attica and Athens: The heart of ancient Greece is in Attica, with Athens as its vibrant center. Athens, renowned for its intellectual and artistic achievements, was a melting pot of different ethnicities. It attracted scholars, artists, and traders from far-flung regions, fostering a cosmopolitan atmosphere. The city's architecture, particularly the Acropolis, reflected the cultural fusion and cosmopolitan character of Athens.

2. Sparta and Laconia: In stark contrast to Athens, the city-state of Sparta in the region of Laconia stood as a symbol of militaristic discipline and conservative values. The Spartans, known for their rigorous training and adherence to tradition, constructed simple and austere buildings. Their architecture mirrored their emphasis on practicality and the collective over individualism.

3. Macedon: To the north, the region of Macedon, under the rule of the formidable Macedonian kings, including Philip II and Alexander the Great, left an enduring mark on Greek history. Macedonian architecture, influenced by neighboring civilizations such as Persia, showcased grandeur and opulence. The city of Pella, the capital of Macedon, boasted splendid palaces, temples, and theaters.

4. Ionian Islands: Off the western coast of Greece lay the Ionian Islands, a cluster of lush and culturally diverse lands. The Ionian cities, including Corfu and Zakynthos, were heavily influenced by Greek, Italian, and even Phoenician cultures. The architecture of the Ionian Islands featured a blend of Greek and Mediterranean styles, characterized by ornate facades, colorful frescoes, and intricate stonework.

Ionian Islands. Thethinkingtraveller.com

5. Aegean Islands: The enchanting Aegean Islands, scattered across the azure waters, were home to distinct communities with their own architectural traditions. Crete, known for its ancient Minoan civilization, boasted labyrinthine palaces and intricate frescoes. Santorini, with its iconic white-washed buildings and blue-domed churches, captured the essence of Cycladic architecture. Each island in the Aegean had its own unique charm and architectural character.

Aegean Islands, Village of Oia in Santorini. Modern Photo. Focusgreece.com

6. Epirus and Thessaly: The mountainous regions of Epirus and Thessaly were inhabited by fiercely independent communities. The architecture of these areas embraced the rugged landscape, with stone structures blending seamlessly with the natural surroundings. Fortresses and defensive walls stood as testament to the turbulent history of these regions.

7. Peloponnese: The Peloponnese Peninsula was an assortment of city-states, each with its own architectural legacy. Corinth, known for its bustling trade and artistic achievements, showcased the architectural influences of various civilizations. Olympia, home to the ancient Olympic Games, boasted grand temples dedicated to the gods.

These ethnic regions and cultural divisions within ancient Greece gave rise to a diverse architectural landscape. From the glory of Athens to the austerity of Sparta, from the opulence of Macedon to the charm of the islands, each region left its unique imprint on Greek architecture. The temples, theaters, and public spaces were not just physical structures but reflections of the beliefs, values, and aspirations of the diverse Greek communities.

HIERARCHIES WITHIN ETHNIC GROUPS AND THEIR IMPACT ON SEGREGATION

Within the ethnic groups of ancient Greece, hierarchies were consequential in shaping social dynamics and contributing to segregation within communities. These hierarchies were based on various factors, including wealth, lineage, occupation, and political power. Let's study the fascinating world of hierarchies within ethnic groups and explore their impact on segregation in ancient Greece.

1. Aristocracy and Elite: At the pinnacle of Greek society were the aristocrats and elite families who held positions of power and influence. These individuals, often descended from noble lineages, enjoyed privileges, wealth, and political authority. They resided in opulent residences, owned vast estates, and were patrons of the arts. The architectural splendor of their palaces and public buildings reflected their status and reinforced their segregation from the rest of society.

Aristocracy and Elite – Nineteenth-century painting by Philipp Foltz depicting the Athenian politician Pericles delivering his famous funeral oration in front of the Assembly. Wikipedia.

2. Free Citizens: Beneath the aristocracy were the free citizens, comprising a broad spectrum of society. These individuals, who had certain rights and privileges, included merchants, artisans, farmers, and professionals. While they enjoyed more freedoms than other social classes, they were still subject to segregation based on economic status and occupation. Free citizens often resided in neighborhoods that reflected their social standing, with wealthier citizens living in well-appointed homes and poorer citizens in more modest dwellings.

Free Citizens in a Greek Society Voting. Only Athenian men could vote. Greekhighdefinition.com

3. Metics: Metics were foreign-born residents of Greek city-states. These individuals, although not citizens, had some legal rights and often played significant roles in commerce and other economic activities. They lived in designated neighborhoods and were subject to certain restrictions and obligations. The metics experienced a level of segregation due to their non-citizen status, yet their contributions to society were recognized and valued.

Metics in Ancient Athens could also refer to immigrants invited by citizens. By Dr. Nathan Smith, Professor of Economics at Fresno Pacific University. Brewminate.com

4. Slaves: Slavery was prevalent in ancient Greece, and slaves occupied the lowest rung of the social hierarchy. They were considered property rather than citizens and were subject to the whims and commands of their owners. Slaves performed a wide range of tasks, from domestic work to agricultural labor and skilled trades. They were segregated from the free population, often residing in cramped quarters or separate slave quarters within larger households. The architecture of slave quarters reflected their marginalized status and provided minimal living conditions.

5. Women: In ancient Greece, women held a subordinate position in society, and their roles were primarily confined to the domestic sphere. They were subject to strict social norms and were often segregated from public life. Women resided within the confines of their households and had limited access to public spaces. The architecture of homes reflected the gendered divisions, with separate areas designated for women's activities and private spaces.

Women in ancient Greece: Different social classes of women in Ancient Greece. Greektraveltellers.com

These hierarchies within ethnic groups contributed to social divisions and segregation in various ways. Aristocrats and elites maintained their privileged status through exclusive access to resources, education, and political power. The segregation between the wealthy and the rest of society was evident in the stark differences in architectural styles and living conditions. Free citizens experienced segregation based on economic disparities, with distinct neighborhoods reflecting social stratification. Metics faced segregation based on their non-citizen status, even though they made valuable contributions to the city-states. Slaves endured the most extreme form of segregation, as they were considered property and subjected to harsh living conditions.

While there were divisions within ethnic groups, it is important to note that there were also instances of interaction, cooperation, and social mobility. Festivals, religious ceremonies, and other public gatherings provided opportunities for people from different social classes to come together. Additionally, individuals could rise in status through military service, wealth accumulation, or acts of valor.[14]

The impact of hierarchies and segregation on ancient Greek society was reflected not only in the architecture of the time but also in the social, economic, and political structures that shaped people's lives. Exploring the remnants of ancient Greek architecture allows us to unravel the complexities of these hierarchies and gain insights into the aspects of segregation and social divisions in this remarkable civilization.

SEGREGATION IN THE MAYAN CIVILIZATION

The emergence of the Mayan Civilization around 700 BCE marked a pivotal epoch in human history. The earliest known Mayan settlement, the city and Temple Complex of Chacchoben, stood as a testament to the immense capabilities and intellectual prowess of this early civilization. Influenced by earlier Mesoamerican cultures, such as the Olmec around 1500 BCE, the Zapotec, and the Teotihuacan, the Mayans took existing cultural paradigms and advanced them into uncharted territories. They developed sophisticated systems of governance with Kings and Queens at the helm, acting as intermediaries between the common folk and their divine pantheon. The architectural style was unique, utilizing local materials to construct impressive edifices decorated with vivid murals that narrated tales of battles, rulers, and spiritual themes. More so, their approach to urban planning revealed a deep understanding of astronomy, which informed the radial pattern of their city layouts.[15]

Mayan Government Structure and Influence of Rulers

At the heart of Mayan society was a well-defined government structure, central to which were the rulers, often Kings and Queens.

They exercised authority over their respective city-states, with each city-state functioning as a separate political entity. The ruler, known as the "Kuhul Ajaw" or "Holy Lord," was regarded as a semi-divine figure, the intermediary between the people and their gods. The ruler's main duties involved leading in warfare, performing religious rituals, and dictating laws. Their influence was pervasive, penetrating all aspects of Mayan life from political affairs to cultural practices.

Succession typically followed a patrilineal line, with the ruler's eldest son usually ascending the throne. However, exceptions were not uncommon, with women sometimes taking on leadership roles in the absence of a male heir. The ruling class was further bolstered by a class of nobles who assisted the ruler in administrative duties and war strategies.

Mayan Architectural Style and Use of Local Materials

Mayan architecture was a reflection of their advanced understanding of construction, design, and aesthetics. The primary materials used were locally sourced, mainly limestone and sandstone. The majority of the structures were straight with sharp angles, concrete construction with cement mortar being the common mode of construction. The exterior surfaces were coated with stucco, providing a smooth surface that artists embellished with elaborate carvings and vividly colored murals. These depictions ranged from religious themes to illustrations of rulers and scenes from battles.

Despite their utilitarian simplicity, Mayan buildings were breathtakingly grand, often comprising tall stepped pyramids, palaces, and ball courts. The Pyramid of Kukulkan at Chichen Itza and the Palace of Palenque are examples of the intricate stone carvings and towering structures that defined Mayan architecture. Even Frank Lloyd Wright's prairie school style of architecture in Oak Park was influenced by the

Mayans use of horizontal lines, flat roofs, stucco, organic connection with the land, and rectangular forms.[16]

The Pyramid of Kukulkan at Chichen Itza. Photo by Alastair Rae, Wikimedia.

The Palace of Palenque (Unesco World Heritage List, 1987), Chiapas, Mexico, Mayan civilization, 7th-8th century. De Agostini / Archivio J. Lange / Getty Image.

Urban Planning and Radial Pattern in Mayan Sites

The Mayans displayed an exceptional understanding of urban planning. Their cities were carefully laid out in a radial pattern, oriented along a north-south axis. Notably, this arrangement was not random. Instead, it reflected the Mayans' deep-seated interest in astronomy, with buildings often positioned to align with solar and other celestial events.

Wide plazas formed the central hub, surrounded by key structures like the royal palace, temples, and administrative buildings. Around these central areas were residential districts, markets, and smaller temples. They also incorporated natural elements into their planning, with buildings sited to take advantage of natural panoramas or to mimic the view itself, such as in the ballcourt at Copan.

The ball court of the Mayan city of Copan. The game was popular across Mesoamerica and the objective was to put a rubber ball through a hoop placed on the side walls. By Adalberto Hernandez Vega. WorldHistory.org

Possible Segregation Within Mayan Society Based on Social Hierarchy

Like most early civilizations, Mayan society was stratified, likely leading to some form of social segregation. At the top was the ruler, followed by the nobility, who were typically high-ranking officials, warriors, and priests. Next came the merchant class and skilled laborers such as artisans and scribes. The majority of the population were peasants who farmed the land and paid taxes to the ruling class.

Distinctive architectural features and spatial organization within Mayan cities provided physical manifestations of this hierarchical segregation. Rulers and nobles resided in grand palaces near the city center, while commoners lived in simple huts on the outskirts. Public spaces, like the central plaza, allowed for interaction among different social classes, but there were likely limitations on access to certain areas and participation in religious or political events.

Mayan civilization displayed a multifaceted social and spatial dynamic reflecting its complex societal hierarchy. From government structures to urban planning, every facet was influenced by the prevailing social order, inextricably linking the spatial and the social in Mayan civilization.

In summary, this chapter introduced some of the earliest civilizations on record known to modern man. With each thriving community and society, there was always a need to create a social hierarchy, and there were constant efforts to stratify the population. It's inherent that people want to exert a form of dominance over others, especially if they are different in religion, culture, ethnicity, and social status. Architecture has reinforced this logic and reasoning to enforce divisions and validate segregation. From ancient civilizations to ancient Egypt, the Greek Empire to the Great Roman Empire, and Native Americans to Mesoamericans, there was always a need to have slaves, servants, the working class, the wealthy class, aristocrats, and monarchies to fuel the economy, and the structures they inhabited reflected their role in society.

09

"Class structures are a luxury that we cannot afford."

H. Rap Brown

ARCHITECT AS NATION BUILDER

FORMATION OF NATIONS AND SEGREGATION

The formation of nations is a complex process embedded in the annals of history, entwined with sociopolitical evolution, cultural growth, economic expansion, and conflict resolution. However, this process has often been accompanied by the unsightly facet of societal organization - segregation. The systemic division of people into distinct groups based on attributes such as race, religion, socioeconomic status, or ethnicity has been an unfortunate byproduct of nation-building. It is essential to understand how nations were formed, and the role segregation has played in shaping our global society.

Nations are political entities with definitive geographic boundaries governed by a central authority. Their formation can be traced back to ancient times when nomadic tribes began to settle in specific regions, eventually forming communities bound by shared cultures, religions, and languages. Over time, as these communities expanded, evolved, and interacted with neighboring communities, they adopted more complex social structures. This progression led to the creation of city-states and, eventually, nations.

The process of nation formation accelerated during the period known as the Age of Discovery (15th to 17th century), as European explorers "discovered" new lands. Often, these discoveries were followed by colonization, where the colonizing nation imposed its culture, language, and governance structures upon the colonized peoples.[1] This process of political, social, and cultural assimilation was a significant driver of nation formation during this period.

In more recent times, the formation of nations has often been spurred by struggles for independence or self-determination. A notable example is the decolonization period following World War II, during which many African and Asian countries gained independence from their European colonizers.

The unfortunate reality of segregation has often been intertwined with the formation of nations. When different cultural, ethnic, or religious groups coexist within a nation, there can be a tendency for dominant groups to enact laws and practices that discriminate against minority groups. This systemic bias can manifest in various forms, including racial segregation, religious intolerance, or class disparity.

One of the most notorious examples of state-sanctioned segregation was the Apartheid system in South Africa, a policy of racial segregation and economic discrimination against non-whites. Similarly, the Indian caste system, although not state-sanctioned, has perpetuated extreme social stratification and discrimination based on one's caste or social class.

In some cases, segregation has served as a catalyst for the formation of new nations. For instance, the Partition of India in 1947, which led to the creation of Pakistan, was largely driven by religious segregation between Hindus and Muslims.[2]

The Partition of India – People exercise in an Indian refugee camp to stave off despair in the wake of the 1947 Partition of India and Pakistan. Kurukshetra was home to one of the largest camps due to its proximity to the hastily drawn border that carved two independent states out of the former British colony. Photograph by henri cartier-bresson, magnum. National Geographic.

Yet, it is important to note that nations are capable of moving beyond segregation, even if the process can be slow and fraught with challenges. Laws can be amended, attitudes can change, and societies can evolve to become more inclusive. Indeed, the fight against segregation has led to some of the most significant civil rights movements in history, further shaping the nations as we know them today.

In essence, understanding the formation of nations and the role of segregation is crucial to grasping the world's socio-political landscape. The history of nations is a rich tapestry, marked not only by the progress of societies but also by their struggles to ensure justice, equality, and unity amidst diversity.

A. Migration and Formation of Nations in Europe, Africa, and the Middle East

Migration has always been a fundamental aspect of human existence, and its impacts are felt far and wide, contributing significantly to the formation and development of nations across continents. In this section, we will explore how migration influenced the formation of nations in Europe, Africa, and the Middle East.

- **Europe**

In Europe, the movement of people and cross-interaction of nationalities changed the course of history and the development of nations in that region of the world. This historical trend extends from ancient times, such as the migrations of the Roman and Greek civilizations that contributed to the expansion and consolidation of their empires, to more recent movements influenced by political, economic, social factors, and warring factions.

One of the most remarkable and transformative periods of migration in European history occurred during the Migration Period,[3] spanning from the 4th to the 6th century CE. This era, often referred to as the "Barbarian Invasions," witnessed the movement of Germanic tribes such as the Goths, Vandals, and Lombards. These tribes traversed vast distances, entering and reshaping the once-mighty Roman Empire. The impact of these migrations was profound, leading to significant shifts in political dynamics and ultimately contributing to the emergence of these diverse nations across Europe including the Franks and Anglo-Saxons.

Barbarian Invasions. The Huns, whose movement westward off the Eurasian Steppe may have triggered migrations into the Western Roman Empire; with The Favorites of the Emperor Honorius by J. W. Waterhouse, 1883. The Collector.com

Notably, the Migration Period played a pivotal role in redefining the geopolitical landscape of the continent. The influx of different groups triggered political upheaval, as new power structures formed and existing empires weakened. This complex interplay of migration and political change laid the foundation for the montage of nations that characterize Europe today such as France and the British Isles.

Fast-forwarding to the 19th and 20th centuries, Europe experienced further waves of migration that were driven by the tumultuous events of the World Wars, the dissolution of empires, and the eventual establishment of institutions like the European Union. The aftermath of these historical events reshaped national boundaries and prompted the emergence of new states while causing others to dissolve.

These instances of migration-driven nation formation underscore the intrinsic connection between human movement and the establishment of political entities. The intertwined narratives of migration and nation-building reveal how the movement of people with various cultural and ethnic differences has continually shaped the map of Europe, forming permanent markers on its history, culture, and societal dynamics.

- **Africa**

In Africa, migration has exerted a powerful influence on the continent's socio-political fabric and economic dynamics. Ancient Bantu migrations, dating back centuries, have left a memorable mark on Sub-Saharan Africa's linguistic and cultural prolificacy. These migrations not only facilitated the spread of cultural practices and languages but also influenced the diverse identities that characterize the region.

Moving into the 19th century, the Scramble for Africa by European colonial powers further underscored the significance of migration in the formation of nations. This period witnessed a tumultuous interplay between European colonial interests and the indigenous populations. The colonial boundaries imposed during this era often disregarded the intricate social and ethnic landscapes that had evolved over centuries. This disruption led to complex challenges related to identity and self-determination for many African communities.

The Post-World War II decolonization era marked a pivotal juncture in African history. As nations gained independence, demographic shifts ensued as previously colonized regions navigated the process of nation-building. Conversely, during the 8th-15th centuries, the influence of Moorish architecture becomes especially pertinent.

The Moors, who originated from North Africa and are renowned for their architectural accomplishments, spawned an unprecedented endowment upon the architectural landscape of Spain and North Africa. This was influenced by Middle Eastern Islamic traditions and Roman, Byzantine, and Visigoth styles and evolved into a distinctive style that featured geometric patterns and highly detailed interior building surface designs. The architectural legacy of the Moors left an unforgettable imprint with intricate designs, complex forms, and innovative structural techniques that continue to influence the aesthetics and construction methods in these regions.⁴

In Spain, the Moors' architectural contributions are manifest in the intricate details of buildings such as the Alhambra in Granada, where the fusion of Islamic and Spanish architectural elements created a unique and captivating synthesis. This blending of architectural styles speaks to the multicultural influences that have shaped Spain's architectural heritage that is unique in the world.

Dawn on Charles V palace in Alhambra, Granada, Spain. Wikipedia.

In North Africa, the Moors' architectural style served as a testament to their advanced engineering, artistic prowess, and intellectual contributions. Many scholars charge that the Moors "awakened" parts of Europe and brought them out of the dark ages. Structures like the Great Mosque of Cordoba stand as enduring examples of the Moors' architectural ingenuity, characterized by ornate embellishments and sophisticated design principles.

Great Mosque of Cordoba, Spain, begun in 786 and enlarged during the 9th & 10th centuries. Wikimedia.

The architectural heritage left by the Moors serves as a vivid reminder of the interconnectedness of cultures and civilizations, demonstrating how migration, trade, and shared knowledge have shaped architectural expressions across geographical and historical boundaries.

- The Middle East

The Middle East's history is steeped in migratory movements, from the ancient Semitic peoples who formed some of the earliest civilizations to the Arab conquests of the 7th and 8th centuries that spread Islam and the Arabic language across the region.[5]

In the 20th century, migration due to political conflicts, such as the Israeli-Palestinian conflict and the displacement caused by various wars, has significantly shaped the region's nations. The influx of refugees has impacted the demographic landscape and contributed to the ongoing political complexities.

The interplay between migration and the formation of nations is evident across these three continents. This relationship is complex and multifaceted, underscoring the essential role migration plays in shaping our world. As we continue to witness significant migration trends, it's crucial to understand this historical context to address contemporary issues effectively.

B. Ethnic Groups and Their Segregation Within Nation-States

The formation of nations and the consequent segregation of ethnic groups within nation-states is a fascinating, albeit complex, phenomenon. Ethnic groups are usually bound by commonalities such as language, culture, religion, or shared history, which distinguish them from other groups. Nation-states, on the other hand, are political entities with defined territorial boundaries, within which the ethnic groups live. The interaction between different ethnic groups and the state can often lead to various forms of segregation. This segregation can be a product of systemic discrimination, socio-economic disparities, historical conflicts, or political maneuvering.

Europe and Ethnic Segregation

In Europe, one of the most striking examples of ethnic segregation is seen in the Balkan Peninsula, which is known for its complex patchwork of ethnic groups. After the collapse of Yugoslavia, newly formed nation-states like Bosnia, Herzegovina, Serbia, and Croatia saw significant ethnic segregation, often fueled by nationalist sentiments and historical grievances. This segregation often led to ethnic conflicts, as witnessed during the Yugoslav Wars of the 1990s.[6]

Effect of the 1991- 1995 Yugoslav War on the class struggle. Spassmaschine August 25, 2009.

Ethnic Segregation in Africa

In Africa, ethnic segregation within nation-states often had its roots in the colonial era when arbitrary borders were drawn without consideration for the ethnic compositions of the regions. This led to a mix of various ethnic groups within newly formed nations, often leading to tensions and conflicts, such as the Hutu-Tutsi conflict in Rwanda and Burundi.

Middle East and Ethnic Groups

In the Middle East, a similar pattern is visible where nation-states like Iraq and Syria house a variety of ethnic groups, including Arabs, Kurds, Turkmen, Assyrians, and more. Historical tensions and political manipulation have often led to ethnic segregation and conflicts, as witnessed in the Kurdish struggle for autonomy in several nations in the region.

The Complexity of Ethnic Segregation

However, it's essential to note that the story of ethnic segregation within nation-states isn't always one of conflict and division. Often, it's also a story of coexistence, integration, and mutual influence. In many places, different ethnic groups have enriched their nations with a mosaic of languages, cuisines, music, and traditions.

The relationship between ethnic groups and their segregation within nation-states is complex and multifaceted. It is often influenced by historical, socio-political, and economic factors and varies significantly from one region to another. By understanding these dynamics, we can work towards mitigating conflicts, promoting coexistence, and appreciating the cultural richness that these ethnic groups bring to their nations.

C. Impact of Segregation on Power Dynamics and Social Divisions

Power dynamics and social divisions within societies are often profoundly shaped by segregation, the systemic separation of people into different areas based on their racial, ethnic, or social background. Drawing on examples from earlier chapters, including the hierarchical social structure of the Mayan civilization and the segregationist policies in modern nations, this section will delve into the effects of segregation on the distribution of power and social divisions within communities.

Segregation, in its different forms, perpetuates and exacerbates inequalities by reinforcing socio-economic disparities and stigmatizing certain social groups. This process significantly impacts the power dynamics within societies by consolidating control and resources in the hands of a specific social group, often at the expense of others.

Take, for instance, the Mayan civilization, where the spatial segregation based on social hierarchies fostered a stratified society, with the ruling elites living in grand palaces and temples at the center of cities while the commoners dwelled in modest houses in the periphery. This geographical segregation mirrored and reinforced many undercurrents, with the elites commanding vast resources, wielding political authority, and maintaining spiritual leadership.

Ancient Mayan House, Mexico. Courtesy of Bowden, Martha. January 4, 2008.

Modern societies are not exempt from such disparities, albeit in subtler forms. In many contemporary nation-states, segregation based on ethnic or racial lines can lead to a concentration of power in certain social groups. These divisions can result in unequal access to resources like education, healthcare, and economic opportunities, thereby reinforcing the status quo and sustaining the social and economic dominance.

For instance, in South Africa under apartheid or in the racially segregated neighborhoods in the United States during the Jim Crow era, minority groups were deprived of resources and opportunities, which entrenched the socio-economic disparities and ensured the continuation of a power imbalance favoring the dominant group.

Moreover, the institutionalization of segregation often contributes to stigmatizing perceptions of marginalized groups, fueling stereotypes, and fostering prejudice. These social divisions can undermine social cohesion, breed conflict, and perpetuate social inequality, thus impacting societal stability and progression.

Segregation significantly affects hierarchies and social divisions within societies, perpetuating systemic inequalities, and hindering social integration. The legacy of segregation, as witnessed in both ancient and contemporary societies, emphasizes the importance of pursuing inclusive and equitable policies to foster unity and social justice.

10

"Power tends to corrupt, and absolute power corrupts absolutely."

Lord Acton

A BRAVE NEW WORLD

THE ARCHITECTURE OF INSTITUTIONALIZED RACISM

Overview of Generational Slavery and the Transmigration of Subjugated Persons

As we study the exploration of the architects of institutionalized racism, it's essential to understand the underlying historical context that propagated and sustained these structures of oppression. This chapter delves into the phenomena of generational slavery and the transmigration of subjugated persons, focusing on two significant instances: the destruction of the native peoples of North America and the diaspora of African people through the Triangular Slave Trade.

A. The Destruction of Native Peoples of North America

From the 15th century onwards, the arrival of European explorers and colonists in the New World marked the beginning of a tumultuous period in the history of the indigenous peoples of North America. This interaction would set off a chain of events that culminated in the extensive devastation of native populations, primarily through the introduction of diseases, warfare, displacement, and forced labor.

The encounter between European settlers and the native inhabitants had catastrophic consequences, largely due to the introduction of diseases that the indigenous peoples had no immunity against. Epidemics like smallpox, influenza, germ warfare, and other illnesses swept through native communities, resulting in staggering death tolls. In some regions, these diseases led to a devastating reduction in native populations by as much as 90%, drastically altering the demographic landscape.[1]

Additionally, the colonial powers, including the English, French, and Spanish, engaged in conflicts with the native tribes to exert control over the newly discovered territories. This often resulted in subjugation, captivity, and enslavement of indigenous individuals. Many native peoples were subjected to forced labor within the colonies or sold as slaves in overseas markets, further eroding their societies and cultures.

Concurrently, the dispossession of native lands pushed these communities into a cycle of displacement, causing profound social disruption and loss of life. This process of forced land seizure and enslavement can be seen as a manifestation of institutionalized racism, rooted in the belief in European racial superiority and the justification of conquest via Manifest Destiny.[2]

It's important to recognize the diversity of native cultures across North America and the distinct architectural forms that emerged from these societies. For instance, the Cherokee and Creek nations in the southwestern region of North America exhibited intricate social structures that contributed to the well-being of the entire community. The architectural manifestations of these cultures varied widely, ranging from caves nestled within the Appalachian Mountains to forts constructed using wood and thatch.

Spiritual beliefs were of the utmost importance in shaping the architectural practices of many native cultures. Structures like burial mounds served as both places of reverence and symbols of their connection to the earth and the cosmos. These mounds, found predominantly in the eastern regions of North America, were designed as elaborate earthen structures that contained tombs and significant artifacts, embodying the concept of life's cyclical nature.[3]

Mound C at Etowah Indian Mounds. Georgia Dept. of Economic Development.

In the northwest, the Iroquois, Wampanoag, and Sioux crafted their dwellings using distinct materials and techniques that reflected their environments and lifestyles. In the western regions, nomadic cultures such as the Navajo, Cheyenne, Apache, Comanche, and Hopi developed shelters like teepees that accommodated their mobility and resource needs.

It is important to mention that many sophisticated civilizations existed in North America prior to colonial expansion. One of the largest Native American societies was that of Cahokia. This was a Pre-Columbian society that existed around 1,050 AD. This location was located near south-western Illinois. The size of this society was nearly 2,200 acres and maintained a population of around 15,000 people based on archeological evidence. This civilization left over 120 earthen mounds in various configurations and dimensions. This site is now a National Historic Landmark.[4]

A Shoshone encampment in Wind River Mountains of Wyoming, Photo by W.H. Jackson, 1870.

Particularly striking is the architectural ingenuity of the Hopi people, who inhabited mountainous terrain. They constructed Kivas, unique circular underground structures, within rocky formations. These Kivas held deep cultural significance, serving as ceremonial spaces and reflecting their spiritual relationship with the land.

Interior of a Kiva at Mesa Verde National Park. Wikimedia.

As we examine the architectural diversity and the impact of colonization on native societies, it becomes evident that the destruction of native peoples in North America was not just about the physical devastation but also the erosion of cultural practices, architectural heritage, and spiritual connections that had thrived for generations. This history highlights the intricate interplay between architecture, culture, and the complex dynamics of colonization.

B. The Diaspora of African People Through the Triangular Slave Trade

Parallel to the events unfolding in North America was another tragedy of equally monstrous proportions—the African slave trade. A significant part of this took place through the Triangular Slave Trade, a complex and horrific network of transatlantic human trafficking that played an integral role in the diaspora of African people.

The Triangular Trade involved three regions: Europe, Africa, and the Americas. European ships loaded with goods like guns, textiles, and alcohol would set sail for Africa, where these items would be traded for enslaved Africans. These individuals were then transported across the Atlantic under horrific conditions in a journey known as the Middle Passage. On reaching the Americas, the enslaved Africans were sold and the ships were loaded with American products like sugar, tobacco, and cotton to be taken back to Europe.

This system facilitated the forced migration of millions of Africans to the New World, where they were subjected to a life of brutal servitude. The architecture of this oppressive system was underpinned by a deeply entrenched belief in racial superiority and the dehumanization of the African people.

The experiences of the native peoples of North America and the African diaspora reflect a pattern of dehumanization, exploitation, and racism that shaped and sustained these structures of oppression.

The architecture of this separation due to race and culture manifested in distinctly different ways. The White population constructed structures referencing English traditional styles and building techniques. In stark contrast, the African population, who were forcibly brought to the Americas, created shelters using the available resources while adhering to methodologies rooted in their cultural heritage.

A prime example of African architectural influence can be seen in the design of slave quarters, which often featured a distinctive architectural typology known as the "Shotgun House." This type of house is characterized by its long and narrow footprint, with the front door opening directly into a public or formal living space. The kitchen typically occupied the middle of the house, while the private and informal bedroom area was situated at the rear. The name "Shotgun" derives from the unobstructed front-to-back circulation through the house, where one could walk directly from the front door to the rear without obstruction.

Shotgun house in the Fifth Ward neighborhood of Houston, Texas, 1973. Wikipedia.

It's essential to note that the level of finishes and comfort in these Shotgun Houses was significantly inferior to the lodgings of the Slave Owner's home. This marked a clear distinction in architectural standards that reinforced the hierarchy of slavery.

On the other end of the spectrum, the architectural style of the Plantation Home emerged as a new typology, characterized by its imposing façade and grand presence. This style often featured a long and elevated front porch with a colonnade spanning the entire front elevation. Such houses projected dominance and authority, symbolizing that the rules and regulations of the plantation were established and enforced from within.

Annandale Plantation in Mannsdale, Mississippi. Built from 1857 – 59. Mississippi Archives.

Studying the architecture of Antebellum Houses provides valuable insights into the society of that era and the architects who designed these structures. The architectural choices made during this time were intricately linked to the social hierarchy perpetuated by slavery.

Plessy v. Ferguson and the Legalization of Segregation

The case of Plessy v. Ferguson, decided by the U.S. Supreme Court in 1896, remains one of the most infamous rulings in American history. It effectively legalized racial segregation, perpetuating systemic racism and deepening racial disparities. The court's decision and its subsequent implications resulted in a marked dark chapter of U.S. history.

Homer Plessy, a man of mixed race (an "Octoroon" in the parlance of the day), intentionally challenged Louisiana's Separate Car Act of 1890 by refusing to leave the "whites only" car on a train journey. Arrested and convicted, Plessy's subsequent appeal became the basis for the case that would reach the Supreme Court. Plessy argued that the Act violated the 13th Amendment (ratified 1865), which abolished slavery, and the 14th Amendment (ratified 1868), which granted equal protection of the laws to all U.S. citizens.[4]

C. The Supreme Court Decision and Its Impact on Racial Segregation

In Plessy v. Ferguson, the Supreme Court was asked to consider the constitutionality of a Louisiana law that mandated separate railway carriages for blacks and whites. The plaintiff, Homer Adolph Plessy, who was of mixed-race but considered black under Louisiana's "one-drop rule," deliberately violated the law as part of a planned challenge to its constitutionality. Plessy was arrested, and his case eventually found its way to the Supreme Court.

The justices ruled in a 7-1 decision that the Louisiana law did not violate the 14th Amendment's Equal Protection Clause. They argued that as long as the separate facilities for blacks and whites were equal, their segregation did not constitute unlawful discrimination. This landmark decision upheld the principle of "separate but equal," thereby legally sanctioned racial segregation across the United States. The impact was immediate and far-reaching, touching every aspect of life, from education and housing to transportation and public accommodations.[5]

THE CIVIL WAR AND THE FORMATION OF SEPARATE AND UNEQUAL

The doctrine of "separate but equal" became the legal groundwork for many other laws and ordinances mandating racial segregation. The court held that segregation itself was not a violation of the 14th Amendment, which guarantees all citizens equal protection under the law, and provided that the separate facilities and services for blacks and whites were ostensibly equal.

However, in practice, the "separate but equal" doctrine became a means to justify gross racial disparities. The facilities and services provided to African Americans were habitually inferior to those provided to White Americans, both in terms of quality and access. Schools, hospitals, parks, and even public transportation were all subject to this grossly unjust policy. This system upheld an inherently unequal social order, perpetuating socioeconomic disparities that have lingered even into the modern era.

D. The Establishment of Jim Crow Segregation Laws

The Plessy decision helped to accelerate the proliferation of state and local laws enforcing racial segregation, now known collectively as Jim Crow laws. These laws, named after a black character in minstrel shows, were enacted from the late 19th century through the first half of the 20th century.

The Jim Crow laws dictated a system of segregation in virtually all public spaces, including schools, buses, trains, restaurants, and even drinking fountains. Beyond just spatial segregation, these laws also sought to disenfranchise African Americans, making it extremely difficult for them to vote through tactics like poll taxes and literacy tests.

The effect of these laws on buildings and the workforce, especially within federally financed and operated establishments and edifices, was profound. In 1913, President Woodrow Wilson's administration introduced policies that emboldened Jim Crow practices, effectively giving Presidential authorization to racial segregation. This dealt a significant blow to African Americans' efforts to fully integrate into American society following the era of slavery. Prior to Wilson's election, Black Americans held positions at all levels of the federal government.

Despite Wilson's campaign promise of equal treatment, many African Americans, including prominent figures like W.E.B. DuBois, supported his candidacy. However, after taking office, Wilson swiftly implemented segregation across various aspects of society under his control, appointing Southern Democrats who supported segregationist policies.[5]

The initial segregation of federal facilities started with postal offices and the treasury department, creating separate spaces for African Americans and White Americans. These policies proliferated throughout the United States, affecting public facilities ranging from places of lodging, transportation, restaurants, schools, and banks to churches and doctor's offices. Buildings were retrofitted to accommodate segregated areas for Whites and Blacks, extending even to spaces like movie theaters and water fountains.

Examples of public segregated facilities included separate waiting rooms in train stations, designated seating areas in buses, and separate entrances for Whites and Blacks in various public buildings. Since the rail transportation system in the U.S. was the primary form of traveling long distances in the late eighteen hundreds and early nineteenth century, many train stations were designed and modified to reinforce this law. The Byrd Street Station in Richmond, VA (1914) and Tampa Union Station in Tampa, FL (1912) illustrates designated spaces to limit and control the movements of White and Black patrons within the same place for the same function.[6]

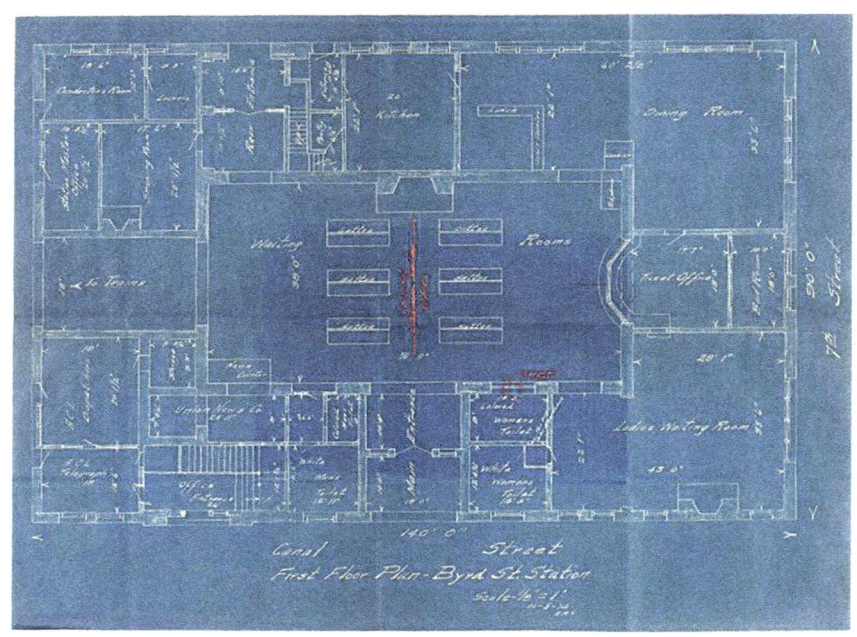

Original floor plan for Byrd St Station, Library of Virginia, and Library of Congress.

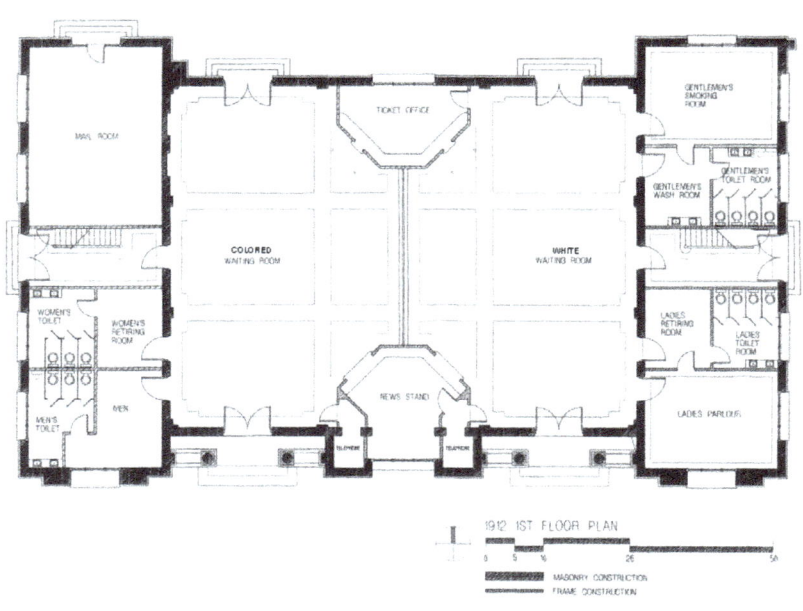

Original floor plan for Tampa Union Station, FTUS, Rowe Architects.

Additionally, examples of buildings designed and constructed with segregated areas were prevalent. For instance, the Pentagon, one of the most iconic government buildings, was designed to contain separate cafeterias and restrooms in accordance with Virginia's racial segregation laws. The construction engineer, Captain Clarence Renshaw, faced the challenge of complying with these laws, despite President Roosevelt's 1941 Executive Order prohibiting discrimination against government workers. When Roosevelt toured the building while under construction, he questioned the need for four large washrooms on each of the main hallways from the outer ring to the inner ring. After learning about Virginia's segregation laws, he ordered that there should be no signage identifying White or Black occupants in the Pentagon's facilities.[7]

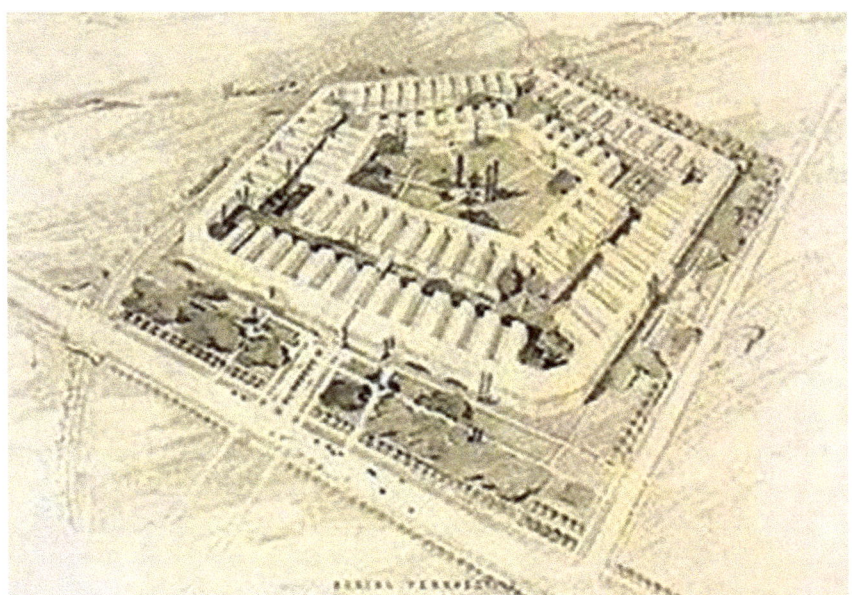

Original sketch for the Pentagon Building, July 21, 1941.

Ultimately, the Plessy v. Ferguson decision and its aftermath deeply entrenched racial discrimination in the United States, institutionalizing racism at the legal level and deeply influencing the design and use of public spaces and federal facilities.

A Brave New World

E. The Civil War and the Formation of Separate and Unequal

The American Civil War, a pivotal event in the country's history, deeply influenced the racial dynamics of the nation. Fought from 1861 to 1865, the Civil War's primary cause was the issue of slavery and the rights of states versus the federal government.

The Role of the Civil War in Shaping Racial Dynamics

Before the Civil War, slavery was deeply embedded in the social, economic, and political fabric of the Southern states. African slaves, taken from their homelands and sold into bondage, formed the backbone of the Southern economy, particularly in cotton production. This practice led to a deeply ingrained racial hierarchy, with whites on top and enslaved Africans at the bottom with Natives Americans.

The Civil War began as a conflict over states' rights, but it was the question of slavery that lit the fuse. The Southern Confederacy feared that the Northern Union, where slavery was less prevalent and was becoming increasingly opposed, would take measures to abolish slavery.

As the war progressed, it shifted from a battle for preserving the Union to a crusade for emancipation. The Emancipation Proclamation issued by President Abraham Lincoln in 1862, although it did not immediately free all slaves, was a clear signal that the end of slavery was a primary war aim for the North. It also allowed for the enlistment of African American men in the Union Army, a significant step toward equality and recognition.[7]

However, the end of the war and the abolition of slavery did not lead to immediate racial equality. The Thirteenth Amendment officially abolished slavery, but it was followed by a backlash from those who were unwilling to see a change in the status quo. The social order had been upended, and many Southern Whites were not ready to accept African Americans as their equals.

This led to a period of violent adjustment as Southern society grappled with a new social reality. While the Civil War ended the institutionalized practice of slavery, it marked the beginning of a new phase in racial dynamics. The end of slavery was not the end of racial subjugation; instead, it was transmuted into different forms that continued to preserve white supremacy and reinforce racial hierarchies. The entrenched racial prejudices, buttressed by pseudo-scientific theories of the time, led to widespread racial discrimination and the birth of institutionalized racism.

The Aftermath of the War and the Rise of Institutionalized Racism

The Civil War, while a catalyst for the emancipation of enslaved African Americans, was not the panacea for racial inequality that many had hoped it would be. In the immediate aftermath of the war, the United States underwent a period known as Reconstruction, during which the federal government attempted to rebuild the Southern states and integrate the freed African Americans into society.

In the early years of Reconstruction, there was significant progress towards racial equality. Freed African Americans were granted citizenship and equal protection under the law by the Fourteenth Amendment and the right to vote by the Fifteenth Amendment. African Americans were elected to public offices, including Congress, in numbers not seen before or since during this period.[8]

However, these advancements were met with violent resistance from Southern Whites who refused to accept this newfound racial equality. The Ku Klux Klan, founded in 1865, began a campaign of terror against African Americans and their white allies, using violence to suppress black political activity and maintain white supremacy.

Simultaneously, Southern states began to implement a series of laws known as the Black Codes, which were designed to restrict the freedom of African Americans and force them back into a form of quasi-slavery. These codes were precursors to the Jim Crow laws, which would come into effect towards the end of the 19th century.

As federal commitment to Reconstruction waned, the Southern states regained control, and the racial gains made during this period were largely reversed. This era marked the rise of institutionalized racism, where discrimination was encoded into law and permeated every aspect of society, from education to employment to housing.

Institutionalized racism was built on the legacy of slavery, using de facto and de jure methods to enforce racial segregation and inequality. It was a complex system of social, economic, and political structures designed to maintain a racial hierarchy with white people at the top, ethnic groups in the middle, and African Americans at the bottom, with native peoples all but extinct.

This period in history solidified the racial dynamics that continue to influence the United States today. While slavery was abolished, the ideology of racial superiority and the systemic structures built around it were not. This was evident in the legalized segregation and widespread discrimination that followed, which we will explore in the next section on the creation of racially biased laws and policies.

Creation of Racially Biased Laws and Policies

The end of the Civil War and the subsequent Reconstruction era led to significant changes in American society. However, these changes were met with considerable resistance, particularly in the South. The postwar era saw the creation of numerous racially biased laws and policies, enacted with the specific aim of marginalizing the newly freed African American population and maintaining a societal hierarchy that favored whites. These laws effectively institutionalized racism and established a legal framework for racial discrimination, undermining the progress made during Reconstruction and shaping the racial hierarchy of the United States for decades to come.

The Jim Crow laws, as aforementioned, were one of the most notable sets of these racially biased regulations. Many aspects of daily life, from neighborhoods to prisons, from schools to cemeteries, were divided along racial lines.

Voting restrictions, including literacy tests, poll taxes, and grandfather clauses, were implemented to suppress African American political participation despite the Fifteenth Amendment's granting of voting rights to African American men.

The Black Codes, as stated previously, were another form of racially biased laws. Although they varied from state to state, their common goal was to limit the freedom of African Americans and ensure their availability as a cheap labor force. They included vagrancy laws, which allowed African Americans to be arrested for being "idle," and apprenticeship laws, where African American children were forced to work for white employers.

These laws and policies not only limited the opportunities and freedoms of African Americans but also cemented a racial hierarchy that continued to permeate American society. The system of institutionalized racism established during this period would have unyielding effects, the repercussions of which can still be felt today.

Segregation and inequality remained deeply rooted in America, but international criticism forced some changes after World War II. In 1948, President Harry Truman signed Executive Order 9981, which abolished racial discrimination in the military and ended segregation in the armed forces.[9]

As the United States grows and becomes a dominant power in the world, inherent problems persist internally and remain a critical factor that has impacted the ideals that fundamentally birthed this nation.

11

"Never underestimate the power of human stupidity."

Robert A. Heinlein

ARCHITECT AS CULTURAL IDENTITY

RISE OF THE NAZI'S AND JEWISH ISOLATIONISM

A. The Role of Architecture in the Segregation of Jewish Communities

The architecture of segregation in Jewish communities throughout history has been an embodiment of a broader social process that extends beyond bricks and mortar. It is intertwined with politics, culture, identity, and control. The building and design of specific structures, towns, and neighborhoods have played an instrumental role in segregating Jewish populations, providing a unique representation of the societal divisions imposed upon them.

In the Jewish Diaspora, ghettos were developed as a mechanism to segregate Jewish communities from Christian majorities. These were densely populated slum areas of cities inhabited by a socially and economically deprived minority. Ghettos were surrounded by walls and were subject to strict regulations. The walls were closed during Christian holidays to keep Jews from leaving and protect them from Pogroms, organized massacres of the religious ethnic group.[1]

The architecture of these ghettos was indicative of the conditions faced by Jewish communities. Buildings were tightly packed and often in states of disrepair, reflecting the economic deprivation experienced by their inhabitants. The cramped and impoverished conditions of these ghettos underlined the extent of segregation and the marginalization experienced by Jewish communities.

In Central and Eastern Europe, prior to World War II, Jewish populations inhabited towns called "shtetls." The architecture of these towns played a role in maintaining separate lives for European Jews within larger communities through self-segregation. While the younger population integrated more into the majority community and adopted their dress, language, and customs, the architecture of shtetls—distinctive houses, synagogues, and public buildings—helped preserve a unique cultural identity and serve as a physical reminder of their segregation.[2]

However, it was with the rise of the Nazi regime in Germany and the subsequent construction of the Nuremberg Laws in 1935 that architecture's role in the segregation of Jewish communities became most horrifically apparent. The laws subjected the Jewish community to live in their own housing complexes, "the ghettos," and were even forced to wear badges on their clothes to indicate their identity to the public. Jewish citizens were isolated and separated within the same country due to their religious origins, forcing them into overcrowded housing complexes, with narrow streets and impoverished conditions.

Contrastingly, at the same time, the rise of Nationalist Nazi, imperial architecture was underway under Adolph Hitler's appointed head architect, Berthold Konrad Hermann Albert Speer. The architecture conceived under Speer's direction was designed to display Nazi dominance, with grandiose structures like the "Cathedral of Light" above Zeppelinfeld stadium, the New Reich Chancellery, and the World Capital Germania. This was emblematic of the contrasting realities experienced by different communities within the same nation, with architecture serving as a tool to segregate, suppress, and emphasize power dynamics.

In this way, architecture served as an instrument of segregation and persecution. It enforced isolation and separation while also amplifying the divisions within society. But as we delve deeper into this chapter, we must also remember that architecture, like any other tool, can be used for better or worse. In the face of such atrocities, Jewish communities have continuously demonstrated resilience and resistance, utilizing their architecture and urban spaces as places of cultural preservation, identity affirmation, and social solidarity. This narrative of resilience is evidence of the enduring spirit of the Jewish people, even in the face of unparalleled hardship.

Jewish Life in "Shtetls" Before World War II

"Shtetls," small towns populated largely by Jews, were a unique and quintessential part of Jewish life in Central and Eastern Europe before World War II. These settlements were often home to self-contained Jewish communities, who led separate lives within larger societies by way of self-segregation.

Shtetl of Kretinge. 1914. Courtesy of The Lost Shtetl Museum.

In these tight-knit communities, life was profoundly shaped by Jewish customs, traditions, and religious observances. The rhythm of life revolved around the Jewish calendar, with its Sabbaths and holidays. The shtetls often had their own synagogues, bathhouses, and study halls, providing the necessary facilities for the religious practices integral to Jewish life.

A typical shtetl was characterized by its distinct architecture. Houses were often wooden, with a pitched roof and were closely spaced. These modest houses often had a kitchen, living area, and sometimes a separate room for the parents. It was not uncommon for large families to live together in these small spaces, with several generations under one roof. The synagogue, with its distinctive features, often served as the community's architectural landmark and the center of religious life.

The economic life of the shtetl was also distinctive. Many of the Jewish inhabitants engaged in small-scale trade, artisanal crafts, or provided professional services. Tailors, shoemakers, blacksmiths, doctors, teachers, and rabbis were common occupations. Despite the general poverty, there was a robust economy within the shtetl, with market days often being bustling affairs.

The cultural life of the shtetl was rich and varied. Despite their often remote and rural locations, these towns were vibrant centers of Jewish intellectual and cultural life. Yiddish literature, theater, and music flourished in these communities, providing entertainment and intellectual stimulation. Jewish education, particularly the study of the Torah and Talmud, was highly valued.

Socially, these shtetls were often close-knit, with strong communal ties. The life within these communities was intertwined, with people sharing joys, sorrows, and everyday life. However, it is important to note that despite the romanticized image of shtetl life, it was not without its hardships. Economic hardship, anti-Semitism, and social exclusion were a part of life in these communities.

In contrast to the world outside, where Jews were often marginalized and persecuted, the shtetls provided a safe space for Jewish life to thrive. They allowed for self-segregation, which gave Jews the opportunity to live according to their traditions and religious laws, forming a protective cocoon around their distinctive way of life. However, with the changing tides of history and the cataclysmic events of World War II, these unique towns and the way of life they housed were almost entirely extinguished, leaving behind a rich but heartbreaking legacy.

Despite their eventual fate, the shtetls remain emblematic of a significant period in Jewish history. Their memory serves as a poignant reminder of a lost world and as a testament to the rich cultural tapestry that characterized Jewish life before World War II. As we venture further into the architecture of segregation and its profound impacts on Jewish communities, it's important to remember these vibrant spaces of Jewish culture and identity that stood in stark contrast to the impending realities of World War II.[3]

Development of Ghettos in the Jewish Diaspora

In the Jewish Diaspora, the development of ghettos became a distinguishing feature of Jewish life, particularly in Europe. These areas were established to segregate Jewish communities from the larger Christian societies around them, and were subjected to strict regulations. The ghettos formed complex urban spaces of confinement, but within their walls, they also fostered a rich Jewish cultural and religious life.

The term "ghetto" is derived from the Venetian word "getto" or "ghèto," meaning foundry, a reference to the area in Venice where the first Jewish ghetto was established in the 16th century. Over time, the term has come to represent a densely populated urban area inhabited by a socially and economically deprived minority. Ghettos were typically characterized by overcrowded living conditions, poor sanitation, and limited access to resources.

Notably, the architecture within these ghettos reflected both the oppressive external regulations and the resilient internal community life. Overcrowding led to the creation of narrow, winding streets and multistory buildings, often with communal courtyards. Spaces were often subdivided to accommodate growing families, resulting in long, narrow houses. In some cases, houses were as narrow as five feet wide, as was documented in the Jewish ghetto Frankfurter Judengasse in 1868.

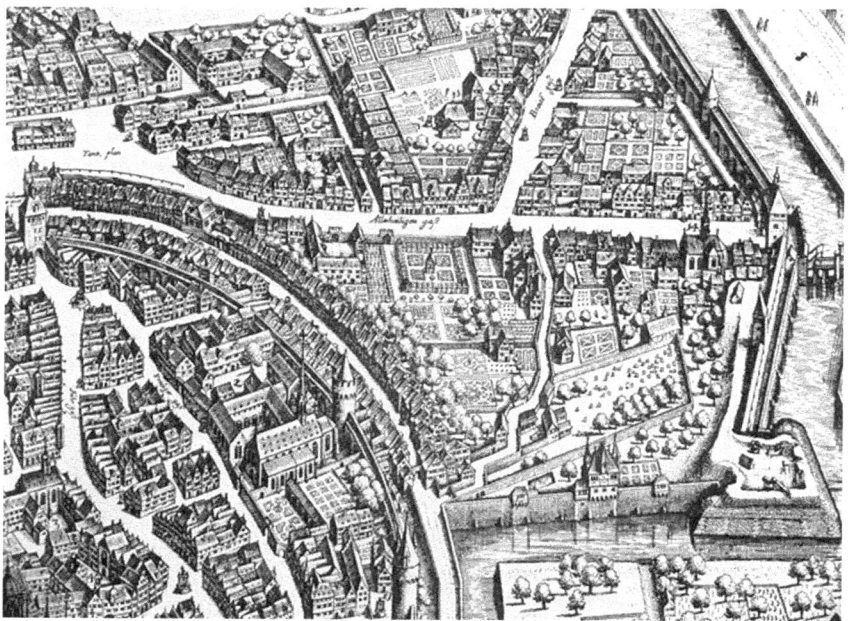

Frankfurt city map 1628, showing the curved Judengasse.(Jewish Ghetto). Wikipedia.

Despite the adverse conditions, these architectural adaptations also testify to the community's resourcefulness and resilience in the face of adversity. The design of these spaces was driven by the necessity of maintaining Jewish life under extremely challenging conditions. They had to be functional, accommodating a high population density and a range of communal activities within limited space.

Overall, the ghettos were both spaces of segregation and suffering, and spaces of cultural endurance and resilience. Their development displays the tenacity of the Jewish community in preserving its identity and traditions in the face of systematic oppression. In our exploration of architecture and segregation, it is imperative to remember these spaces and the complex stories they tell of a people's struggle to survive and thrive amidst adversity.

B. How the Nuremberg Laws Segregated and Marginalized Ethnic Groups in Nazi Germany

The Nuremberg Laws of 1935 marked a devastating period in the history of Jewish segregation. Spearheaded by the Nazi regime, these laws were instrumental in constructing a system of institutionalized racism and discrimination against Jewish people in Germany, which later extended to occupied territories during World War II.

The Nuremberg Laws encompassed two main pieces of legislation: The Reich Citizenship Law and the Law for the Protection of German Blood and Honor. The Reich Citizenship Law stripped Jewish citizens of their German citizenship, reducing them to mere subjects of the state. The Law for the Protection of German Blood and Honor outlawed marriages and extramarital intercourse between Jews and Germans, effectively isolating Jewish individuals and families from the broader society.

The notorious Mischling laws, a component of the Nuremberg Laws, went even further in creating divisions based on blood quantum. This was a classification system defining a person as "mixed race" based on their percentage of Jewish ancestry. These laws effectively categorized citizens into racial hierarchies and prescribed their rights (or lack thereof) based on their so-called "racial purity." [4]

In terms of physical segregation, the Nuremberg Laws subjected the Jewish community to new living conditions. Jewish individuals were then moved into those confined, impoverished ghettos. One of the most notorious aspects of this segregation was the forced use of badges. Jewish individuals were mandated to wear badges, typically the yellow Star of David, on their clothes. This visible mark further isolated them from the rest of society and facilitated their persecution.

As the Nuremberg Laws took effect, the atmosphere within Germany grew increasingly hostile. Jewish people found it difficult to live within such a society, and many sought to leave the country if they could afford it. Tragically, for many, escape was impossible. The laws were just the beginning of a systematic plan to eradicate Jewish life from German society, ultimately culminating in the horrific events of the Holocaust.

The Nuremberg Laws, thus, highlight the devastating potential of legislative power when used to enforce segregation and discrimination. In our examination of architecture and segregation, it is germane to note the significance of these laws. They not only segregated Jewish communities within physical spaces but were part of a wider mechanism of systematic exclusion and dehumanization. The echoes of these laws can still be felt in the collective memory of the Jewish Diaspora, reminding us of the critical need for vigilance against such atrocities in the future.

C. Impact of Nazi Architecture and Ideology

Rise of the Nazis and Adolf Hitler's Vision

The rise of Nazi power in the 1930s signaled a radical shift in Germany's sociopolitical and architectural landscape. Adolf Hitler, the visionary of this transformation, saw architecture as a potent tool in achieving his ambitious agenda. Believing in the inherent political nature of architecture, Hitler leveraged it to shape national identity, propagate Nazi ideologies, and consolidate power.

Appointment of Albert Speer as the Head Architect of the Third Reich

Among Hitler's closest confidants in achieving this vision was Albert Speer, known as the "first architect of the Third Reich." Speer shared Hitler's grandiose vision and was entrusted with manifesting this dream into reality. His architectural designs were emblematic of Nazi ideology, merging elements of tradition with concepts of alpine architecture to conceive a new, totalitarian style. Speer's designs were aimed at portraying an imposing, omnipotent image of the Nazi regime, reflecting their desire for global dominance.

Nazi Architectural Designs and Symbolism

One of the most iconic structures conceived by Speer was the "Cathedral of Light" at the Zeppelinfeld stadium. This creation utilized 152 searchlights to form vertical bars of light that encased the night sky, evoking the sense of an imposing, radiant cathedral. The overwhelming visual spectacle left viewers in awe of the Nazi regime's prowess.

The Cathedral of Light above the Zeppelintribune (1936). Wikipedia.

Speer also proposed the design of "World Capital Germania," which was Hitler's vision for the future capital of the world. It was to feature grand boulevards, colossal buildings, and a huge triumphal arch, epitomizing Nazi power and supremacy. [5]

A model of Adolf Hitler's plan for Germania under the direction of Albert Speer. Wikimedia.

These designs were steeped in symbolism, aiming to portray the Nazi regime as an enduring, timeless force. Speer's structures often incorporated an aesthetic of monumentalism, highlighting Nazi ideals of power, authority, and longevity.

Imperial Style and the Portrayal of Power and Dominance

The imperial style of Nazi architecture was no accident. Hitler and Speer deliberately used architecture as a means of communication to instill wonder, fear, and reverence in the German people and the wider world. The monumental scale and grandeur of Nazi buildings were designed to inspire a sense of national pride and submission to the regime's power.

Legacy and Consequences of Nazi Architecture

The imprint of Nazi architecture and ideology on the landscape was significant, even if much of it never came to fruition or was destroyed after World War II. Speer's concept of "ruin value" highlighted a grim outlook: Nazi buildings should leave aesthetically pleasing ruins that would endure for thousands of years, much like the ancient ruins of Egypt and Greece. This vision expressed a warped sense of permanence, linking the Nazi regime to ancient, revered civilizations.[6]

However, the legacy of Nazi architecture is a double-edged sword. While the remaining structures serve as a haunting reminder of the atrocities committed under the guise of Hitler's ambitions, they also remind us of the dangers of allowing architecture and planning to be wielded as tools of propaganda, manipulation, and division.

After the defeat in World War II, Speer was found guilty of war crimes and crimes against humanity at the Nuremberg Trials and sentenced to twenty years in prison. The irony of this cannot be overstated - the same architect who designed spaces to segregate and discriminate was judged and condemned in a court of law for his role in these heinous acts.

The impact of Nazi architecture and ideology in shaping the Jewish experience cannot be overlooked. The spatial segregation imposed by the Nazi regime amplified the discriminatory practices of the time, lending an architectural expression to the Nazi's perverse vision of racial and cultural supremacy.

12

"In the middle of every difficulty lies opportunity."

Albert Einstein

ARCHITECT AS DESTROYER

WHITE NATIONALISM AND THE PURSUIT OF RACIAL SEGREGATION

DEFINITION AND CHARACTERISTICS OF WHITE NATIONALISM

White nationalism is a socio-political ideology that asserts the belief in the supremacy of the white race, often expressed through a desire for a separate nation or state exclusively for white people. It is founded on a presumption of racial hierarchy where white people are considered superior to other racial groups. White nationalism involves a broad range of beliefs and viewpoints, from calls for the maintenance of white culture and identity to more extreme expressions of racial hatred and calls for violence.

Historical Examples of White Nationalist Movements

Throughout history, several movements have emerged that embody elements of white nationalism. One of the most notorious examples is the Ku Klux Klan, which was established after the American Civil War in the late 1860s. Its members used violence and terror to suppress African Americans and reestablish white dominance in the southern United States. The Klan saw a resurgence in the 20th century, fueled by opposition to civil rights advancements.[1]

In South Africa, the white nationalist ideology was embedded into the government policy known as Apartheid. Instituted in 1948,

Apartheid enforced a system of legal racial segregation that privileged white South Africans while oppressing the majority black population.

In the latter part of the 20th century, white nationalist movements have continued to surface, often in response to societal changes such as immigration and multiculturalism. These movements often employ fear and division to gain support, manipulating narratives to suggest a threat to the white race.

Influence of White Nationalism on the Promotion of Segregation

White nationalism has been a significant force in promoting racial segregation. At its core, it seeks to maintain racial purity and the supposed superiority of the white race. This ideology often manifests as a desire for separate living spaces, educational institutions, and even countries. This drive for racial separation has played out in policies and practices designed to isolate and marginalize racial and ethnic minorities.

In the United States, white nationalism underpinned the Jim Crow laws that mandated racial segregation in public facilities in Southern states. It was a force behind redlining policies that segregated cities and created racial disparities in housing and wealth that persist to this day.

In other parts of the world, white nationalist ideology has led to horrific acts of violence and oppression. The Apartheid system in South Africa was designed to keep the racial hierarchy intact and consolidate political and economic power among the white minority.

In the present day, while explicit, legal segregation is largely a thing of the past, white nationalism continues to contribute to racial divisions and inequities. Through implicit biases, discriminatory policies, and systemic racism, white nationalist ideologies persist, continuing to foster environments of segregation and racial tension. These realities serve as a sobering reminder of the deeply held beliefs of white nationalism and its part in shaping our segregated world.

A. The Holocaust and the Extremes of Segregation

Overview of the Holocaust and Its Historical Context

The Holocaust remains one of the most harrowing periods in human history, a constant reminder of the depths of inhumanity possible under systems fueled by hatred, prejudice, and unchecked power. Lasting from 1933 to 1945, during the thick of World War II, this dark era was marked by the calculated and systemic murder of nine million Jews. The genocide was orchestrated by Adolf Hitler's Nazi Party in Germany and constituted the mass extermination of nearly two-thirds of Europe's Jewish population.

The roots of the Holocaust stretch back to centuries of deeply ingrained anti-Semitic sentiments in Europe. Adolf Hitler and the Nazi Party harnessed these prejudices, using Jews as scapegoats for Germany's struggles. Jews were blamed for Germany's economic hardships during the Great Depression, the Treaty of Versailles' terms seen as too harsh, and the nation's defeat in World War I.[3]

When Hitler ascended to power in 1933, he weaponized these prejudices and transformed them into state policy. The regime began enacting discriminatory laws, progressively isolating and marginalizing Jews. The Nuremberg Laws of 1935 formalized this anti-Semitic policy, stripping Jews of their civil rights and segregating them from the rest of German society.

The infamous Kristallnacht (Night of Broken Glass) in November 1938 marked a significant escalation in the state-sanctioned violence against Jews. Synagogues were burned, Jewish businesses were vandalized, and thousands of Jews were rounded up and sent to concentration camps.[4]

As World War II commenced, the systematic persecution of Jews worsened, ultimately leading to the implementation of the "Final

Solution," a Nazi plan intended for the complete extermination of Jews. They were forced into ghettos, deported to concentration and extermination camps, and subjected to mass shootings and gas chambers. This genocide was not limited to Germany but extended throughout the territories occupied by the Nazis, reflecting Hitler's vision of racial purity.

The Holocaust ended only with the fall of Nazi Germany in 1945. Its traumatic legacy has reverberated across generations, prompting extensive reflection on the nature of hate, the consequences of unchecked power, and the urgency of preventing such horrors from ever occurring again. The Holocaust was a grim reminder of the horrific potential of segregation, racism, and xenophobia when they were institutionalized and propagated by those in power.

Role of Segregation in the Implementation of Nazi Policies

Segregation was a key tool employed by the Nazis to implement their genocidal policies. In the years leading up to the Holocaust, the Nuremberg Laws enacted by the Nazi regime segregated Jews from German society. Jews were stripped of their citizenship and civil rights, including the right to work in certain professions, to marry non-Jews, and even to own property.

With the onset of World War II, Jews were forced into ghettos in major cities where they were isolated from the rest of society. Living conditions in these ghettos were dire, with overcrowding, starvation, and disease rampant. The ghettos not only served to dehumanize and degrade the Jewish population, but also facilitated the Nazis' Final Solution by making it easier to transport Jews to concentration and extermination camps.

Impact of the Holocaust on Future Perceptions of Segregation

The Holocaust had disheartening effects on global perceptions of segregation, and racial and ethnic discrimination. The atrocities committed during this period exposed the extreme consequences of state-sponsored segregation and led to international outcry and the establishment of human rights norms designed to prevent such horrors from recurring.

The Nuremberg Trials, held after World War II, highlighted the criminality of the genocidal policies pursued by the Nazi regime. The trials underscored the dangers of segregation and the doctrines of racial superiority that often underlie it to an international audience.[5]

The lessons of the Holocaust continue to influence discussions on segregation and racial discrimination today. It serves as a stark reminder of the potential consequences of intolerance, hatred, and division. Despite these lessons, however, instances of segregation and discrimination continue to occur, underscoring the importance of maintaining vigilance and promoting values of inclusion, tolerance, and equality.

B. Migration of Europeans to the United States

Overview of European Migration Waves to the U.S.

The history of the United States is fundamentally a story of immigration, marked by several significant waves of migrants, primarily from Europe, who sought to build new lives on American soil. European migration to the United States has transformed the demographic, cultural, and economic environs of the nation and continues to shape its identity.

The initial wave of European migration was dominated by explorers, traders, and colonists from Spain, France, and England during the late 15th and 16th centuries. These early migrants founded the first

European settlements in the New World, setting the stage for centuries of subsequent immigration.

The largest influx of European immigrants, however, came in the 19th and early 20th centuries, a period known as the Great Wave. This era was marked by massive demographic changes in the United States as millions of Europeans made the journey across the Atlantic. The majority of these immigrants hailed from Germany, Ireland, and the United Kingdom, driven by a combination of political turmoil, religious persecution, and economic hardships in their home countries. They sought the promise of economic opportunity and religious freedom that the United States represented.[3]

The Irish, in particular, were escaping the devastating effects of the Great Famine (1845-1849). Germans migrated in large numbers following political unrest and economic difficulties in the German Confederation. British immigrants were often motivated by the opportunities for land ownership and social mobility, seemingly more accessible in the U.S. than in class-stratified Britain.

Later in the 19th century and into the early 20th century, the primary sources of European immigration shifted from Northern and Western Europe to Southern and Eastern Europe. Italians, Poles, and Russian Jews, among others, arrived in vast numbers, escaping poverty, pogroms, and political instability. This shift changed the ethnic and cultural makeup of American society.

The implementation of the Immigration Act of 1924 significantly reduced the inflow of European immigrants, as it imposed strict quotas favoring immigrants from Northern and Western Europe, reflecting a resurgence of nativist sentiments.[4]

Post-World War II saw another notable influx of Europeans, including a significant number of displaced persons and Holocaust survivors. Many Eastern Europeans also arrived during this period, fleeing the political climate of the Cold War and the imposition of Soviet control.

In more recent decades, the nature of immigration to the United States has changed once again, with a higher proportion of immigrants now coming from Asia and Latin America. Nevertheless, the impact of European migration remains permanent, having shaped the United States in meaningful and consequential aspects.

Examples of European Ethnic Groups and Their Experiences

Understanding the experiences of various European ethnic groups who migrated to the United States provides a comprehensive picture of the challenges, adaptation strategies, and cultural transformations during this significant period in history. Let's delve into the experiences of a few distinct European groups: the Irish (Gaelic/ Gael), Italians (Latin/ Falisci/ Greek), Germans (Saxon/ Franks), and Polish (Slavic).

1. Irish Immigrants

The Irish made up one of the largest groups of immigrants in the 19th century, particularly during the Great Famine (1845-1849). Upon arrival, they often faced discrimination based on their Catholic faith and were viewed as competition for low-skilled jobs, leading to economic marginalization and social segregation. The Irish overcame these challenges through strong community bonds and formed powerful political and social organizations. Over time, they successfully integrated into American society, with many rising to positions of influence in politics and other fields.[5]

2. Italian Immigrants

Italian immigration to the U.S., peaking at the turn of the 20th century, was primarily fueled by economic hardship in Italy. Italian immigrants often worked in unskilled jobs in the construction and service industries, and they faced significant prejudice and stereotyping. Yet, their strong sense of community and their contributions to American food, music, and other aspects of culture eventually led to greater acceptance and integration.

3. German Immigrants

German immigrants started arriving in the U.S. in large numbers in the mid-19th century due to political unrest and economic difficulties in their homeland. Germans brought a rich cultural heritage, influencing American cuisine, holiday traditions, and education. They established numerous German-language newspapers, schools, and churches, maintaining a strong cultural identity. Despite facing discrimination during the World Wars due to anti-German sentiment, they successfully integrated into American society and constitute one of the largest self-reported ancestry groups in the U.S. today.

4. Polish Immigrants

Polish immigrants primarily arrived in the late 19th and early 20th century, escaping political oppression and seeking better economic opportunities. They often worked in the industrial cities of the Midwest, in factories and mines. Like other immigrant groups, they faced language barriers and cultural differences, leading to initial segregation. However, their resilience and strong community values facilitated their assimilation into American society. Today, Polish-Americans are recognized for their contributions to America's labor movements and cultural richness.

Each of these groups, despite facing significant challenges upon arrival in the U.S., gradually found ways to contribute to and thrive within the fabric of American society. Their experiences highlight the quintessential immigrant narrative of struggle, adaptation, and eventual integration, underlining the important role immigration has played in shaping the United States.

Factors Contributing to the Formation of Ethnic Enclaves

Ethnic enclaves, also known as ethnic neighborhoods, have been a prominent feature of immigration experiences worldwide. They represent geographical areas with a high concentration of a specific ethnic group and are generally characterized by unique cultural, social, and economic dynamics. A variety of factors drives the formation of such enclaves:

1. Social and Cultural Factors

When individuals migrate to a new country, they often seek out others who share their language, culture, and traditions. This leads to the establishment of communities that provide a sense of familiarity and comfort in an unfamiliar environment. Ethnic enclaves provide a space where immigrants can practice their cultural traditions, speak their native language, and maintain their unique identities.

2. Economic Factors

Economic factors play a significant role in the formation of ethnic enclaves. Many immigrants, especially those with limited resources or language skills, find it easier to find employment within their communities. Some enclaves become economic hubs for specific types of businesses that cater to the cultural preferences of the ethnic group, thus providing employment opportunities.

3. Housing and Discrimination

Housing discrimination and restrictive covenants have historically played a significant role in the formation of ethnic enclaves. Immigrants often faced discrimination in housing markets, leading them to settle in specific neighborhoods with other individuals from their home country. Over time, these neighborhoods evolved into ethnic enclaves.

4. Chain Migration

Chain migration refers to the social process by which migrants from a particular town or region follow others from that area to a particular destination. As more people from a specific ethnic group settle in an area, they create a support network that attracts further migration to the enclave.[5]

5. Social Support and Networks

Ethnic enclaves often provide a network of support to new immigrants, making it easier for them to navigate the challenges of immigration. These support networks can provide essential resources such as help with job searches, housing, and navigating government bureaucracy.

Understanding the factors that contribute to the formation of ethnic enclaves can provide important insights into the dynamics of immigration and integration, as well as the social, cultural, and economic fabric of societies.

RISE OF MIGRANT COMMUNITIES

Introduction to the Concept of Migrant Communities

Migration has been a fundamental aspect of human society throughout history. People have moved across continents and oceans, driven by diverse factors such as political instability, economic opportunities, environmental changes, and the desire for a better life. These movements have led to the creation of vibrant and diverse migrant communities in various parts of the world.

A migrant community refers to a group of individuals who have relocated from their native regions and established a new community in a different geographical location. These communities are characterized by a shared sense of identity, often linked to their common place of origin, and can include first-generation immigrants as well as their descendants.[6]

The concept of migrant communities is rooted in the broader process of migration, which involves the movement of people from one area to another with the intention of settling, permanently or temporarily, at a new location. These communities often form in response to the challenges and opportunities presented by migration.

Migrant communities can be found in virtually every country around the globe. From the Chinese communities in the United States to the Turkish communities in Germany, from the Indian communities in the United Kingdom to the Italian communities in Argentina, these communities contribute significantly to the social, economic, and cultural landscapes of their host countries.

Migrant communities often provide a support network that helps newcomers adjust to their new environment. They may offer resources like language classes, job placement services, and cultural events, all of which can ease the transition for new immigrants. Additionally, these communities can act as a form of social protection, providing a sense of belonging and security for individuals in an unfamiliar environment.

At the same time, the formation of migrant communities is also shaped by the host society's response to newcomers. Factors such as immigration policies, societal attitudes, and economic conditions can influence the development and integration of these communities. Understanding the dynamics of migrant communities is therefore crucial for addressing key issues related to migration, diversity, and social cohesion in today's increasingly interconnected world.

Case Studies: Germantown, Chinatown, Little Italy, and Little Haiti

Migrant communities can be seen all over the world, but the United States serves as a unique melting pot due to its rich history of immigration. This nation is home to various vibrant social groups, each with a distinctive cultural identity, reflecting the diverse origins of its inhabitants. We can better understand this phenomenon through the examination of four well-known migrant communities: Germantown, Chinatown, Little Italy, and Little Haiti.

Germantown

One of the earliest examples of a migrant community in the U.S. is Germantown, located in Philadelphia, Pennsylvania. It was founded in the late 17th century by German Quaker and Mennonite families seeking religious freedom. Over the years, Germantown developed into a cultural and commercial center, with many of its residents maintaining German customs, language, and institutions. Today, Germantown retains its historical charm and continues to be an important cultural hub, further cementing the contribution of early German immigrants on the American landscape.

Chinatown

When it comes to the most recognizable migrant communities, Chinatowns located in various cities across the U.S. certainly stand out. The first Chinatown was established in San Francisco during the California Gold Rush in the mid-19th century. Here, Chinese immigrants, many of whom were laborers working on the Transcontinental Railroad, clustered together as a way of coping with racial prejudice and discriminatory laws. These communities served as beacons for later arrivals, offering a familiar environment where the Chinese language, customs, and culinary traditions were preserved. Today, Chinatowns continue to be vibrant centers of Chinese-American life and are popular tourist destinations due to their unique cultural offerings.

Little Italy

Another prominent migrant community in the United States is Little Italy. These neighborhoods, commonly found in cities like New York and Chicago, are a testament to the substantial migration of Italians to the U.S. during the late 19th and early 20th centuries. However, while these neighborhoods are often associated with Italian heritage, they also hold a significant place in the history of Irish Americans.

Little Italy neighborhoods emerged as immigrants sought to establish a sense of belonging and cultural familiarity in their new homeland. These areas allowed communities to retain their native language, Catholic religious practices, and culinary traditions, which provided a vital support network for newcomers.

However, it's important to note that Little Italy neighborhoods were not exclusive to Italians alone. Irish Americans, who also played a vital role in shaping America's urban landscape, were closely intertwined with these communities. Both Irish and Italian immigrants faced similar challenges and sought solace in these neighborhoods.

Over time, as many descendants of the original immigrants moved away, Little Italy neighborhoods have evolved. However, they still symbolize the rich heritage of both Italian and Irish Americans, reflecting their ideals and ways of life on the cultural fabric of the United States.

The architecture of Little Italy neighborhoods often reflects a blend of Italian and Irish design influences. Buildings may incorporate elements reminiscent of both Italian and Irish architecture, and community spaces may feature symbols and imagery that connect residents to their cultural roots. This architectural influence serves as a poignant reminder of the multicultural journey that both Italian and Irish Americans have embarked upon, enriching the mosaic of the American urban vernacular.

Little Haiti

Located in Miami, Little Haiti stands as a strong hold for the large wave of Haitian refugees who fled political instability and natural disasters from the 1980s onwards. As the first neighborhood in the U.S. to be officially recognized as a Haitian enclave, Little Haiti is a vibrant cultural hub, brimming with Creole-speaking residents, colorful murals, Haitian art galleries, and restaurants offering traditional Haitian cuisine. The community continues to serve as a magnet for new immigrants, facilitating their adaptation to American society while preserving their unique cultural heritage.

Each of these communities exemplifies the ways in which migrants can significantly impact their host society, not only enriching the cultural tapestry but also contributing to economic growth and development. Whether through Germantown's enduring historical presence, the cultural vibrancy of Chinatown and Little Italy, or the resilience embodied by Little Haiti, these communities reveal the complex interplay between migration, identity, and belonging.

Factors Influencing the Formation and Development of Migrant Communities

1. Economic Opportunities: Migrants often gravitate towards areas with ample job opportunities, which often dictate where these communities establish their roots. For instance, the development of Chinatowns was influenced by work opportunities on the Transcontinental Railroad and in California's gold mines during the mid-19th century.

2. Social and Cultural Cohesion: Migrants tend to settle in areas where their compatriots have already established a presence. This fosters a sense of belonging and cultural familiarity, helping migrants retain their traditional customs and languages while adapting to their new surroundings.

3. Historical and Political Factors: Immigration policies and geopolitical events significantly influence the formation of migrant communities. For example, Little Haiti in Miami emerged in response to the large number of Haitians fleeing political turmoil in the 1980s.

4. Availability and Affordability of Housing: Migrant communities often form in areas with affordable housing options. This enables migrants, especially those with low income or newly arrived, to establish themselves without undue financial pressure.

5. Support Systems: The presence of immigrant support services, such as legal aid, language classes, and job placement services, can also encourage the formation of migrant communities. These services not only provide crucial assistance but also create an environment conducive to immigrant integration.

6. Chain Migration: This refers to the social process whereby immigrants from a particular town or region follow others from that area to a particular city or neighborhood, creating a chain of migration. These chains can significantly shape the formation and growth of migrant communities.[6]

The formation and development of migrant communities are influenced by a complex mix of economic, social, cultural, and historical factors. Understanding these can help provide valuable insights into the dynamics of migration and the multicultural fabric of host societies.

13

*"Not everything that is faced can be changed,
but nothing can be changed until it is faced."*

James Baldwin

ARCHITECT AS ENFORCER

LEGALIZED SEGREGATION AND ARCHITECTURE

A. Eldridge Cleaver and the Perpetuation of Racism

Understanding Cleaver's Perspective on Racism in America

Eldridge Cleaver, a prominent figure in the Black Panther Party and an influential voice of the Civil Rights Movement, has provided thought-provoking perspectives on racism in America. Born in 1935, Cleaver witnessed firsthand the violent bigotry and harsh racial segregation of mid-20th-century America. This exposure to rampant racism shaped his views, subsequently reflected in his poignant and fiery rhetoric and writings.

Cleaver's perspective on racism was greatly influenced by his tumultuous life experiences. These included his time in prison, where he wrote his best-known work, *Soul On Ice* (1968). This collection of essays provides a candid, stark look into the structural racism ingrained in American society. According to Cleaver, racism was not just an ideological stance or a personal prejudice. Instead, he saw it as a fundamental part of the American social, economic, and political systems.[1]

His experiences of inequality and prejudice colored his perspective and fueled his activism. Cleaver did not shy away from stating that America was constructed on a foundation of systemic racism, with structures in place to sustain white supremacy and perpetuate racial inequality. This outlook was far from pessimistic; rather, it was an indictment, a critique intended to incite change and progress towards racial justice.

Cleaver advocated for radical societal restructuring as a solution to this systemic problem. As a prominent member of the Black Panther Party, he worked tirelessly towards this end, believing in the need for revolutionary change to dismantle racist structures. He saw the struggle against racism as inherently linked with the fight against economic inequality, imperialism, and the militarization of the police.

While Cleaver's views were radical for his time and remain so today, they continue to inform ongoing discussions about racial inequality and social justice. His critical insights, derived from his lived experiences and intellectual reflection, have had a long-lasting impact, challenging us to confront the harsh realities of racism and strive for a truly equitable society.

Next, let's explore the implications of one of Cleaver's most potent symbolic expressions: the Cherry Pie Metaphor.

Implications of the Cherry Pie Metaphor

Eldridge Cleaver's "Cherry Pie" metaphor, found in his book *Soul On Ice*, serves as a vivid illustration of the systemic racism within American society. While seemingly simple on the surface, the metaphor provides a profound critique of the racial disparities and discrimination prevalent in the United States.

In this metaphor, Cleaver describes America as a cherry pie, with different slices representing the different races, religions, and economic classes within the society. The pie, as a whole, represents the American dream—the promise of prosperity, equality, and liberty for all. Yet, not all slices of the pie are the same. The slices are not evenly divided, and some are more desirable—more filled with cherries—than others.

The "cherries" within the pie symbolize the privileges, opportunities, and benefits associated with living in America, such as quality education, gainful employment, adequate housing, and basic human rights. However, Cleaver asserts that these cherries are unequally distributed, with some sections of the pie—those representing white, wealthy Americans—enjoying a disproportionately large share.

On the other hand, slices representing marginalized groups, particularly Black Americans, have fewer cherries. This uneven distribution signifies the systemic barriers and discrimination that these communities face, inhibiting their access to opportunities and making the American dream elusive.

The implications of the cherry pie metaphor are vast. This metaphor underscores how systemic racism is not just about individual prejudices but is embedded within the very structure of society, affecting resource distribution, social mobility, and opportunities for different racial and socioeconomic groups. It also suggests that achieving true racial equality requires more than just non-discrimination; it demands actively working towards fair distribution of the "cherries."

Cleaver's Cherry Pie Metaphor continues to resonate in contemporary conversations about racial and socioeconomic disparities. It serves as a compelling critique of systemic racism and a powerful call to action for a more equitable society. The metaphor underscores the importance of recognizing these deep-seated inequalities and working collectively toward comprehensive systemic reform. This is a challenge that remains relevant today as we continue striving for social justice and racial equality.

B. Brown v. Board of Education and the Challenge to Segregation

One of the most transformative moments in American civil rights history came in the mid-20th century with the landmark case, Brown v. Board of Education. This Supreme Court case would play a pivotal role in the fight against racial segregation in the United States, particularly within the education system.

The case originated in Topeka, Kansas, in 1951 when Oliver Brown, an African American father, attempted to enroll his third-grade daughter, Linda, in an all-white public school. Despite the school being considerably closer to their home, Linda was denied admission solely on the grounds of her race. She was instead expected to attend a segregated Black school further away.

Incensed by the blatant racial discrimination, Oliver Brown joined forces with the local National Association for the Advancement of Colored People (NAACP) branch to challenge the segregation policy. The NAACP, at the time, was actively seeking out plaintiffs to challenge the segregationist doctrine of "separate but equal" established by the Plessy v. Ferguson case in 1896.

Brown v. Board of Education was not a single case but a consolidation of five similar cases from different states (Delaware, South Carolina, Virginia, and the District of Columbia in addition to Kansas) that the Supreme Court heard together. The other cases were Briggs v. Elliott (South Carolina), Davis v. County School Board of Prince Edward County (Virginia), Gebhart v. Belton (Delaware), and Bolling v. Sharpe (District of Columbia).[2]

Argued by NAACP lawyer and future Supreme Court justice Thurgood Marshall, the case challenged the constitutionality of segregation in public schools, asserting that it violated the 14th

Amendment's Equal Protection Clause, which guarantees all citizens equal protection under the law.

The Brown case, named for Oliver Brown as a legal strategy to have a man lead the plaintiff roster, went to the U.S. Supreme Court, where it was combined with four other cases to create the seminal Brown v. Board of Education. The consolidated cases encompassed over 200 plaintiffs and represented a broad swath of the United States, thereby ensuring that the decision would have a nationwide impact.

Role of Architecture in Segregated School Buildings

The role of architecture in segregated school buildings was significant and demonstrative of the wider societal system that supported and enforced racial segregation. The architectural designs of these buildings served as stark visual embodiments of the unequal distribution of resources, opportunities, and access between white students and their black counterparts.

In the era of segregation, "separate but equal" was the legal doctrine that upheld racial segregation, stipulating that as long as the separate facilities provided to different races were equal, segregation did not violate the Fourteenth Amendment. However, in practice, the separate facilities for African American students were far from equal.

Architecturally, the schools built for Black students were often markedly inferior to those for White students. They were typically underfunded, overcrowded, and in poor repair. Schools for Black children were often constructed with substandard materials and with less attention to aesthetic or functional design, reflective of the lesser value placed on Black education. Many lacked adequate facilities like libraries, science labs, or even basic heating in colder climates, and many had to use outdated and worn textbooks handed down from White schools.

School built for Black students in 1952. The Emory School in Hale County, Alabama. A part of the Rosenwald School Program. Photographed by Andrew Feiler.

Conversely, schools for White children were more likely to be constructed with higher quality materials and modern architectural designs, often featuring well-equipped classrooms, libraries, and laboratories. They were generally better maintained, with investments made in their expansion and improvement, reflecting the higher societal value placed on White education.

Schools built for White students. Farmville High School, VA. (Courtesy of Richmond Times-Dispatch.)

The physical disparities between Black and White schools were a daily, tangible reminder of the profound inequities in American society. The architecture of segregated schools visually and spatially enacted the racial hierarchy and served to maintain the racial status quo. It was a physical manifestation of the ideology of white supremacy, subtly communicating the message of racial inequality to students, teachers, parents, and the wider community.

In this context, the architectural design of segregated schools was more than just a backdrop to the education process; it was an active participant in the systemic racism of the time, shaping students' educational experiences and opportunities in deeply consequential ways. The fight to desegregate schools, therefore, was not just about sitting next to White students; it was about gaining access to the substantially better resources and environments of the White schools.

Images of Segregated Buildings

A photo of Massachusetts Ave. near Union Station in 1935. Photo by Carl Mydans. Resettlement Administration. Ghosts of DC.org

Chicago slums, 1954. Photographer: Fritz Goro, Life Magazine.

African American man drinks from a water fountain marked "colored" at a streetcar terminal in Oklahoma City, Oklahoma in 1939. Photograph by Bettmann. National Geographic.

Leland, Mississippi, the Delta Area. Photographer: Dorothea Lange, 1939. Library of Congress.

Negro man entering movie theater by "Colored Entrance," Belzoni, Mississippi, 1939. Black movie goers were directed to separate seating areas, usually in the balconies of theaters, such as this one in Mississippi. Source: Marion Post Wolcott, Oct. 1939, Library of Congress Prints.

Architect as Enforcer

"The Miseducation of the Negro" by Carter G. Woodson: An Analysis

In his seminal 1933 work "The Miseducation of the Negro," Carter G. Woodson argued that African Americans were being culturally indoctrinated, rather than taught, in American schools. This, he contended, was not accidental but a strategic ploy to maintain the racial hierarchy.

The primary focus of "The Miseducation of the Negro" is the examination of the Western education system, particularly its effects on African Americans. Woodson was highly critical of an educational system that, he believed, often perpetuated a "white supremacist" agenda and alienated African Americans from their rich cultural heritage. He saw the education system as a primary tool used by the dominant culture to propagate racism and reinforce a subservient mentality among African Americans.

Woodson held that the American education system provided African Americans with an education that made them despise their own history and culture, encouraging them to aspire to standards and norms set by a society that marginalized and devalued their race. African American students were led to believe that their history and culture were primitive and irrelevant, and that they should instead look towards Europe as the beacon of "civilization" and culture.[3]

Woodson argued for a new kind of education that would empower African Americans by teaching them their own history, accomplishments, and contributions to society. This, he believed, was essential for fostering racial pride and a strong sense of identity, ultimately challenging and changing the racial status quo.

Woodson's views are particularly relevant when considering the role of education in shaping racial dynamics in segregated societies. His critique of the education system as a tool of racial oppression resonates with the experience of many African American communities in the era of segregation and resonates still today. "The Miseducation of the Negro" has thus become a cornerstone in discussions on racial equality in education.

The ideas outlined in the book remain a critical guide for analyzing the impact of education on racial segregation and the propagation of discriminatory practices. Woodson's call for an educational paradigm that values, includes, and propagates the histories and cultures of all races remains an essential vision for achieving an egalitarian society. The examination of these views in our current context underscores the vital connection between education, self-perception, and societal roles in the context of racial segregation.

Desegregation and Its Aftereffects: Consequences of Forced Integration in Schools and Communities

When the landmark case Brown v. Board of Education of Topeka concluded in 1954, the Supreme Court's unanimous decision signaled the formal end of racial segregation in public schools. However, desegregation was not an immediate or smooth process, and it gave rise to a variety of complex social and political consequences that we continue to grapple with today.

The years following the Brown ruling were marked by widespread resistance, particularly in the South. Many Southern states launched what came to be known as the "Massive Resistance," a coordinated effort to resist integration. Some schools, rather than integrate, chose to shut down altogether, leading to the rise of segregation academies—private schools set up for White students.[4]

Forced integration led to significant demographic changes in schools and communities. One immediate consequence was the phenomenon known as "white flight," where white families, in an attempt to avoid integrated schools, moved from urban centers to suburbs, leading to a further socio-economic segregation. This reorganization often stripped resources from urban schools and communities, creating new forms of de facto segregation even as de jure segregation was being dismantled.

The forced integration of schools also brought about substantial psychological and social impacts. African American students, who were sent to previously all-white schools, often faced intense racial hostility and violence, epitomized by events like the Little Rock Nine incident in 1957, where nine Black students needed the assistance of federal troops to safely attend school.

Despite these obstacles, desegregation also resulted in some critical positive shifts. Many African American students gained access to more resources and better-funded schools due to integration. The interaction between races in an educational setting also encouraged familiarity and understanding, helping to break down some racial stereotypes and prejudices.

In the long run, the forced integration of schools laid the groundwork for more significant societal changes. It was a critical precursor to the broader Civil Rights Movement, and it set legal and moral precedents that helped challenge other forms of segregation and discrimination.

However, the aftereffects of desegregation are complex and layered. Many scholars argue that the legacy of forced integration is a mixed one. While it undeniably helped challenge the norms of racial segregation and opened up new opportunities for Black students, it also sparked backlash and resistance that morphed into new forms of segregation and racial disparity, particularly in terms of wealth and education. Today, many American schools remain segregated in practice, if not in law, demonstrating the perpetual challenges of achieving true racial integration and equality in the United States.

Urban Renewal and Destruction of Black Communities

Urban renewal, initially conceived as a strategy to improve the physical conditions of American cities and stimulate economic growth, had significant and often detrimental impacts on Black communities across the United States in the mid-20th century.

The process began in the 1940s and extended into the 1960s and 1970s under the auspices of improving "blighted" urban landscapes. However, these projects often led to the displacement of Black communities and destruction of their neighborhoods, causing an alarming level of socioeconomic disruption and perpetuating racial inequality.

Blighted Urban. Blog.Bluebeam.com/what-causes-urban-blight-and-what-can-be-done-about-it/

The Federal Housing Act of 1949 provided funding for city-based renewal projects, which led to the demolition of many older, economically depressed urban neighborhoods to make way for highway projects, public housing units, shopping centers, and various other new developments. These areas were predominantly populated by Black residents who had limited political power to oppose the damaging consequences of these initiatives.

The beginning of the end: The Housing Act of 1949. West End post-demolition looking south toward Customs House, c. 1962 (Johnathan Kaiser, The West End Museum Archives).

In many instances, urban renewal equated to what James Baldwin famously referred to as "Negro removal." It forced the displacement of countless African American families from their long-established communities, scattering them into public housing projects that quickly became isolated ghettos or to other areas often characterized by poverty, crime, and limited opportunity.[5]

It is important to note that due to these conditions experienced by minorities, a new form of expression was created to provide a voice or outlet to the greater population and eventually the entire nation. This new art form was called "Hip Hop" or "Rap" music in which musical artists became a sounding board of their experiences. One such Hip Hop group was named, "Grandmaster Flash and the Furious Five" with their groundbreaking song called, "The Message."

Queensbridge Houses. Veron Blvd. Queensboro Bridge and Ravenswood power plant. Wikimedia.

Moreover, the process of urban renewal often contributed to gentrification. After original neighborhoods were destroyed and their residents displaced, wealthier, predominantly White residents began to move into these newly renovated areas, causing property values and costs of living to rise significantly. As a result, the original residents were priced out, and their former communities lost much of their cultural and historical identity.

From an architectural perspective, urban renewal resulted in the loss of a significant amount of historically Black architecture, erasing a tangible connection to the past. This led to a collective sense of loss within these communities and a disconnection from their cultural and historical roots.

While urban renewal was promoted as an effort to improve living conditions and stimulate economic growth, the net effect was often destructive for Black communities. Despite the adverse impacts, these episodes of urban renewal forced a greater awareness of the need for urban policies and planning practices that are equitable and considerate of all communities. This recognition has influenced modern approaches to urban development, although the historical legacy of these urban renewal projects remains a source of ongoing debate and remediation.

ROLE OF THE DEPARTMENT OF HOUSING AND URBAN DEVELOPMENT (HUD) AND ITS IMPACT

The Department of Housing and Urban Development (HUD) was established in 1965 during the administration of President Lyndon B. Johnson as part of his "Great Society" program. Its mission was to create strong, sustainable, inclusive communities and quality, affordable homes for all.

HUD has played a significant role in the U.S., especially in terms of housing policy and urban development. Over the years, it has developed a variety of programs designed to improve the housing situations of the poor and disenfranchised. However, its impact on communities, particularly Black and minority communities, has been mixed and has evolved significantly over time.

Initially, HUD continued the urban renewal policies of the 1950s and early 1960s, funding city-based projects that often led to the displacement of minority communities. The agency financed the construction of public housing projects, many of which became isolated, crime-ridden, and mired in poverty, effectively creating more segregation within urban landscapes.

However, in the 1970s, HUD began to shift its policies under the influence of civil rights activism and legislation, as well as growing recognition of the failures of past strategies. The agency began promoting desegregation efforts, including the implementation of the Section 8 voucher program, which provided rental assistance to low-income families, the elderly, and the disabled, enabling them to seek housing in a wider array of neighborhoods.

HUD has also been instrumental in enforcing fair housing laws, which prohibit discrimination in housing on the basis of race, color, religion, sex, disability, familial status, or national origin. The Fair Housing Act of 1968, which HUD is charged with enforcing, was a landmark law aimed at ending racial segregation in housing.

Despite these strides, HUD has faced criticism for not doing enough to combat housing discrimination and segregation. Some argue that the agency has failed to adequately enforce the Fair Housing Act, leading to ongoing patterns of residential segregation.

HUD's role in affordable housing provision and urban development has been, and continues to be, essential. Its policies and programs have evolved over time, often reflecting broader societal attitudes towards race, poverty, and the role of government in addressing these issues. Despite some significant achievements, the agency's legacy is complicated by instances of failure and unintended consequences, and its future role remains an important part of ongoing discussions about racial and socioeconomic inequality in America.[6]

Federal Measures and Programs to Desegregate Facilities

The United States has undertaken significant federal measures and implemented various programs in an effort to desegregate public facilities and counteract the harmful effects of racial segregation. Many of these measures were enacted during the Civil Rights Movement in the 1950s and 1960s, a period marked by an intensified struggle for racial equality.

1. Brown v. Board of Education (1954): This Supreme Court decision declared that state laws establishing separate public schools for Black and White students were unconstitutional, overturning the "separate but equal" precedent established by the Plessy v. Ferguson ruling. The ruling called for the desegregation of schools across the nation.

2. The Civil Rights Act of 1964: This landmark legislation outlawed discrimination based on race, color, religion, sex, or national origin. Title II of the Act specifically prohibited segregation or discrimination in places of public accommodation engaged in interstate commerce, including hotels, motels, restaurants, theaters, and all other public accommodations.

3. The Voting Rights Act of 1965: This act aimed to overcome legal barriers at the state and local levels that prevented African Americans from exercising their right to vote under the 15th Amendment. By ensuring voting rights, it empowered Black communities to influence the operation of public facilities in their localities through their elected representatives.

4. The Fair Housing Act of 1968: Part of the Civil Rights Act of 1968, the Fair Housing Act prohibited discrimination concerning the sale, rental, and financing of housing based on race, religion, national origin, and since 1974, gender. The Act has been crucial in the fight against residential segregation.

5. The Busing Measures of the 1970s: To speed up the desegregation of public schools, court-ordered busing policies were implemented to transport students to schools outside of their local districts. These measures were controversial and met with resistance in many communities, but they served as an important tool in breaking down segregated schooling structures.

6. The Section 8 Housing Choice Voucher Program: Launched in the 1970s by the Department of Housing and Urban Development, this program provides rental assistance to low-income families, the elderly, and the disabled to afford decent, safe, and sanitary housing in the private market. The program wanted to break up concentrated areas of poverty and provide opportunities for residents to live in a variety of communities.[7]

These federal measures and programs represent significant efforts to desegregate facilities and public spaces in the United States. Their effects have been mixed, with many challenges persisting even after their implementation. Nevertheless, they laid a crucial foundation for ongoing efforts to promote racial equality and integration.

ARCHITECTS AS POLICYMAKERS: INFLUENCE OF ARCHITECTS IN SHAPING POLICIES AND REGULATIONS

As stewards of the built environment, architects possess significant potential to effect meaningful changes in societies. Architects have the opportunity, and indeed the obligation, to apply their unique skills and perspectives in the policy-making arena.

1. Influencing Urban Planning and Development: Architects play a crucial role in urban planning and development. Their input can guide the formation of zoning laws, building codes, and land use policies. These elements of urban planning can significantly affect a community's quality of life and socioeconomic dynamics. For example, zoning laws can either encourage or discourage diversity and integration, and architects can influence these outcomes.

2. Promoting Sustainability and Environmental Policy: Architects are at the forefront of designing energy-efficient buildings and promoting sustainable practices in the construction industry. They can advise policymakers on regulations and incentives that encourage sustainable design, contributing to the fight against climate change.

3. Advocating for Affordable Housing: Architects understand the constraints and opportunities in constructing affordable housing. They can provide valuable insights into policies that either facilitate or hinder the development of affordable homes. Their expertise can inform measures such as inclusionary zoning or housing voucher programs, and they can advocate for design solutions that make efficient use of space and resources.

4. Preserving Cultural Heritage: Architects often engage in efforts to preserve historical buildings and cultural heritage sites. In doing so, they influence policies around preservation and the integration of new development with historical context.

5. Accessibility and Universal Design: Architects can champion the importance of accessible design for individuals with disabilities. By advising on regulations pertaining to accessibility, they ensure that the built environment caters to all users, promoting inclusivity.

By wielding their influence in these and other policy areas, architects serve as crucial advocates for better buildings, better cities, and better societies. They shape not just the physical world, but the policies that govern it, wielding significant influence over how societies grow and develop.

Role of Architects in Promoting Equality and Inclusion

1. Designing for All: Architects can foster equality by adhering to principles of universal design, which aim to create spaces accessible and usable by all people, regardless of age, ability, or status. For example, incorporating ramps alongside stairs, ensuring doorways are wide enough for wheelchair users, or designing multi-sensory environments for visually impaired individuals can make spaces more inclusive.

2. Promoting Social Integration: Residential and urban planning can be used as tools to prevent segregation and encourage social integration. Mixed-use developments that combine residential, commercial, and public spaces promote interaction among a diverse range of people. By advocating for integrated, multi-income housing and designing communal spaces that encourage interaction, architects can help break down social barriers and foster a sense of community.

3. Advocacy and Representation: Architects can use their influence to advocate for marginalized communities, ensuring their needs are considered in the design and planning process. This might involve engaging communities in the design process to understand their needs and preferences better, or advocating for policies that promote fair housing and prevent discriminatory practices.

4. Sustainability and Equity: By promoting sustainable design, architects can also contribute to social equity. Low-income communities are often disproportionately affected by environmental issues like poor air quality or lack of green space. Sustainable design approaches can help to mitigate these impacts and create healthier, more livable environments for all residents.

5. Educational Role: Architects often have opportunities to educate clients, the public, and policymakers about the importance of inclusive design. By raising awareness of these issues, they can help to shift attitudes and influence policy in a way that prioritizes inclusivity.

6. Reflecting Diversity in Design: Architecture can celebrate cultural diversity and heritage by incorporating design elements that reflect the local community's history and values. This approach can help communities feel more connected to their built environment, fostering a sense of belonging and inclusivity.[8]

In these ways and more, architects play a vital role in promoting equality and inclusion. Through thoughtful, inclusive design, they can help to create a built environment that respects and celebrates the diversity of its users.

14

*"Conformity is the jailer of freedom
and the enemy of growth."*

John F. Kennedy

ARCHITECT AS POLICYMAKER

THE THIRD WAVE OF MIGRATION

Migration of Asians, Mexicans, and Central Americans to the U.S.

The late 20th and early 21st centuries ushered in a significant shift in American migration patterns. This period, often referred to as the "Third Wave," was characterized by a substantial influx of immigrants from Asia, Mexico, and Central America. A rich tapestry of history, culture, and personal stories weaves together to form this wave, with its formidable impact resonating through the fabric of modern-day America.

During the post-World War II era, a marked shift in American immigration policy culminated in the Immigration and Nationality Act of 1965, abolishing the national-origins quota system that had been in place since the 1920s. The quota system had significantly restricted immigration from non-European countries. With its elimination, the floodgates were opened for a new era of diversity.

Asian immigrants were among the first to take advantage of this opportunity. Initially, many came from China, India, and the Philippines, later joined by Vietnamese and Korean immigrants after the Vietnam and Korean Wars. For Mexicans and Central Americans, the proximity to the United States and long-standing economic and political relationships led to large-scale migration. The Bracero Program, established during World War II, allowed millions of Mexican workers to come to the United States temporarily to work, setting a precedent for future immigration patterns.

The Third Wave brought with it significant diversity in culture, skills, and perspectives. With each new immigrant came a story of hope, aspiration, or survival, adding to the rich cultural tapestry of America. From the vibrant Latino communities in Los Angeles and the bustling Chinatowns that popped up in major cities to the proliferation of Indian and Pakistani restaurants and markets in places like New York and Chicago, the influence of this wave of migration is evident.

THE EVERLASTING EFFECTS OF SEGREGATION

The Third Wave of migration occurred against a backdrop of significant racial tension and civil rights struggles in the United States. Even as new immigrants from Asia, Mexico, and Central America who sought opportunities for a better life, they faced the deep-seated and systemic barriers that are the legacies of racial segregation. These barriers have had profound and irreversible repercussions on the lives of these immigrants and their descendants, affecting both individuals and communities in many unforeseen ways.

Psychological Impacts on Individuals and Communities

The history of racial segregation in America, although formally abolished, continued to affect new immigrants. Experiences of racial and ethnic discrimination can have profound psychological impacts on both individuals and communities. Despite their diverse backgrounds, many Asian, Mexican, and Central American immigrants found themselves classified under broad racial or ethnic categories and subjected to stereotypes and prejudice.[1]

Moreover, the struggle to balance cultural preservation with assimilation often posed challenges. The pressure to assimilate, coupled with the discrimination faced by these immigrants, resulted in feelings of otherness, alienation, and stress.

Social and Economic Conditions Under Segregation

The legacy of segregation also had significant influences on the social and economic conditions faced by these new immigrants. Despite the promise of the American dream, many immigrants found themselves confined to low-wage jobs, limited by language barriers, lack of recognition for foreign credentials, and outright discrimination.

In many urban areas, patterns of residential segregation emerged as immigrants settled into ethnic settlements. While these communities often provided support and a sense of belonging, they also often reflected the social and economic inequities experienced by these groups, such as limited access to quality education, healthcare, and other public services.

Moreover, the racial wealth gap, a direct result of historic segregation and discriminatory practices, also affected immigrant populations. Despite their often significant contributions to the American economy, many Asian, Mexican, and Central American immigrants and their descendants continue to face economic disadvantage and marginalization.[2]

Understanding the Third Wave of migration in the context of the lasting effects of segregation provides crucial insights into the challenges faced by these immigrant groups. It sheds light on the ongoing struggle for equity and inclusion, and underscores the continued relevance of confronting America's history of racial segregation.

THE RISE OF GATED COMMUNITIES

In the latter part of the 20th century and into the 21st, another trend emerged within the patchwork of American communities—the rise of gated communities. These private, fenced, and often luxuriously appointed neighborhoods represented a shift in how people choose to live, spurred by various societal factors and fundamentally changing the nature of residential communities across the United States.

Emergence and Popularity of Gated Communities

The first gated communities began appearing in the 1960s and 1970s in places like California and Florida. Their growth was spurred by a mix of factors, including a desire for increased safety, privacy, and exclusivity. However, the rapid proliferation of gated communities in the 1990s and beyond reflected deeper societal shifts.[3]

Security was one significant driving factor in their popularity. Amid increasing reports of crime and social disorder in the late 20th century, many people sought the perceived safety of enclosed communities, where entry could be monitored and controlled.

The second factor was exclusivity. Gated communities were, and continue to be, associated with a certain level of prestige. They often include high-end homes, top-notch amenities, and landscaped grounds—offering a lifestyle of comfort and luxury that many aspire to.

Finally, there was the appeal of controlled environments. Gated communities provided a sense of order, with enforced community rules and standards maintaining the aesthetics and property values within the gates. This sense of order, in combination with the other factors, made gated communities an attractive proposition for many people—despite their often higher costs.

Gated Communities. Condocontrol.com

Implications for Social Integration and Segregation

While the rise of gated communities has been a significant trend in the American landscape, their implications for social integration and segregation are great. On one hand, these communities often provide a safe, secure, and aesthetically pleasing living environment for their residents. On the other hand, they can exacerbate social inequalities and create divisions within broader society.

Gated communities, by their very nature, create physical and symbolic barriers between their residents and the wider community. The gates, walls, and security measures that define these communities serve to separate residents from the "outside world," both literally and figuratively. This segregation can limit interactions between people of different socio-economic statuses, races, and ethnicities, and contribute to a lack of understanding or empathy for those who live "outside the gate." [4]

Moreover, the rise of gated communities can contribute to economic and racial segregation. These communities are often populated by those with higher incomes who can afford the real estate prices and maintenance fees. As a result, gated communities can become districts of wealth, segregating their residents from lower-income populations. Similarly, they can also reflect racial segregation, particularly if socio-economic status is correlated with race or ethnicity, as is often the case in the United States.

While gated communities offer many advantages to their residents, their rise also presents challenges for societal integration and inclusivity. They reflect a society increasingly divided along socio-economic and racial lines, a manifestation of the wider issues that stem from historic patterns of segregation.

The rise of gated communities is thus not just a trend in housing preferences but a significant socio-cultural phenomenon that warrants a closer examination. Understanding this trend and its implications is crucial for grappling with issues of social integration and segregation in contemporary America.

SELF-SEGREGATION OF RACES AND ETHNIC GROUPS

The United States is famously known as a "melting pot" of cultures and ethnicities, a nation where individuals from all corners of the globe converge to form a diverse and complex society. Yet, beneath this broad tapestry of diversity, there exists a nuanced phenomenon that sometimes goes overlooked—self-segregation among races and ethnic groups.

Separate and Equal: Understanding Self-Segregation

Self-segregation is the process by which individuals of the same race or ethnic background voluntarily cluster together, creating communities that reflect their shared culture, experiences, and often, language. This phenomenon is prevalent across different racial and ethnic groups, seen in various forms such as ethnic neighborhoods in cities, culturally specific retirement communities, or even social media groups and online communities.[5]

To understand self-segregation, it's crucial to separate it from the enforced segregation of the past. Unlike historic examples of segregation, which were mandated and enforced by discriminatory laws and policies, self-segregation is typically a voluntary choice. It is driven by the desire for community, the comfort of cultural familiarity, and the necessity of mutual support.

Self-segregation can manifest as residential patterns where neighborhoods become predominantly inhabited by one ethnic or racial group. Examples include the vibrant Chinatowns, Little Italys, and Latino barrios found in many American cities. Here, languages, traditions, foods, and festivals from the homeland are preserved and celebrated, providing a sense of belonging and continuity for residents.

On one hand, self-segregation has positive aspects. It allows for the preservation of cultural heritage, provides a sense of community, and can offer a safe space for individuals who may feel marginalized or discriminated against in broader society. Such communities can provide social, emotional, and even economic support to their members. For immigrants, in particular, these communities can serve as crucial networks that help them navigate their new surroundings and mitigate the challenges of acculturation.

However, self-segregation also has its drawbacks. While it can reinforce a sense of identity and community, it can also reinforce cultural divides, limiting interactions between different racial and ethnic groups. This can foster a lack of understanding or even perpetuate stereotypes as interactions with those outside one's racial or ethnic group become limited. Self-segregation can also lead to economic isolation and may inadvertently reinforce socio-economic disparities.

In a broader context, the phenomenon of self-segregation reflects the complexity of racial and ethnic dynamics in the United States. It underscores the persistent impact of race and ethnicity on individuals' lived experiences, social networks, and community structures. Understanding self-segregation is crucial for comprehending the depth and nuances of America's racial and ethnic landscape, an essential component in addressing the broader issues of segregation and integration in American society.

The Edward Scissorhands Effect on Communities

The term "Edward Scissorhands Effect" may seem peculiar in the context of discussing self-segregation and community formation. Still, it holds significant relevance. Inspired by Tim Burton's 1990 film, Edward Scissorhands, the term has been adopted in the social sciences to describe a particular kind of social and spatial isolation within communities.

In the film, Edward Scissorhands, portrayed by Johnny Depp, is a synthetic man with scissors for hands who lives on the outskirts of a uniform suburban neighborhood. Despite his unusual appearance and manners, Edward becomes an object of fascination for the locals until a series of unfortunate incidents lead to his ostracization and subsequent return to his secluded existence.

This narrative in the film is metaphorically seen in real-life communities where visible or invisible "scissors" separate individuals or groups from the larger community. The "scissors" in this case represent factors like race, ethnicity, social class, or even distinct lifestyles that result in self-segregation or imposed segregation.[6]

The Edward Scissorhands Effect on communities. The ice cream colors fail to distinguish the homes of individual families in this cookie-cutter suburb. Medium.com, 20th Century Fox.

The Edward Scissorhands effect is significant in understanding how neighborhoods and communities evolve and function. Here's how this plays out in communities:

1. Homogeneity and Exclusion: Just like the suburb in the film, many communities today are built around homogeneity, whether it's socio-economic status, race, or lifestyle. While this can foster a strong sense of community among like-minded or similar individuals, it can also create an environment of exclusion for those who don't fit the mold.

2. Fascination Turning into Fear: As seen in the film, the "different" or the "other," represented by Edward, initially sparks fascination but eventually turns into fear and exclusion. In real-world communities, this can manifest as xenophobia, racism, or classism when the "other" is perceived as a threat, leading to their further marginalization.

3. Retreat to Self-Segregation: The film concludes with Edward retreating back to his castle, an act of self-segregation in response to the community's rejection. This resonates with how some individuals or groups in society retreat into enclaves of their own, seeking solace and acceptance among those who share their identity, experiences, or circumstances.

The Edward Scissorhands effect brings to light the sometimes harsh realities of community formation and segregation. It emphasizes the need for inclusivity, tolerance, and understanding in communities. Overcoming the Edward Scissorhands effect entails recognizing and challenging our prejudices, ensuring diverse representation in community planning and development, and fostering an environment that values differences and promotes social cohesion.

The Seaside Community Phenomenon

The Seaside community phenomenon is an interesting concept that emerged in the context of urban planning and community development, particularly in the United States. Seaside, a small resort community in Florida that was founded in 1981, came to represent a distinctive and influential approach to building communities, leading to what's now known as "New Urbanism."

Entrance sign to Seaside, Florida, Wikipedia.

Understanding the Seaside Community Phenomenon

The community of Seaside, Florida, was designed with an intentional focus on walkability, mixed-use development, and architectural unity. It was conceived as a reaction to the car-centric suburban sprawl that had become the norm in American city planning.

Seaside was designed to promote a strong sense of community through its urban design and architectural principles. These are some of the key characteristics that define the Seaside community phenomenon:

1. Walkability and Connectivity: Seaside was designed to promote walking over driving. The town features a network of narrow streets, ample pedestrian paths, and communal spaces within easy walking distance of homes and businesses. This facilitates daily interaction among residents and helps foster a close-knit community.

Areas easily accessible by walking. USDN, Sustainableconsumption.usdn.org

2. Mixed-Use Development: Seaside incorporates a mix of residential, commercial, and communal spaces. Homes, shops, schools, and parks are interspersed throughout the community, facilitating a blend of public and private life. This mixed-use approach encourages a vibrant street life and allows for more social interaction among residents.

Mix of residential and commercial space, Seaside, FL. SoWal.com

3. Architectural Unity: While each building in Seaside is unique, they all adhere to a cohesive architectural style that gives the town a unified and distinctive identity. This architectural cohesion contributes to a sense of belonging and community identity.

Architectural Unity, Seaside, FL. Poshbeachrealty.com

Implications of the Seaside Community Phenomenon

The Seaside community phenomenon has had significant implications for urban planning and community development.

First, it sparked the New Urbanism movement, which advocates for the creation of walkable, mixed-use neighborhoods as an alternative to suburban sprawl. This movement has influenced urban planning principles not only in the United States but also in other parts of the world.[7]

Example of a mixed-use neighborhood, Missoula, MT. Homeword.org

Second, the Seaside community phenomenon has reshaped ideas about what constitutes a strong community. It has highlighted the importance of communal spaces, walkability, and architectural unity in fostering a sense of belonging and community spirit.

However, it's also important to note the criticisms associated with the Seaside community phenomenon. These include concerns about exclusivity, lack of diversity, and high costs of living, which have led some critics to label Seaside and similar communities as utopian enclaves that may inadvertently foster social segregation.

The Seaside community phenomenon is an experiment of the power of urban design in shaping community dynamics. It presents valuable insights but also cautionary tales about the role of urban planning in creating social integration or segregation.

EX-PATRIOTS AND REFUSAL TO INTEGRATE

Ex-patriots, or expatriates, are individuals who choose to live outside their native country and present a unique facet to the study of integration and segregation. While expatriates can foster cultural exchange and contribute to the diversity of their host country, there are instances where they show a reluctance or outright refusal to integrate into the local society. This can result in forms of self-segregation, creating distinct expatriate communities that can impact the customs, culture, and social dynamics of the host country.

Images of Self-Segregated Facilities

Restaurant in Dearborn, Michigan. Flickr, Sharghzadeh. Detroit MetroTimes.

Koreatown in Atlanta, GA near I-85 corridor to Northeast Atlanta. Quora.com

Understanding Ex-Patriot Refusal to Integrate

Living in a foreign country, expatriates often face language barriers, cultural differences, and other challenges that can make integration difficult. Some individuals choose to embrace these challenges, immersing themselves in the local culture and language as part of their overseas experience. Others, however, may opt to stick with what is familiar, forming expatriate communities with fellow nationals and maintaining their home country's customs and traditions.[8]

Isolationism as a Form of Self-Segregation

This choice to stay within familiar circles can lead to isolationism, a form of self-segregation where expatriates live, socialize, and even work within the confines of their own community. This phenomenon is not uncommon in countries with significant expatriate populations. For example, in cities like Dubai or Singapore, it's not unusual to find entire neighborhoods predominantly inhabited by expatriates from a specific country.

While such communities can offer a comforting slice of home in a foreign land, they can also create a bubble that separates expatriates from the local population. This isolation can exacerbate cultural misunderstandings, reinforce stereotypes, and hinder the mutual exchange of ideas and experiences that is often an enriching aspect of multicultural societies.

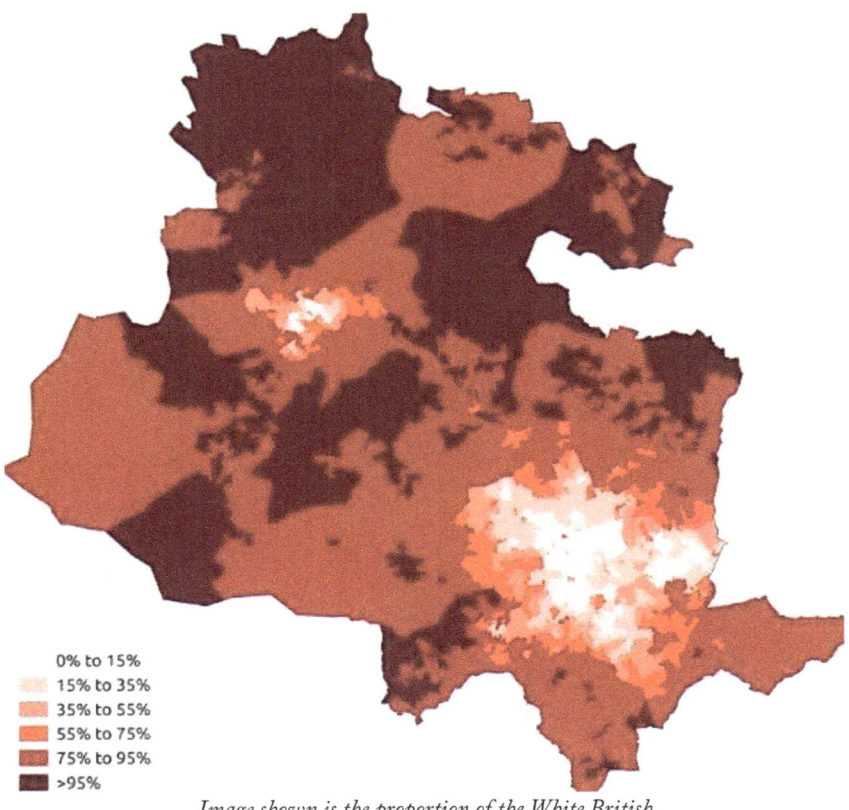

Image shown is the proportion of the White British population in 2011 in Bradford. Wikipedia.

Impact on Customs, Culture, and Social Dynamics

The refusal of expatriates to integrate can have significant effects on the customs, culture, and social dynamics of the host country.

On one hand, the presence of large, non-integrating expatriate communities can lead to cultural fragmentation. This can widen the gap between different sections of society, leading to misunderstandings and reinforcing cultural and social divides.

On the other hand, these communities can also contribute to cultural diversity and cosmopolitanism. They introduce new cuisines, traditions, and perspectives, enriching the host country's culture. However, this potential benefit is often only fully realized when there is a degree of cultural exchange and integration between expatriates and the local population.

The phenomenon of expatriates and their refusal to integrate poses complex issues for multicultural societies. While the formation of expatriate communities can bring cultural diversity and vibrancy, a lack of integration can also perpetuate social segregation. Striking a balance between preserving cultural identity and encouraging integration is a challenging task, but is crucial to ensuring the harmonious coexistence of different cultures in a shared social space.

SOUTH AMERICA AS A MODEL

In the quest to achieve a racially and ethnically harmonious society, we must explore the models presented by different regions across the globe. An interesting region in this context is South America, with Brazil as a notable example, where the historical blending of indigenous, African and European cultures has resulted in an ethnically diverse and vibrant society.

Brazil's Integration of Races

Brazil, often referred to as a "racial democracy," offers an intriguing model of racial integration. It is one of the most ethnically diverse countries in the world, a result of centuries of intermarriage between Indigenous Brazilians, Portuguese colonizers, African slaves, and immigrants from Europe, the Middle East, and Asia.

The concept of "mestiço," or mixed-race identity, is central to Brazilian self-understanding. Unlike the "one-drop rule" applied historically in the United States, which categorized anyone with even a trace of African ancestry as Black, Brazil's spectrum of racial identities is varied and fluid. It has over a hundred terms for different skin shades, a testament to its racial diversity.[8]

However, this does not mean that Brazil is without racial issues. Socioeconomic disparities along racial lines are evident, and racism, though less overt than in other parts of the world, is a systemic issue. Nonetheless, Brazil's racial integration and fluid understanding of race present an alternative perspective to the often-polarized racial discourses in many other regions of the world.

Lessons and Potential Solutions from South America

The South American model, as exemplified by Brazil, provides crucial insights for other multicultural societies grappling with issues of racial integration and segregation. Here are a few key lessons:

1. Embrace Racial Fluidity: Rather than rigid racial categorizations, a more fluid understanding of race can promote integration. It encourages the blending of cultures and reduces the "us versus them" mentality often associated with distinct racial groups.

2. Encourage Cultural Exchange: South America's vibrant culture is evidence of the power of cultural exchange. The mutual sharing and appreciation of different cultural practices can encourage understanding and unity among diverse racial and ethnic groups.

3. Address Systemic Inequities: The persistence of racial inequities in Brazil serves as a warning that racial harmony is not merely about cultural integration but must also involve addressing socioeconomic disparities.

4. Prioritize Education: An educated populace is better equipped to challenge racial prejudices and stereotypes. Education should highlight the nation's racial and cultural diversity, reinforcing pride in the country's multicultural identity.

5. Legislation: Effective anti-discrimination laws and equal opportunity policies can help mitigate racial disparities. Brazil, for instance, has implemented affirmative action policies in university admissions to promote educational equity.

South America's racial dynamics, particularly Brazil's, provide a fascinating model of integration. While not without its challenges, it offers valuable lessons in understanding race beyond rigid binaries and promoting a culture of inclusivity and mutual respect. These lessons could be potential solutions for societies worldwide grappling with their own racial and ethnic complexities.

GENTRIFICATION OF NEIGHBORHOODS

Gentrification, a significant phenomenon in urban neighborhoods, has considerable implications for racial segregation, community dynamics, and economic disparities. The process of gentrification involves an influx of more affluent individuals into an economically disadvantaged neighborhood, causing a rise in property values, and often displacing the original inhabitants.

Reasons Behind Gentrification

Gentrification is a complex process driven by several interlinked factors. Here are some of the key reasons:

1. Economic Development: Urban renewal initiatives and public policies aimed at attracting investment often set the stage for gentrification. The establishment of new businesses, restaurants, and entertainment venues can increase a neighborhood's attractiveness to wealthier individuals.

2. Housing Demand: Rapid urbanization and the desire for proximity to city centers can increase demand for housing in certain neighborhoods, driving up property prices and attracting wealthier residents.

3. Cultural Shift: Changes in lifestyle preferences, such as a preference for urban living, historic homes, or walkable neighborhoods, can attract more affluent individuals to certain neighborhoods.

4. Speculative Investment: Real estate developers and investors can contribute to gentrification by purchasing and renovating properties in "up-and-coming" neighborhoods, expecting that the area's property values will increase.

Remaking of Ybor City with increasing density of high-end multifamily developments. Photo by Jerel McCants in 2024.

Effects on Segregation and Community Dynamics

Gentrification can profoundly reshape the social, economic, and racial landscape of neighborhoods with far-reaching implications.

1. Displacement: As property values and rents rise, long-term residents, often racial or ethnic minorities, may be priced out of their neighborhoods. This displacement can further exacerbate racial segregation by pushing marginalized communities into fewer and fewer neighborhoods.

2. Change in Local Culture: As new, typically wealthier, residents move in, the local culture and character of the neighborhood can change. Small businesses, local markets, and community centers that once served the original residents may be replaced by more upscale establishments, as experienced in southwest Atlanta in the mid-2000s.

3. Economic Inequality: While gentrification can increase property values and bring new amenities to a neighborhood, these benefits often accrue to new, wealthier residents rather than the original inhabitants. This can widen economic disparities within communities.

4. Social Tension: Gentrification can create social tension between new and long-term residents. These groups may have different values, priorities, and levels of influence in community decision-making, leading to conflicts and a sense of alienation among original residents, such as the transformation of Harlem during the early 1990s.

Tension in a Gentrifying Neighborhood. Thecityateyelevel.com

5. Polarization: As gentrification progresses, a neighborhood may become economically polarized. With the influx of wealthier residents, the cost of living rises and the neighborhood may split into distinct areas of wealth and poverty as noticed in Miami's Overtown district since the creation of the Wynwood Arts District.

In essence, gentrification is a double-edged sword. On one hand, it can lead to the revitalization of neighborhoods, attracting new investments, and potentially reducing crime rates. On the other hand, if not carefully managed, it can conflagrate racial and socioeconomic segregation, disrupt community cohesion, and lead to the displacement of the original inhabitants. As such, understanding and addressing the effects of gentrification is crucial for promoting equitable and inclusive urban development.[9]

THE FUTURE OF SEGREGATION

The future of segregation remains a critical and complex issue in societies worldwide, bearing significant implications for psychological well-being, social cohesion, and economic equality. Forecasting this future is a daunting task, as it must take into account numerous variables, from shifts in public policy and demographic trends to the effects of global events and the role of technology in society.

Predictions and Challenges

1. **Increasing Urbanization and Gentrification:** The continued urbanization trend could expound racial and economic segregation if it leads to more gentrification without adequate policies to protect vulnerable populations. We may see increased polarization within cities, with affluent enclaves existing alongside marginalized communities.

2. **Virtual Segregation:** In our increasingly digitized world, new forms of segregation might emerge. Algorithmic bias and the digital divide might lead to a new kind of segregation, where access to resources and opportunities is dictated by digital literacy and access to technology. This form of segregation could further redefine inequalities and segregation in physical space.

3. **Migration and Global Events:** The continued effects of climate change and geopolitical events could stimulate increased migration, leading to more multicultural societies. Without effective integration policies, these societies could face increased segregation and social tension.

4. **The Future of Education:** The trend of school segregation, whether due to economic, racial, or other factors, is concerning. If left unchecked, educational segregation could perpetuate inequality for future generations, leading to a deeply divided society.

Implications for Societies Worldwide

The persistence of segregation has significant implications for societies.

1. Economic Inequality: Persistent segregation often results in a lack of access to quality education and job opportunities for marginalized groups, perpetuating a cycle of poverty and economic inequality.

2. Social Cohesion: High levels of segregation can lead to increased social tension, misunderstanding, and conflict between different racial, ethnic, or economic groups.

3. Political Polarization: As societies become more segregated, different groups may become more entrenched in their views, leading to increased political polarization and instability.

4. Health Disparities: Segregation can result in significant disparities in health outcomes, with marginalized communities often having less access to quality healthcare and facing higher levels of stress and poorer health outcomes.

Psychological Effects of Segregation

Segregation has far-reaching psychological effects on individuals and communities.

1. Stress and Mental Health: Living in segregated, disadvantaged neighborhoods has been linked to higher levels of stress and mental health problems, including depression and anxiety.

2. Stereotyping and Prejudice: Segregation can foster stereotyping and prejudice, as it reduces opportunities for meaningful interaction between different racial and ethnic groups.

3. Internalized Racism: For marginalized racial and ethnic groups, living in segregated societies can lead to internalized racism, where individuals come to believe in the negative stereotypes about their own group, with harmful effects on self-esteem and mental health.

4. Identity and Belonging: For those in segregated communities, there can be feelings of alienation and a lack of belonging in the wider society, which can impact mental well-being and social development.

To say the least, as we move toward the future, it's clear that the challenge of segregation remains deeply relevant. Only through inclusive policies, open dialogues, and intentional effort can societies hope to address these challenges and create more equitable, integrated communities. As we grapple with these issues, it's essential to remember that our shared futures are intertwined. The benefits of addressing segregation will accrue to all as societies become more equitable, inclusive, and cohesive.

There is a lot to unpack and examine in understanding the migrant movement to the United States, legal and illegal, to the indestructible grasp of segregation and its various forms and rebirths: Gated Communities, Self-Segregation, Ex-Patriots Refusal to Integrate, South America's Model, Gentrification, and the look forward to segregation in the future.

The policies influenced by segregation are irreversible. To quote actor and activist, Michael J. Fox, in his role as Mike Flaherty on the sitcom, "Spin City," "Once bread has become toast…It can never go back to being bread again!"

15

"He has put a knife on the things that held us together and we have fallen apart."

Chinua Achebe, *Things Fall Apart*

ARCHITECT AS GATEKEEPER

SOCIOECONOMIC SEGREGATION

Impact on Architecture

Socioeconomic segregation, which refers to partitioning people into neighborhoods based on their social and economic status, has left an undeniable imprint on architecture in urban areas. This trend has been propelled largely by widening income inequality and patterns of residential clustering.

Architecture, both as a profession and a cultural artifact, has played an integral role in mirroring and often reinforcing this segregation. High-income neighborhoods often feature buildings with high-end construction materials, more open space, and innovative design elements. In contrast, lower-income areas are typically marked by denser housing structures with fewer amenities and resources.

Kowloon Walled City Dense Housing Structures in British Hong Kong in 1993. Wikipedia.

The impacts are multifaceted. For one, this segregation alters the physical landscape, resulting in urban areas where class distinctions are starkly visible in the built environment. But more significantly, it influences the lived experiences of residents, their access to opportunities, and their interactions with the city and with each other. In lower-income neighborhoods, residents often endure limited access to public services and green spaces, and poor housing conditions, which collectively diminish their quality of life.

Gentrification and Its Role in Exacerbating Segregation

Gentrification, the process by which lower-income urban areas experience an influx of higher-income residents and corresponding investment, has become a defining feature of contemporary urban life. While it brings apparent benefits, such as improved infrastructure, increased property values, and more services, it has been heavily criticized for its role in exacerbating segregation.

In terms of architecture, gentrification is often marked by a stark contrast in building types within a relatively small area. Often, historic buildings are renovated with a luxury touch, and new condominiums or apartments built with modern design principles are juxtaposed against the older, typically less-maintained architecture of pre-gentrification buildings. This architectural discrepancy creates visible markers of economic disparity.

Gentrification with old and new homes side by side in Old East Dallas. Wikipedia.

From a socioeconomic perspective, gentrification can lead to displacement of original residents as rising property values and rents often make it unaffordable for them to stay. Consequently, they're pushed into less desirable areas, leading to a concentration of poverty elsewhere—a phenomenon known as "displacement-induced segregation." The communities that emerge from gentrification are often less racially and economically diverse than those they replace, which further entrenches segregation.[1]

This pattern of gentrification thus contributes to a "tale of two cities" within the same urban area, where the prosperity enjoyed by some contrasts starkly with the hardship endured by others. Such segregation, visible in the architectural and socioeconomic landscape, challenges notions of urban cohesion and shared prosperity. Consequently, it raises critical questions about the role of policy, planning, and architectural practices in mitigating or exacerbating these trends.

A Tale of Two Cities. Mydissentproject.wordpress.com

Segregation in Education and Its Architectural Implications

School zoning, the practice of assigning students to schools based on their residential location, has had effects on racial and economic segregation. It plays an influential role in perpetuating racial and economic segregation. This is particularly evident in urban settings, where residential segregation often translates into school segregation. As wealthier families and families of a particular race or ethnicity cluster in certain neighborhoods, the schools in those zones become similarly homogeneous.

Architecturally, this is reflected in the facilities and resources available to schools in different zones. Schools in wealthier zones typically have access to better funding and can afford modern, well-maintained facilities. In contrast, schools in poorer zones often contend with outdated facilities in need of repair. The difference in these environments can greatly impact the quality of education and the students' sense of belonging and motivation.

Furthermore, the architecture of these schools often mirrors the socio-economic status of the families it serves. Schools in wealthier neighborhoods are likely to have state-of-the-art buildings, expansive sports facilities, and well-stocked libraries. In contrast, schools in lower-income neighborhoods may face overcrowding, with multiple students sharing a single desk and schools operating in shifts to accommodate all students.

Designing Inclusive Educational Environments

Designing inclusive educational environments can be a potent tool for challenging and reducing segregation. It involves creating spaces that are physically and socially accommodating to all students, regardless of their race, socio-economic status, or other characteristics.

At a basic level, inclusive design entails ensuring that all schools are well-equipped, well-maintained, and suitable for learning. All students should have access to adequate classrooms, libraries, laboratories, and outdoor spaces. The architecture should inspire learning, foster interaction, and promote a sense of community among diverse students.

Inclusive design also involves thinking about the finer details that shape students' experiences. For example, are there spaces where students from different backgrounds can come together and interact? Do the artworks, symbols, and other elements reflect the diverse cultures of the students? Even seemingly small decisions, like the layout of classrooms or the choice of decorations can send strong messages about inclusivity and belonging.[2]

Inclusive educational environments are not just about reducing segregation but also about promoting equity and social cohesion. They offer an opportunity to challenge the existing disparities and to ensure that all students, regardless of their background, have the opportunity to thrive. The task is complex and challenging, but it is a critical step towards a just society for the 21st century learning environments and beyond.

16

*"Never lookin' back or too far in front of me;
the present is a gift and I just wanna be."*

Common

ARCHITECT AS INTEGRATOR

"WHO GOT IT RIGHT?"

Inclusive Design

Creating environments that welcome and cater to all individuals, regardless of their backgrounds or abilities, is at the core of inclusive design. In the context of urban planning and architecture, it signifies designing spaces that are accessible, safe, and comfortable for everyone. As we explore the design process of inclusive design and Universal Design, we will consider how it can be leveraged to address segregation and reinvent perceptions of community and belonging among diverse groups.

Universal Design and Accessibility

Universal design goes beyond merely providing access; it is about designing spaces and buildings that everyone can use intuitively and independently, irrespective of age, ability, or status. Universal design puts people at the center of the design process and caters to the broadest range of users from the outset, resulting in buildings and spaces that are functional, user-friendly, and aesthetically pleasing.

Accessibility + Universal Design = Value. Uxness: UX Design, Usability Articles.

The concept of universal design was first proposed by the architect Ronald L. Mace who was a wheelchair user and devoted his career to improving accessibility in architecture. His work highlights seven principles that form the foundation of universal design: equitable use, flexibility in use, simple and intuitive use, perceptible information, tolerance for error, low physical effort, and size and space for approach and use. These principles echo many of the principles of inclusive design, emphasizing a human-centered approach to architectural planning.[1]

Accessibility is a critical part of universal design. It is not just about physical access to buildings but also involves making environments, products, services, and interfaces work for people of all abilities in all situations. It requires a thoughtful understanding of various impairments (mobility, sight, hearing, and cognitive) and ensures that these factors are considered from the start of the design process. For instance, a universally designed building might include ramps and tactile flooring for those with mobility or visual impairments, clear signage with large print, braille for those with visual impairments, and quiet spaces for those with sensory sensitivities.[2]

1. Accessibility: One of the foundational principles of inclusive design is accessibility. An inclusively designed space should be easy to navigate for all individuals, including those with mobility, visual, or hearing impairments. This encompasses physical attributes such as ramps, wide doorways, tactile paving, and audible signals, as well as cognitive aspects like simple and intuitive signage.

Tactile paving can assist the visually impaired as they walk.

2. Flexibility: Flexibility allows spaces to be useful to people with diverse abilities. Adjustable fixtures, modular furniture, and multi-use areas cater to various needs and preferences, and can evolve over time as those needs change. For example, adjustable lighting can accommodate individuals with visual impairments, while multi-use spaces can facilitate both community events and quiet solitude.

Lighthouse for visually impaired people. Photograph by Razorfrog; The Herbst Foundation, Inc.

3. Simple and Intuitive Use: Regardless of the user's experience, knowledge, language skills, or concentration level, inclusive design ensures that spaces are easy to understand and use. This means that the design must be straightforward, consistent, and predictable.

Exit Sign that is "Simple and intuitive." Universaldesignmeetstheexitsign.com

4. Perceptible Information: Information necessary for using the space effectively should be presented in multiple ways—visual, auditory, and tactile—to ensure it's perceivable by all users. This could involve multilingual signage, Braille, or audible announcements.

5. Tolerance for Error: Good design minimizes hazards and adverse consequences of accidental or unintended actions. In other words, the design should anticipate misuse and incorporate safety measures to reduce potential harm.

6. Low Physical Effort: Users should be able to use the space efficiently and comfortably with a minimum of fatigue. This involves considering the physical effort required to navigate the space or use its features, and seeking to minimize this where possible.

Baotou Vanke Central Park in China. ZAP Associates, LLC. Photo by Ren Yi/ Qiu Ripei.

7. Size and Space for Approach and Use: Adequate space should be provided for all users, regardless of their body size, posture, or mobility. This can involve considerations for personal space, pathways wide enough for wheelchair users, and amenities within easy reach for all users.

Enabling Village by WOHA in Singapore. Photo by Edward Hendricks.

By incorporating these principles of inclusive design, we can begin to dismantle the architectural aspects of segregation, creating spaces that not only accommodate but also celebrate diversity. Beyond physical design, these principles also encourage a broader societal shift towards inclusivity, emphasizing that every individual has a valuable role to play in the construct of a community.

Incorporating Diverse Perspectives in Architectural Decision-Making

The inclusive design process values diversity and seeks to involve a range of voices in architectural decision-making. Too often, architectural decisions are made by a small group of people who may not represent the broad spectrum of users who will engage with the space. By incorporating diverse perspectives, architects can ensure that the built environment responds to a wider array of needs and preferences.

This approach involves engaging various stakeholders, including potential users, community members, and experts in fields such as accessibility, sustainability, and cultural heritage. This might look like workshops, interviews, or consultations conducted throughout the design process to gather insights and feedback. These perspectives can inform everything from the overall layout of a space to the small details that make a space feel welcoming and intuitive to use.

It's also crucial to consider historical, cultural, and social contexts in design decisions. Architecture does not exist in a vacuum; it's a reflection of the society in which it is created. By understanding these contexts, architects can create spaces that respect and celebrate cultural diversity, promoting social cohesion and community identity.[3]

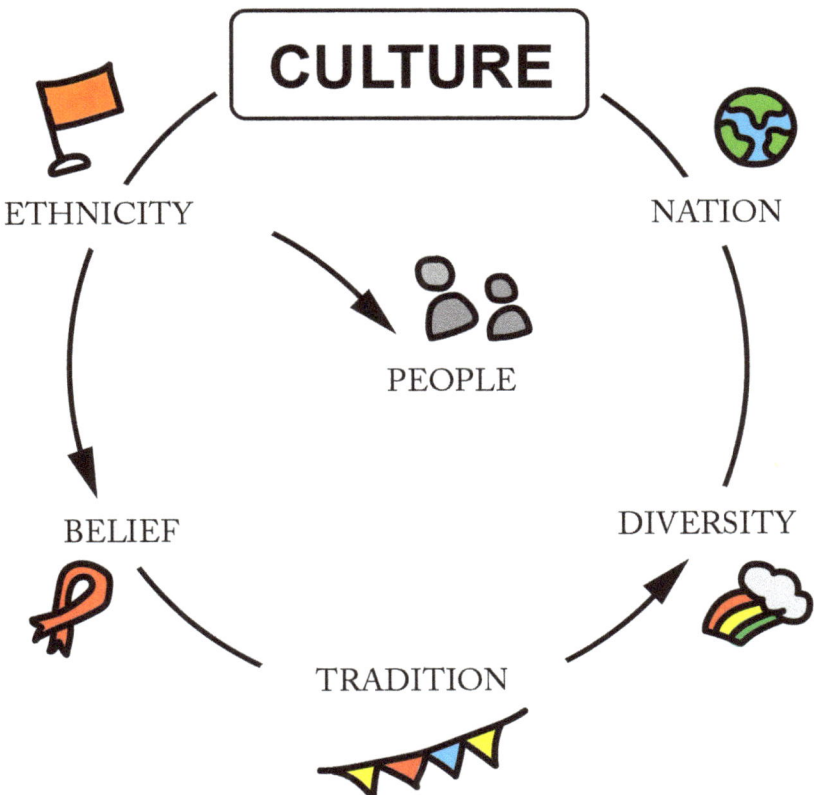

Integration of culture in design. DaevasDesign.com

In the context of segregation, incorporating diverse perspectives becomes even more important. It provides a platform for marginalized groups to express their needs and preferences, spawns a sense of ownership among all community members, and helps to ensure that the resulting environments promote integration rather than perpetuating divisions.

CASE STUDIES OF INCLUSIVE ARCHITECTURE

Successful Examples of Breaking Down Segregation Through Design

1. High Line, New York City:

The High Line in New York City is a fascinating example of how inclusive architecture can help to bridge societal divides and breeds a sense of community. Once an abandoned railway line, the High Line was transformed into a 1.45-mile-long elevated linear park that cuts across several neighborhoods on the west side of Manhattan.

The park, designed by architects Diller Scofidio and Renfro, and landscape architect James Corner, Field Operations, was constructed with universal design principles in mind. It is fully wheelchair accessible, features clear signage, and has various entry points to cater to different mobility needs. Various artworks and community programs make it a vibrant, welcoming space for all.[4]

Visitors stroll the first section of the High Line Park, over the 18th Street crossing. Wikimedia.

While initially criticized for causing gentrification in surrounding areas, the High Line now serves as a model for how to create inclusive urban green spaces. The project's success has inspired similar initiatives in other cities around the world, demonstrating the potential for design to ignite social inclusion and community connection.

2. The Hiroshima Nishi Fire Station:

Japanese Architect and 2024 Pritzker Architecture Prize Laureate, Riken Yamamoto, has focused his career designing spaces for community and family, and to create opportunities for people to meet. "For him, a building has a public function even when it is private." His design for this fire station included a transparent glazing and interior walls made of glass, where the public can see into the lives of the daily activities of firefighters and make a connection with "those who are protecting the community." The firefighters train in a central atrium where many people come to see and interact.[5]

Hiroshima Nishi Fire Station. Facebook.com/Pritzker Architecture Prize.

What sets this fire station apart is Yamamoto's ideas on community and exploration of his mediations of "threshold," between public and private space. The result is a building that doesn't just accommodate the 24-hour, daily life of the firehouse but celebrates its challenging traditional notions of what a fire station means to the community.[6]

3. Quinta Monroy Housing, Iquique, Chile:

Designed by Chilean architect Alejandro Aravena, the Quinta Monroy Housing project presents a novel approach to low-income housing and urban segregation. Aravena's firm, Elemental, was tasked with rehousing a community of nearly 100 families living in informal settlements within the same neighborhood on a tight budget.

Their solution was to create "half a good house" - core structures that met all legal requirements and provided a decent living environment but could be easily expanded by the residents themselves when they had the means. This design empowered residents and catered to their evolving needs, promoting a sense of ownership and community.[7]

Quinta Housing. Photographed by Cristobal Palma / Estudio Palma. ArchDaily.com/ Rethinkingthefuture.com

While these case studies represent a range of contexts and approaches, they share a common understanding of architecture as a tool for social integration and inclusion. They highlight the need for architects to engage with users and communities, embrace diversity, and challenge traditional norms and standards in their quest to create more inclusive built environments.[8]

The Role of Community Engagement in Creating Inclusive Built Environments

Community engagement in the design and planning process is critical to creating inclusive built environments. It is the process by which architects and planners interact with community members to understand their needs, aspirations, and concerns about their built environment. By involving local residents and stakeholders, architects can create designs that not only respond to the specific needs of the community but also provides encouragement of ownership and belonging among its members.[9]

1. Understanding Local Needs

Every community is unique, with its own set of cultural practices, social norms, and individual needs. Community engagement allows architects to understand these intricacies. It helps them to understand how people interact with their environment, what they value about it, and what they wish to change. This insight can guide the design process, ensuring that the final outcome is not only functional but also respects and enhances the local culture and way of life.

2. Fostering a Sense of Ownership

When community members are involved in the design process, they are more likely to feel a sense of ownership over the final result. This sense of ownership can promote stewardship and long-term care of the built environment. Moreover, it can also invoke feelings of pride and identity among community members, enhancing social cohesion and the overall quality of life.

3. Promoting Inclusivity and Equity

Community engagement can help to ensure that the voices of all members of a community, including those that are often marginalized, are heard and considered in the design process. This can lead to more equitable outcomes, as the built environment can be designed to meet the needs of diverse populations. It can also challenge existing power structures as it gives community members a direct say in shaping their environment.

4. Facilitating Long-Term Success

Projects that are developed with community engagement are more likely to succeed in the long term. This is because they are more likely to have local support and meet the real, identified needs of the community.

Case Study - The Via Verde Housing Project, The Bronx, New York

The Via Verde project in the South Bronx, New York, is a prime example of community engagement done right. The project was born out of a design competition aiming to create affordable, sustainable housing. Community members were actively involved in the design process, attending workshops and providing input on design decisions.

The result is a mixed-income housing development that not only meets the community's needs but also promotes healthy living through a series of green roofs and courtyards. The success of Via Verde has been largely attributed to the community engagement process, which ensured the design was deeply rooted in the context and values of the community.[10]

Typically, these types of projects are a combination of the local municipality, a quasi-governmental agency (Housing Authority) and the developer/ builder. This collaboration is commonly known as a Public Private Partnership (PPP). What has been missing and what makes these projects more successful is the fourth "P," the People. A new term should be coined as (PPPP) to create and manifest a quadruple bottom line.

Via Verde green community roof garden. Melrose, Bronx, NY. Grownyc.org

Community engagement is not just a tool for gathering information. It's a transformative process that can lead to more inclusive, equitable, and successful design outcomes. It recognizes community members as experts in their own lives and values their knowledge and input in shaping their built environment.

17

"Life is like a bowl of chili, it has beans and it has spices."

9th Grade Math Teacher

CONCLUSION

THE NEW REPUBLIC

This extensive exploration of segregation and architecture from historical to contemporary societies affirms the intricate and profound relationship between the two. The narrative of this book, woven across 16 thought-provoking chapters, illuminates the architectural echoes of human segregation over centuries and across civilizations.

Our journey commenced with early civilizations and the societal hierarchies depicted in their architectural designs (Chapters 1-7). Through the elaborately planned palaces of Crete and Assyria to the expansive Roman villas, we saw how architecture mirrored, enforced, and perpetuated social divisions and cultural identities. These ancient structures bear testimony to a bygone era, yet their influence lingers.

As we moved to Chapters 8-10, the book unraveled how the formation of nations and the rise of institutionalized racism profoundly shaped architectural landscapes. The transformation from smaller ethnic communities to larger nation-states fostered stark architectural manifestations of power imbalances and segregation. The examination of white nationalist movements laid bare the architectural symbols of dominance and the disturbing power of design to reinforce discrimination.

Chapters 11 and 12 highlighted the extreme manifestations of segregation through the lens of Jewish isolationism and the Holocaust. From the self-segregated Jewish "shtetls" to the ghettos enforced by the

Nuremberg Laws, architecture became a stark reminder of oppression and systemic discrimination. The architectural remnants of these eras serve as solemn monuments to the destructive force of segregation.

In Chapter 13, the lens focused on Eldridge Cleaver's insights into racism, exploring the psychological aftermath of racial segregation. The chapter painted a striking picture of the destruction of Black communities through urban renewal projects and the devastating effects of forced integration.

Chapter 14 transitioned us to the modern challenges of segregation. The exploration of the Third Wave of migration, the rise of gated communities, self-segregation, and gentrification offered a multifaceted view of contemporary segregation.

Our exploration extended into Chapter 15, probing the architectural implications of contemporary urban spaces and educational institutions. The socioeconomic segregation and gentrification, coupled with school zoning and design, provided a comprehensive understanding of the spatial dimensions of today's segregation.

The final chapter, Chapter 16, embarked on a hopeful note, focusing on the transformative potential of inclusive design. It underscored the importance of accessibility, diverse perspectives in architectural decision-making, and community engagement in creating inclusive built environments.

The narrative journey traversed in this book is a testament to the perpetual impact of architecture on societal segregation. As we look back on history's architectural monuments to segregation, we are reminded of the pivotal role architects, policymakers, and society as a whole play in shaping our collective future. As we step into the future, this book urges us to envision and create architectural spaces that promote inclusivity, social justice, and integration rather than division. Let this be our architectural legacy for generations to come.

REFLECTION ON THE ROLE OF ARCHITECTURE IN PERPETUATING OR CHALLENGING SEGREGATION

As we reflect upon the role of architecture in perpetuating or challenging segregation, it's important to acknowledge the unfading influence it holds. Throughout history, architecture has served as a tangible manifestation of societal norms, ideologies, and power structures. By defining spaces, assigning purposes, and dividing communities, architecture has often emboldened segregation—whether consciously or unconsciously. However, it's also important to note that architecture has the potential to challenge and change these patterns, offering an opportunity to shape a more inclusive and equitable society.

The architecture of segregation has been etched into our urban landscapes in numerous ways. From the stratified housing of ancient civilizations, the imposing white nationalist buildings, to the ghettos of the Holocaust, architecture has been wielded as a tool of power and control. It has encoded societal hierarchies into brick and mortar, thus defining and delineating social boundaries. In contemporary societies, this legacy continues with segregated neighborhoods, the proliferation of gated communities, and the gentrification of urban spaces.

However, while architecture has often been complicit in underpinning segregation, it also possesses the potential to challenge and disrupt these patterns. As architects, urban planners, and decision-makers, we wield the power to reshape our built environments to reflect values of inclusivity, accessibility, and social justice. Architecture can serve as a platform for fostering social integration and bridging divides, a notion that becomes increasingly relevant as we confront the spatial dimensions of modern segregation.

The principles of inclusive design and universal accessibility outlined in the book provide a roadmap towards achieving this goal.

By considering diverse perspectives in architectural decision-making and engaging communities in the design process, we can ensure our built environments cater to all users irrespective of their race, economic status, or abilities. As seen in the case studies of inclusive architecture, integrating these principles into our designs can break down barriers of segregation.

Furthermore, the role of architecture extends beyond the physical realm; it influences our mental landscapes and our perceptions of others. A move towards inclusivity in design can foster a sense of belonging and unity, challenging the stereotypes and biases that underpin segregation.

While architecture's role in promoting segregation is undeniable, it's crucial to recognize its capacity to challenge segregation as well. It can serve as a powerful instrument for social change, transforming the very fabric of our societies. The future of architecture lies in leveraging this potential, transforming segregated spaces into platforms for connection and community. This reflection serves as a call to action for architects, planners, and policymakers to harness the power of design to challenge segregation and create a more inclusive and equitable civilization.

A. Call to Action for Architects to Prioritize New Paradigms in Their Designs

In light of the critical insights and historical lessons that have surfaced through the exploration of the relationship between architecture and segregation, a call to action is paramount. Architects, as the curators of our built environments, wield the power to challenge the legacy of segregation and to promote social integration and inclusivity.

Firstly, architects must acknowledge the profound influence of their designs on the social canvas. The built environment is not merely a physical entity but a living, breathing organism that nurtures our interactions, frames our experiences, and shapes our societal structures. Recognizing this interplay is the first step towards inclusive design. This can be studied through the field of Ekistics, which is the science of examining all kinds of human settlements and drawing on research and experience of professionals in the fields of architecture, engineering, sociology and urban design. This field is focused on achieving a balance between the inhabitants and their physical and sociocultural environments.[1]

Next, architects should strive to understand the diverse needs and experiences of the communities they serve with ekistics as a basis of design. This involves reaching beyond standard architectural considerations and delving into the sociocultural, economic, and psychological aspects that affect people's relationship with spaces. This could involve ethnographic studies, community consultations, or collaboration with social scientists.[2]

Designs should focus on promoting accessibility, champion interaction, and respecting cultural diversity. This entails developing environments that are physically and socially accessible to people of all ages, abilities, and cultural backgrounds. Moreover, public spaces should be designed to encourage social interactions that bridge the societal divides. A new term can be discussed to embody the tenants of approaching design without inherent borders; Aequitas means equity in Greek, which is used to reference the origin of classical orders in temple buildings. We take this term and apply it to the notion of expanding one's design ideals while adding to the field of architectural study. We now have a term to describe this design methodology:

"Aequo-Tectura" – To design with equity as a principle.

This inclusive design paradigm also means respecting and validating the rich tapestry of cultural expressions and values that can be derived through ekistics. Architecture can act as a powerful medium to reflect and celebrate diversity rather than diluting or marginalizing it either intentionally or from unintended consequences.

Architects have a responsibility to challenge the status quo. This means actively pushing against discriminatory practices, questioning entrenched biases, and advocating for policies that promote social equality and integration. It is about more than creating beautiful spaces; it's about using architecture as a tool for social change.

The call to action for architects is clear: Prioritize Aequotectura in design. Embrace diversity. Challenge segregation. Shape a more integrated and inclusive world, one space at a time. This is not merely a professional obligation, it is a moral imperative that, when embraced, can shape the future of societies and the world at large.

B. Importance of Ongoing Research and Dialogue on the Topic of Segregation and Architecture

The exploration of the intertwined relationship between architecture and segregation has shed light on some crucial dimensions of our societal framework. However, it is vital to emphasize that the conversation is far from over. The ongoing research and dialogue on this topic are of utmost importance for multiple reasons.

First, the dynamics of segregation are in constant flux. As societal norms and demographics evolve, so do the forms and consequences of segregation. To ensure that our understanding of the issue remains relevant and robust, we must continuously update our knowledge. Further research allows us to track these changes, understand their implications, and devise appropriate strategies to address them.

Second, architecture, as a discipline and a practice, is continually evolving, influenced by technological advancements, environmental concerns, and shifting societal values. Therefore, research that monitors these changes can help us uncover new opportunities and challenges in designing spaces that promote integration and equality.[3]

Third, the dialogue surrounding segregation and architecture is integral to raising awareness about the issue. Continued conversation encourages an opportunity to utilize Aequotectura and challenge the biases and systems that perpetuate segregation. It equips architects, urban planners, and policymakers with the knowledge they need to create more equitable and inclusive spaces.

Finally, ongoing research fosters innovation. The exploration of new ideas, strategies, and solutions can revolutionize how we approach the design of our built environment. Whether it's reimagining urban housing, developing inclusive public spaces, or leveraging technology to promote accessibility and new form-making, research pushes the boundaries of what's possible.

The importance of ongoing research and dialogue on the topic of segregation and architecture cannot be overemphasized. This continuous exploration is a powerful tool for challenging segregation and creating a new republic of thoughtful designers. By keeping the conversation alive, we continue to learn, innovate, and progress towards a better future.

C. In Closing

Recalling my memories as a child, traveling with my family on a frequent trip to visit our Grandparents, my father told those familiar stories of his own childhood, back in "Those Days." I along with my brother and sisters listened and wondered in amazement and apprehension at the same time. Although the Jim Crow Laws no longer exist in my reality, there still remains remnants of that era that will permeate indefinitely.

REFERENCES

CHAPTER 1

1. Merriam-Webster. (2024). Segregation. In Merriam-Webster.com dictionary. Retrieved from https://www.merriam-webster.com/dictionary/segregation
2. Turner, Margery Austin & Greene, Solomon (2020, November 01). "Structural Racism Explainer Collection: Causes and Consequences of Separate and Unequal Neighborhoods". From https://www.urban.org/racial-equity-analytics-lab/structural-racism-explainer-collection/causes-and-consequences-separate-and-unequal-neighborhoods
3. Wikipedia contributors. (2024, May 7). Architecture. In Wikipedia, The Free Encyclopedia. Retrieved May 29, 2024, from https://en.wikipedia.org/wiki/Architecture
4. Britannica. (2024, April 11). Gestalt psychology. The Editors of Encyclopedia Britannica, Retrieved May 29, 2024, from https://www.britannica.com/science/Gestalt-psychology

CHAPTER 2

1. Longley, Robert. (2021, December 6). What Is De Jure Segregation? Definition and Examples. Retrieved from https://www.thoughtco.com/de-jure-segregation-definition-4692595, Cox, B. (2010). De Facto Segregation. In T. C. Hunt (Ed.), Encyclopedia of Educational Reform and Dissent (Vol. 1, pp. 260-261). SAGE Reference.
2. Longley, Robert. (2021, December 6). What Is De Jure Segregation? Definition and Examples. Retrieved from Wikipedia contributors. (2023, November). History of urban planning. In Wikipedia. Retrieved March 2024, from https://en.wikipedia.org/wiki/History_of_urban_planning
3. Lesso, R. (2022, May 9). What Were Homes Like in Ancient Rome? Retrieved from https://www.thecollector.com/what-were-homes-like-in-ancient-rome/

4. Wikimedia Commons. (2007, March 1). File:Ostia_Antica-strada01-modified.jpg. Wikimedia Commons. Retrieved from https://commons.wikimedia.org/wiki/File:Ostia_Antica-strada01-modified.jpg

5. Wikipedia contributors. (2024, May 18). Haussmann's renovation of Paris. In Wikipedia, The Free Encyclopedia. Retrieved May 29, 2024, from https://en.wikipedia.org/wiki/Haussmann_27s_renovation_of_Paris

6. Wikipedia contributors. (2024, May 13). White flight. In Wikipedia, The Free Encyclopedia. Retrieved May 29, 2024, from https://en.wikipedia.org/wiki/White_flight

CHAPTER 3

1. (2024, May). Ordering principles in architecture. [Web log post]. Retrieved December 2023, from https://murattyavuz.wordpress.com/2014/05/21/ordering-principles-in-architecture/-3

2. Parmar, R. (2017, July 24). Transformation of Building in Architecture. Gharpedia. Retrieved December 2023, fromhttps://gharpedia.com/blog/transformation-of-building-in-architecture/

3. Susan Stanburg (2017, July 6) Mental health and architecture - St. Elizabeth mental hospital (R. Denise Everson, architect). NPR article

CHAPTER 4

1. South African History Online. (n.d.). A History of Apartheid in South Africa.https://www.sahistory.org.za/article/history-apartheid-south-africa

2. Wikipedia contributors. (2024, April 24). George Town, Chennai. In Wikipedia, The Free Encyclopedia. Retrieved May 29, 2024, from https://en.wikipedia.org/wiki/George_Town,_Chennai

3. Wikipedia contributors. (2024, May 17). The Troubles. In Wikipedia, The Free Encyclopedia. Retrieved May 29, 2024, from https://en.wikipedia.org/wiki/The_Troubles

4. Wikipedia contributors. (2024, May 8). Hostile architecture. In Wikipedia, The Free Encyclopedia. Retrieved May 29, 2024, from https://en.wikipedia.org/wiki/Hostile_architecture

5. Ockman, Joan. (2011). What is Democratic Architecture? The Public Life of Buildings. Dissent Magazine. http://www.dissentmagazine.org/article/what-is-democratic-architecture-the-public-life-of-buildings

6. Irshad, Dania. (2022). Why architecture needs a social conscience. Rethinking The Future. http://www.Rethinkingthefuture.com/rtf-fresh-perspectives/a3026-why-architecture-needs-a-social-conscience

7. Wikipedia contributors. (2024, May 26). District Six. In Wikipedia, The Free Encyclopedia. Retrieved May 29, 2024, from https://en.wikipedia.org/wiki/District_Six

8. Wikipedia contributors. (2024, March 24). Israeli West Bank barrier. In Wikipedia, The Free Encyclopedia. Retrieved May 29, 2024, from https://en.wikipedia.org/wiki/Israeli_West_Bank_barrier

9. Wikipedia contributors. (2024, May 22). Green Line (Israel). In Wikipedia, The Free Encyclopedia. Retrieved May 29, 2024, from https://en.wikipedia.org/Green_Line_(Israel)

10. Andrews, Farah. (2020). Banksy in Palestine: A look at the street artist's work in Gaza and the West Bank. Art & Design. http://www.thenationalnews/arts-culture/art/banksy-in-palestine-a-look-at-the-street-artist-s-work-in-gaza-and-the-west-bank

11. Cancino, Alejandra. (2021, December 15). Cabrini-Green: A History of Broken Promises. Block Club Chicago. http://www.blockclubchicago.org/2021/12/15/cabrini-green-a-history-of-broken-promises

CHAPTER 5

1. A&E Television Networks. (2018, January 12). Neolithic Revolution. History.com. Retrieved from https://www.history.com/topics/pre-history/neolithic-revolution

2. The Impact of Urbanization on Architectural Design. (n.d.). Title of the Website. https://alens.tistory.com/entry/The-Impact-of-Urbanization-on-Architectural-Design

3. Various Contributors. (2021, December 15). The Connection between Architecture and Culture. Indus University. http://www.indusuni.ac.in/the-connection-between-architecture-and-culture.php

4. Balazs, Rebeka Dora. (2021, August 26). Architecture and Society in Interaction, The duty of architects. ABUD. http://www.abud.hu/blog-architecture-and-society-in-interaction

5. Wikipedia contributors. (2024, April 29). Bessemer process. In Wikipedia, The Free Encyclopedia. Retrieved May 30, 2024, from https://en.wikipedia.org/wiki/Bessemer_process

6. Wikipedia contributors. (2023, December 18). Roman roads. In Wikipedia, The Free Encyclopedia. Retrieved December 19, 2023, from https://en.wikipedia.org/wiki/Roman_roads

CHAPTER 6

1. Pitts, F. W. (1999). Segregation and the Bible. Mercer University Press.
2. Kranz, Jeffrey. (2022, October 23). The 12 Tribes of Israel in the Bible: a Quick, Illustrated Guide. Overviewbible. http://www.overviewbible.com/12-tribes-israel
3. Genesis. New International Version (NIV). Bible Gateway. from https://www.biblegateway.com/passage/?search=Genesis%201&version=NIV
4. Britannica. (2024, May 9). Year of Jubilee. The Editors of Encyclopedia Britannica, Retrieved May 11, 2024, from https://www.britannica.com/topic/Year-of-Jubilee
5. Abrahamus. (2010, November 30). HCSBSB: Iron Age Israelite Home. The Guide of Bezalel. https://guildofbezalel.blogspot.com/
6. Flecther, Elizabeth. (2006). Houses in Bible Times. Houses in Ancient Times. https://womeninthebible.net/bible-archaeology/ancient_houses/
7. Wikipedia contributors. (2024, January 24). Solomon's Temple. In Wikipedia, The Free Encyclopedia. Retrieved May 30, 2024, from https://en.wikipedia.org/wiki/Solomon%27s_Temple

CHAPTER 7

8. Wikipedia contributors. (2023, July 8). Ancient Egyptian architecture. In Wikipedia, The Free Encyclopedia. Retrieved 09:56, July 27, 2023, from https://en.wikipedia.org/w/index.php?title=Ancient_Egyptian_architecture&oldid=1164304305
9. Quora contributors. (2020, June 15). What kind of residences did the Egyptian Pharaohs live in? In Quora. Retrieved May 31, 2024, from https://www.quora.com/What-kind-of-residences-did-the-Egyptian-Pharaohs-live-in-Are-there-ruins-of-any-of-their-palaces
10. Touman, Ibrahim A & Al-Ajmi, Farraj F. (2017, January). Ancient Egyptian architecture. Research Gate. Retrieved June 2023, from https://www.researchgate.net/figure/a-An-ancient-rural-Egyptian-houses-20-th-century-shown-practice-of-typical-storing_fig4_321362642
11. Fiorini, Marco V. (2012). The Egyptian Architects Unveiled on the Site of The Great Pyramid. Academia. Retrieved June 2023, from https://www.academia.edu/31333451/The_Egyptian_Architects_Unveiled_On_the_Site_of_the_Great_Pyramid
12. Wikipedia contributors. (2023, January 9). List of Egyptian Architects. In Wikipedia, The Free Encyclopedia. Retrieved May 16, 2023, from https://en.wikipedia.org/wiki/List_of_Egyptian_architects05

13. National Geographic Society. (2023, October 19). Greek City-States. National Geographic Education, from https://education.nationalgeographic.org/resource/greek-city-states/
14. Graf, Fritz. (2015, May 9). Festivals in Ancient Greece and Rome. Religion, Oxford University Press, from https://oxfordre.com/religion/display/10.1093/acrefore/9780199340378.001.0001/acrefore-9780199340378-e-58
15. Wikipedia contributors. (2023, August 13). Ancient Greek Architecture. In Wikipedia, The Free Encyclopedia. Retrieved August 2023, from https://en.wikipedia.org/wiki/Ancient_Greek_architecture
16. Wikipedia contributors. (2019, August 13). Category: Ancient Greek Architects. In Wikipedia, The Free Encyclopedia. Retrieved August 2023, from https://en.wikipedia.org/wiki/Category:Ancient_Greek_architects
17. Wikipedia contributors. (2023, August 30). Appian Way. In Wikipedia, The Free Encyclopedia. Retrieved August 2023, from https://en.wikipedia.org/wiki/Appian_Way
18. Mouritsen, Henrik & Fantin, Joseph D. (2014, July 1). The Freedman in the Roman World. Voice Dallas Theological Seminary. Cambridge University Press, from https://voice.dts.edu/review/freedman-roman-world-mouritsen/
19. Silver, Sandra Sweeny. (2018, September 05). Ancient Roman Villas. Early Church History. From https://earlychurchhistory.org/daily-life/ancient-roman-villas/
20. Athanasiou, Christina (2024, March 2024). The insulae: The apartment buildings of the ancient Romans. Roman Empire Times, from https://romanempiretimes.com/the-insulae-the-apartment-buildings-of-the-ancient-romans/
21. Wikipedia contributors. (2023, March 20). Aurelian Walls. In Wikipedia, The Free Encyclopedia. From https://en.wikipedia.org/wiki/Aurelian_Walls#:~:text=The%20Aurelian%20Walls%20(Italian%3A%20Mura,during%20the%204th%20century%20BC
22. SoCalFelipe. (2013, December 23). The Values of Early Rome, As Exemplified by Cato the Elder. SoCal Felipe. From https://historyissexydotcom2.wordpress.com/category/ancient-history/
23. McLaughlin, Katherine. (2023, June 15). Roman Architecture: Everything you Need to Know. Architecture + Design. From https://www.architecturaldigest.com/story/roman-architecture-101
24. McLaughlin, Katherine. (2023, June 15). Roman Architecture: Everything you Need to Know. Architecture + Design. From https://www.architecturaldigest.com/story/roman-architecture-101

25. Wikipedia contributors. (2023, November 6). Hadrian. In Wikipedia, The Free Encyclopedia. from https://en.wikipedia.org/wiki/Hadrian
26. Wikipedia contributors. (2023, November 5). Vitruvius. In Wikipedia, The Free Encyclopedia. from https://en.wikipedia.org/wiki/Vitruvius

CHAPTER 8

1. Wikipedia contributors. (2023, September 28). Crete. In Wikipedia, The Free Encyclopedia. from https://en.wikipedia.org/wiki/Crete
2. National Geographic Society. (2023, October 19). Assyrian Empire. National Geographic Education, from https://education.nationalgeographic.org/resource/assyrian-empire/
3. Wikipedia contributors. (2023, August 29). Mesopotamia. In Wikipedia, The Free Encyclopedia. from https://en.wikipedia.org/wiki/Mesopotamia
4. King, L. W. (1910). The Code of Hammurabi. Oxford University Press.
5. Mark, Joshua J. (2017 September 21). Social Structure in Ancient Egypt. World History Encyclopedia. from https://www.worldhistory.org/article/1123/social-structure-in-ancient-egypt/
6. Wikipedia contributors. (2023, June 15). Slavery in Ancient Egypt. In Wikipedia, The Free Encyclopedia. from https://en.wikipedia.org/wiki/Slavery_in_ancient_Egypt
7. Wikipedia contributors. (2023, July 24). Dominus. In Wikipedia, The Free Encyclopedia. from https://en.wikipedia.org/wiki/Dominus
8. Wikipedia contributors. (2023, May 16). Culture of Greece. In Wikipedia, The Free Encyclopedia. from https://en.wikipedia.org/wiki/Culture_of_Greece
9. MacDonald, W. L. (1986). The Architecture of the Roman Empire. Yale University Press
10. Wikipedia contributors. (2023, August 12). Maya Civilization. In Wikipedia, The Free Encyclopedia. from https://en.wikipedia.org/wiki/Maya_civilization
11. Hammond, David. (2017, October 1). The Prairie School's Mexican Connection: How Ancient Mayan Architecture Shaped Frank Lloyd Wright. New City Design. from https://design.newcity.com/2017/10/01/impact-of-the-indigenous-on-wrights-prairie-school-how-ancient-mayan-architecture-shaped-frank-lloyd-wright/

CHAPTER 9

1. Wikipedia contributors. (2023, September 1). Age of Discovery. In Wikipedia, The Free Encyclopedia. From https://en.wikipedia.org/wiki/Age_of_Discovery
2. Wikipedia contributors. (2023, August 10). Partition of India. In Wikipedia, The Free Encyclopedia. From https://en.wikipedia.org/wiki/Partition_of_India
3. Wikipedia contributors. (2023, June 1). Migration Period. In Wikipedia, The Free Encyclopedia. From https://en.wikipedia.org/wiki/Migration_Period
4. Wikipedia contributors. (2023, July 10) Moors. In Wikipedia, The Free Encyclopedia. From https://en.wikipedia.org/wiki/Moors
5. Wikipedia contributors. (2023, July 30) History of the Middle East. In Wikipedia, The Free Encyclopedia. From https://en.wikipedia.org/wiki/History_of_the_Middle_East
6. Spassmachine. (2009, August 25). Yugoslavia: from wage cuts to war – Wildcat, Wildcat #18 (Summer 1996). Libcom.org. From https://libcom.org/article/yugoslavia-wage-cuts-war-wildcat

CHAPTER 10

1. Flixico, Donald L. (2023, July 11). When Native Americans Were Slaughtered in the Name of 'Civilization'. HISTORY. A&E Television Networks. From https://www.history.com/news/native-americans-genocide-united-states
2. Woods, William I. (2023, June 21). "Cahokia Mounds". The Editors of Encyclopaedia Britannica Article History. From https://www.britannica.com/place/Cahokia-Mounds
3. National Archives. (2024, April 10). 14th Amendment to the U.S. Constitution: Civil Rights (1868). The U.S. National Archives and Records Administration. From https://www.archives.gov/milestone-documents/constitution
4. Wikipedia contributors. (2023, June 23) Separte but Equal. In Wikipedia, The Free Encyclopedia. From https://en.wikipedia.org/wiki/Separate_but_equal
5. Rothstein, R. (2017, May). The Color of Law: A Forgotten History of How Our Government Segregated America. Liveright Publishing.
6. History.com Editors. (2023, April 11). Jim Crow Laws. HISTORY. A&E Television Networks. https://www.history.com/topics/early-20th-century-us/jim-crow-laws

7. Roulo, Claudette. (2024, April 16). 10 Things You Probably Didn't Know About the Penatgon. U.S. Department of Defense. From https://www.defense.gov/News/Feature-Stories/story/article/1650913/10-things-you-probably-didnt-know-about-the-pentagon/
8. Grimsley, Mark. (2007, June 10) National Security Program, Article: The Social Dimensions of the U.S. Civil War. Foreign Policy Research Institute. From https://www.fpri.org/article/2007/06/the-social-dimensions-of-the-u-s-civil-war/
9. Wikipedia contributors. (2023, August 24) Black Codes (United States). In Wikipedia, The Free Encyclopedia. From https://en.wikipedia.org/wiki/Black_Codes_(United_States)

CHAPTER 11

1. United States Holocaust Memorial Museum. "Pogroms." Holocaust Encyclopedia. From https://encyclopedia.ushmm.org/content/en/article/pogroms
2. Wikipedia contributors. (2023, August 19) Shtetl. In Wikipedia, The Free Encyclopedia. From https://en.wikipedia.org/wiki/Shtetl
3. United States Holocaust Memorial Museum. "The Nazi Rise To Power." Holocaust Encyclopedia. From https://encyclopedia.ushmm.org/content/en/article/the-nazi-rise-to-power
4. United States Holocaust Memorial Museum. "Nuremberg Trials." Holocaust Encyclopedia. From https://encyclopedia.ushmm.org/content/en/article/the-nazi-rise-to-power
5. Milligan, Mark. (2022, February 6). Germania – Hitler's Megacity. Heritage Daily. From https://www.heritagedaily.com/2022/02/germania-hitlers-megacity/142687
6. Wikipedia contributors. (2023, July 17) Nazi Architecture. In Wikipedia, The Free Encyclopedia. From https://en.wikipedia.org/wiki/Nazi_architecture

CHAPTER 12

1. Wikipedia contributors. (2024, March 20). White Nationalism. In Wikipedia, The Free Encyclopedia. Retrieved 02:40, March 31, 2024, from https://en.wikipedia.org/wiki/White_nationalism
2. Wikipedia contributors. (2024, March 21). Ku Klux Klan. In Wikipedia, The Free Encyclopedia. From https://en.wikipedia.org/wiki/Ku_Klux_Klan

3. United States Holocaust Memorial Museum. "Introduction to the Holocaust." https://encyclopedia.ushmm.org/content/en/article/introduction-to-the-holocaust

4. United States Holocaust Memorial Museum. "Kristallnacht." https://encyclopedia.ushmm.org/content/en/article/kristallnacht

5. Bradsher, Greg. (2010, Volume 42, Number 4). United States National Archives and Records Administration. "The Nuremberg Laws." Prologue Magazine. From https://www.archives.gov/publications/prologue/2010/winter/nuremberg.html

6. Wikipedia contributors. (2023, July 23). European immigration to the Americas. In Wikipedia, The Free Encyclopedia. From https://en.wikipedia.org/wiki/European_immigration_to_the_Americas

7. Wikipedia contributors. (2023, August 03). Immigration Act of 1924. In Wikipedia, The Free Encyclopedia. From https://en.wikipedia.org/wiki/Immigration_Act_of_1924

8. Wikipedia contributors. (2023, August 12). Great Famine (Ireland). In Wikipedia, The Free Encyclopedia. From https://en.wikipedia.org/wiki/Great_Famine_(Ireland)

9. Report on the American Workforce. (2001). "Counting "Minorities: A Brief History and a Look at the Future." U.S. Department of Labor. U.S. Bureau of Labor Statistics. From https://data.bls.gov/search/query/results?q=ethnic%20enclaves%20in%20early%2019th%20Century

10. Wikipedia contributors. (2023, August 12). History of immigration to the United States. In Wikipedia, The Free Encyclopedia. From https://en.wikipedia.org/wiki/History_of_immigration_to_the_United_States

CHAPTER 13

1. Cleaver, Eldridge (1968). Soul on Ice. Ramparts Press, Inc.

2. History.com contributors. (2009, October 27). Brown V. Board of Education. From https://www.history.com/topics/black-history/brown-v-board-of-education-of-topeka

3. Woodson, C. G. (1933). The Mis-Education of the Negro. Associated Publishers.

4. Bunch, Lonnie. Our American Story, "The Little Rock Nine". National Museum of African American History & Culture. Smithsonian. From https://nmaahc.si.edu/explore/stories/little-rock-nine

5. Wikipedia contributors. (2023, September 04). Urban Renewal. In Wikipedia, The Free Encyclopedia. From https://en.wikipedia.org/wiki/Urban_renewal

6. Wikipedia contributors. (2023, March 31). Housing and Urban Development Act of 1968. In Wikipedia, The Free Encyclopedia. From https://en.wikipedia.org/wiki/Housing_and_Urban_Development_Act_of_1968
7. Pruitt, Sarah. (2018, May 16). Brown V. Board of Education: A First Step in the Desegregation of America's Schools. From https://www.history.com/news/brown-v-board-of-education-the-first-step-in-the-desegregation-of-americas-schools
8. Interaction Design Foundation - IxDF. (2016, September 13). "What is Design for All?". From https://www.interactiondesign.org/literature/topics/design-for-all

CHAPTER 14

1. Brown, Nicholas P., Bergin, Tom & Heath, Brad. (2023, October 04). "The Racial Wealth Gap: A History of Inequity". From https://www.reuters.com/investigates/special-report/usa-slavery-tennessee-timeline/
2. Lautard, Manon & Galpin, Pierre-Francois. "Gated Communities: a new form of urbanity and a real estate product born or peri-urbanization". Cities Territories Governance. From https://www.citego.org/bdf_fiche-document-1728_en.html
3. Vesselinov, Elena. (2008, July 21). "Members Only: Gated Community and Residential Segregation in the Metropolitan United States". Sociological Forum. From https://onlinelibrary.wiley.com/doi/abs/10.1111/j.1573-7861.2008.00075.x
4. Wikipedia contributors. (2023, August 16). Self-segregation. In Wikipedia, The Free Encyclopedia. From https://en.wikipedia.org/wiki/Self-segregation#:~:text=Self%2Dsegregation
5. Haddon, Cole. (2023, November 21). "Everything You Think You Know About EDWARD SCISSORHANDS Is Wrong". 5AM StoryTalk, Substackcom. from https://colehaddon.substack.com/p/everything-you-think-you-know-about
6. Wikipedia contributors. (2023, August 1). Seaside, Florida. In Wikipedia, The Free Encyclopedia. From https://en.wikipedia.org/wiki/Seaside,_Florida
7. Skerry, Peter. (2000, March 01). "So We Really Want Immigrants to Assimilate?". Brookings Institution, From https://www.brookings.edu/articles/do-we-really-want-immigrants-to-assimilate/
8. Wikipedia contributors. (2023, August 23). Race and ethnicity in Brazil In Wikipedia, The Free Encyclopedia. From https://en.wikipedia.org/wiki/Race_and_ethnicity_in_Brazil

9. Picardo, Elvis. (2022, July 29). Gentrification: Definition, Causes, Pros 7 Cons. Investopedia, Dotdash Meredith. From https://www.investopedia.com/terms/g/gentrification.asp

10. Can, Aysegul. (2020, March 19). "Our City? Galate, Istanbul: Understanding Conflict and Tension in a Gentrifying Neighborhood. The City at Eye Level. From https://thecityateyelevel.com/stories/galata-istanbul-understanding-conflict-and-tension-in-a-gentrifying-neighbourhood

11. Mijs, Jonathan J. B. & Roe, Elizabeth L. (2021, April 07). "Is America coming apart? Socioeconomic segregation in neighborhoods, schools, workplaces, and social networks, 1970 - 2020. Sociology Compass, Vol. 15, Issue 6 e12884. From https://compass.onlinelibrary.wiley.com/doi/full/10.1111/soc4.12884

12. ABC Television Networks. (2023, September 21). Spin City. In Wikipedia, The Free Encyclopedia. from https://en.wikipedia.org/wiki/Spin_City

CHAPTER 15

1. Pansini, Riccardo & Campenni, Marco & Shi, Lei. (2020, March 20). "Segregating socioeconomic classes leads to an unequal redistribution of wealth". Humanities & Social Sciences Communications. Palgrave Commun 6, 46. From https://www.nature.com/articles/s41599-020-0419-2#citeas

2. Wellspring Center Contributors. (2024). "6 Ways To Establish Inclusive Learning Environments". Wellspring Center For Prevention. From https://wellspringprevention.org/blog/how-establish-inclusive-learning-environments/

CHAPTER 16

1. Swan, Henny & Pouncey, Ian & Pickering, Heydon & Watson, Leonie. (2000, March 01). "Inclusive Design Principles". Inclusive Design Principles. From https://inclusivedesignprinciples.org/

2. Sharma, Praveen. (2024). "Accessibility + Universal Design = Value". UX Design, Usability Articles, Course, Books, Events. UXness & Interaction Design Foundation. From https://www.uxness.in/2020/12/accessibility-universal-design-value.html

3. Daevas Design. (2016, April 28). "Integration of Culture in Design". Daevas, Inc. From https://daevasdesign.com/integration-culture-design/

4. Wikipedia contributors. (2023, September 04). High Line. In Wikipedia, The Free Encyclopedia. From https://en.wikipedia.org/wiki/High_Line

5. Noveck, Jocelyn (2024). "Pritzker Prize Goes to Japanese Architect Who Values Community in Spaces Both Public and Private". AP National Writer. From https://apnews.com/article/pritzker-prize-2024-architecture-riken-yamamoto-acd345fe3206318d8b0d075720adc980
6. The Pritzker Architecture Prize. (2024). "2024 Pritzker Architecture Prize Laureate, Riken Yamamoto." Facebook.com. From https://www.facebook.com/PritzkerArchitecturePrize/
7. Aravena, Alejandro. (2024). "Quinta Monroy Housing, Iquique". Arquitecturaviva. From https://arquitecturaviva.com/works/viviendas-quinta-monroy-1
8. Hussey, Sally. (2024). "Why is Community Engagement Important". Granicus. From https://granicus.com/blog/why-is-community-engagement-important/
9. JBPro. (2024, January 29). "Community Engagement in the Planning Process". JBPro. From https://jbpro.com/community-engagement-in-comprehensive-planning
10. Grow NYC. (2024). "Via Verde Rooftop Garden". Grow NYC. From https://www.grownyc.org/openspace/gardens/bx/via-verde

CHAPTER 17

1. Britannica. (2024). "Ekistics". The Editors of Encyclopaedia Britannica Article History. From https://www.britannica.com/topic/ekistics
2. Neumann Smith. (2023, April 18). "Celebrating Diversity in Architecture". Neumann Smith Architecture. From https://www.neumannsmith.com/celebrating-diversity-in-architecture/
3. Jargowsky, Paul A. (2015, August 9). "Architecture of Segregation, Civil Unrest, the Concentration of Poverty, and Public Policy". The Century Foundation. From https://tcf.org/content/report/architecture-of-segregation/